Teaching the Visually Handicapped

Kenneth A. Hanninen

Wayne State University

BLINDNESS PUBLICATIONS

BLINDNESS PUBLICATIONS

International Standard Book Number: 0-675-08775-9

Library of Congress Catalog Card Number: 74-81958

Second Edition

Printed in the United States of America

Foreword

Since the appearance of Dunn's 1968 article which questioned the efficacy of labels and special education programs for mildly retarded children, special educators in all of the categorical exceptional child areas have taken a more critical view of their labels and special educational programs. It soon became apparent that Dunn's concerns developed into a professional bandwagon which was followed or sought after by some and by others merely viewed with caution or rejected as out of tune.

This benchmark article in special education initiated a great deal of discussion, research, publishing, and program development change. In some instances it appears that the classroom teacher and the children were caught up in new categorization schemes, and/or were involved in new and sometimes different educational delivery programs. It is interesting to contemplate that exceptional children, even those with a mild level of involvement, still exhibit significant learning problems and that programs still experience varying degrees of success in helping children reach their maximum potential, however well or poorly that may be defined.

In whatever category or degree of involvement a child by decree or function finds himself, and in whatever delivery system a teacher finds himself responsible for learning direction, there is still a question from both: "What should I do on Monday?" or "What can I do on Monday?" Children, in whatever their class placement, demonstrate very specific characteristics and educational needs, and the teacher must, by his very presence, know what and how to respond to these characteristics and needs.

Dr. Hanninen's book, though related to a highly specific categorical disability, comes as close to avoiding a jump toward a bandwagon or a confrontation and denunciation of the bandwagon as one is likely to see. What is presented here is a broad discussion of the characteristics of children who do not see or who do not see well. Although words such as *blind, visually handicapped,* and other limiting terms are used, one is not struck by an overwhelming self-importance in the terminology. What is stressed in this volume, and ultimately what makes it readily useful to the reader, is the straightforward presentation of what children are like, what they need, and suggestions about how a teacher may meet these needs. Where the discussion about suggested procedures may seem oriented to the teacher of the visually impaired child, a close examination of what is written will reveal the relevance and usefulness of the techniques and procedures for a variety of individuals: the teacher in the self-contained class, the itinerant and resource teacher, the teacher in the integrated regular class, and also the parent.

Readers of this book should assure themselves that they will find and know children who will not be represented by either the characteristics presented or the methodologies suggested. And this is how it is and should be. The uniqueness of us all prohibits the identification of all that is unique.

Gary A. Best
Department of Special Education
California State University
Los Angeles

Preface

While this book is expected to be of particular value to college students preparing to be teachers in the elementary and secondary schools, it should also prove useful to teachers, school administrators, counselors, and special education personnel in the public and private schools. It can serve as a basic textbook in courses in methods of teaching visually handicapped children, as well as a reference for inservice teachers, school administrators, and others who must familiarize themselves with educational practices with blind and partially seeing students.

Considerable stress has been placed on specific instructional methods and materials which have proven useful with visually handicapped children who have been integrated with their normally seeing peers in local schools. Those interested in the prevailing educational practices in the integration of blind and other visually handicapped students with children who have normal vision will find the chapters dealing with adaptations within curriculums and methods of organization for instruction to be of interest. Conventional terminology is used throughout the book, in those instances where this could be identified. The educational practices described are those which are presently popular.

A discussion of the education and training of visually handicapped children with concomitant disabilities is presented because of their increasing presence. In a real sense, this book is one on the state of the art of teaching visually handicapped children and youth.

The generous assistance of many people is gratefully acknowledged. Students too numerous to mention assisted in testing much of the content and organization of the book as they prepared to become teachers of visually handicapped children. Asa J. Brown, Thomas W. Coleman, Jr., Otis N. Nelson, Richard M. Parres, Gwen V. Retherford, William P. Sosnowsky and Hubert P. Watson, all dear friends and colleagues at Wayne State University, provided timely advice and encouragement during the completion of this book. John J. Lee and John W. Tenny attempted to instill neophyte college teachers with proper portions of firmness, affection, and humility in their contact with the "real world" of teaching handicapped children. My own children, Lori, age 8, Brian, age 4, and Lynn, age 3, constantly remind me that all children are priceless. But most of all I wish to acknowledge with special gratitude and affection the many hours of labor in the typing and preparation of the manuscript by my wife, Sylvia.

Thanks are also expressed here to Jonathan McDuffie for his generous assistance in providing photographs which describe some of the methods and material better than words; to the American Foundation for the Blind for the photographs which show visually handicapped children interacting with their peers; and to Frances Margolin for her patient editorial assistance throughout the preparation of the book. Of course, I am responsible for any shortcomings of the book.

Kenneth A. Hanninen

PREFACE TO THE REVISED EDITION

Teaching the Visually Handicapped, originally published by Charles E. Merrill Publishing Company (1975), provides in this revised edition modifications suggested by readers' comments on the first edition. The major change is the addition of the two chapters "Teaching Deaf-Blind Children," and "The Structure and Function of the Eye."

It appeared that any discussion of the education of children with multiple disabilities requires an extensive presentation of methods and material in teaching deaf-blind children. Access to information on teaching children with this combination of handicaps is limited. This is a very small subgroup of blind, however, the methods of instruction suggest techniques useful more generally for children with sensory obstacles to learning.

The second chapter added to this book is an attempt to present a brief, relatively nontechnical, description of eye physiology and some common eye pathologies encountered in the classroom. Objective information on the eye will hopefully dispel some of the debilitating stereotypes concerning visual impairment. This chapter does not purport to be a substitute for a textbook on this topic. It should, however, relieve the reader of the necessity of requiring a separate reference source in order to follow the methods discussion as it relates to eye physiology.

The purpose of the book remains the same as was true for the first edition. To provide a reasonably concise source of information about the methods and material useful in teaching visually impaired children.

Kenneth A. Hanninen

Contents

Introduction

1

DEFINITION

"Visually handicapped" as used in this book applies to those children who have no vision or whose visual acuity is so limited after optical correction that special teaching methods and materials are necessary in order to achieve some degree of educational success. This definition does not include children whose visual acuity can be improved to near normal levels through use of common eyeglasses or spectacles, thus enabling them to participate fully in the regular school program without further modification. While it has been recognized for many years that visually handicapped children have the same basic physical, intellectual, and emotional needs as all children (American Foundation for the Blind, 1957, p. 13), it is also true that the restrictions imposed by their limited visual acuity create special needs. It is the special needs of these children which will dictate the unique features of their school curriculum, instructional methods, and the design of educational material. The extent to which the educator can adapt to these needs will determine the degree of school success the child will enjoy in becoming a mature, independent, and contributing adult.

1

Specifically, for legal purposes "blindness" is defined in the United States as "visual acuity for distance vision of 20/200 or less in the better eye, with best correction; or . . . field of vision . . . no greater than 20 degrees." "Partially seeing" is defined as "visual acuity greater than 20/200 but not greater than 20/70 in the better eye after correction." (National Society for the Prevention of Blindness, 1966, p. 10.) Since these definitions do not provide a useful distinction for educational purposes, "blindness" in this book will refer to the student who does not have sufficient vision to learn to read print and must use braille as the reading medium. The "partially seeing" is defined here as the student who must have either enlargement of print or use of optical aids in reading print. When blind and partially seeing are discussed as a single group, the term "visually handicapped" will denote them.

DEVELOPMENT OF EDUCATION
OF BLIND CHILDREN

Organized education of blind children dates back to 1784 when Valentin Hauy began the first school for the blind in Paris, France. Schools for the blind were initiated in several other cities in Europe during the succeeding decades. In 1832 Samuel Gridley Howe inaugurated the first school for blind in the United States. This school and those which began proliferating across the country during the nineteenth century were residential schools in which the children were boarded and given child care as well as education. The best method of organization for education of blind was considered to be the residential school and practically no attempt was made to provide an education for blind in the local public schools. Today there are fifty-five residential schools in the United States, and every state has state residential school programs or sends students to other state programs when residential placement is considered necessary. Not until 1900 did the first classes for blind children appear in local public schools (Farrell, 1956, p. 56). These local school programs for blind grew slowly, until the rapid increase of these programs in the 1950s when the visually handicapped population increased dramatically with the increased incidence of retrolental fibroplasia and the accompanying desire of parents to have their blind and partially seeing children remain at home while receiving an education (Misbach and Sweeney, 1970, p. 2).

Recognition of the unique needs of partially seeing children occurred first with the opening of the Myope School in London, England, in 1908. It had become apparent to some educators of blind by this time that

some of the methods and material used in teaching blind were not appropriate with children who had some residual vision. Hence, separate classes for the two types of students were initiated. During the early part of the twentieth century several local public schools in the United States had initiated programs specifically for the education of partially seeing children (Hathaway, 1959, p. 8). Initially these programs were ones in which these children were taught in special rooms and were separate from the normally seeing children in the schools. However, by 1963 more than two-thirds of the local school programs for partially seeing enrolled these children in the regular classrooms (Jones and Collins, 1966, p. 16). Supplemental instruction and service were provided by a special teacher for visually handicapped.

PHILOSOPHY AND POLICY

A basic philosophy which has dictated the recent development of local school programs for visually handicapped is that these children should be provided education locally so that they may live at home while attending school. *The Pine Brook Report* (1957), which articulated a philosophy for educating blind and other severely visually handicapped with their sighted peers, states:

> The education of blind with sighted children in public and private schools is predicated upon the basic philosophy that all children have a right to remain with their families and in their communities during the course of their education; that a blind child has a right to be counted as one of the children of the family and of the community; and that both the family and the community have an obligation to provide for the blind child, as a minimum, the equivalent of what he might have had if sighted (p. 13).

There will continue to be children who require residential school placement away from home, but local schools should provide instruction for these children within the local school system unless there are compelling reasons to seek placement away from home.

The spirit of *The Pine Brook Report* has been reaffirmed by the *Policy Statement* on the provision of educational services issued by the American Foundation for Blind (1969), which states that the visually handicapped child must be provided certain educational services under specified conditions. Among the conditions are: (1) a continuum of types of programs from which a program best suited to the child's needs may be selected, (2) appropriate materials, techniques of instruction, curriculum, and qualified teachers to make the educational experiences meaningful, (3) an educational placement made on the basis of individual needs and abilities, and (4) parent counseling to insure appropriate follow-up at home as well as planning for the child's education. The obligation of local school authorities to provide for not only visually handicapped, but for all other exceptional children, is nowhere stated more explicitly than in "Basic Commitments and Responsibilities to Exceptional Children" (1971):

> The concept of universal education includes exceptional children as well as others. Efforts should be strongly supported to make explicit the obligations of local state and provincial governments to educate exceptional children (p. 182).

The fact that local school officials have the responsibility to educate visually handicapped means that some information must be available concerning methods of identifying these children and organizing for their instruction. Fortunately printed sources of information are available (Jones, 1969; Scholl, 1968) along with consultation with state education agencies concerning specific options available for educating the visually handicapped child. The chapters which follow will provide information directly related to facilitation of instruction of visually handicapped children.

References

American Foundation for the Blind. *The Pine Brook Report.* New York, 1957.

American Foundation for the Blind. *Policy Statement: Provision of Educational Services to Children Who Are Blind or Visually Handicapped.* New York, 1969.

Basic commitments and responsibilities to exceptional children. *Exceptional Children, 38,* 1971, 181–87.

Farrell, G. *The Story of Blindness.* Cambridge, Harvard University Press, 1956.

Hathaway, W. *Education and Health of the Partially Seeing Child.* New York, Columbia University Press, 1959.

Jones, J. W. *The Visually Handicapped Child.* Washington, D.C., U.S. Government Printing Office, 1969.

Jones, J. W. and Collins, A. P. *Educational Programs for Visually Handicapped Children.* Washington, D.C., U.S. Government Printing Office, 1966.

Misbach, D. L. and Sweeney, J. *Education of the Visually Handicapped in California Public Schools.* Sacramento, California Department of Education, 1970.

National Society for the Prevention of Blindness. *Fact Book.* New York, 1966.

Scholl, G. T. *The Principal Works with the Visually Impaired.* Arlington, Virginia, Council for Exceptional Children, 1968.

2

Adjustment of Blind Children in School

Blind children mature through the same developmental process as their sighted peers. They have the same need for a positive self-concept as children without handicaps. They must grow up in a reassuring atmosphere, knowing that they will be accepted. In order to develop personality integrity, children without vision must have appropriate parent and teacher relationships, they must have respect from others, and they must learn to function independently in their social environment

REASONS FOR MALADJUSTMENT

The blind do have some unique adjustment problems. It has not been established whether they have more problems, or problems of a more serious nature, then do sighted people; however, they do have some problems uniquely different from their sighted contemporaries.

There has been considerable stress in literature on the fact that the maladjustment of the blind is not due to the actual visual impairment, but rather due to the attitudes of the sighted toward the blind and also due to the emotional stress placed on them by the sighted in social situations (Sommers, 1944; Harth, 1965; Zahren, 1965). Cutsforth (1951) very succinctly concludes that:

Adjustment of Blind Children in School

> ...vestigations into the life of the blind show that the characteristic emotional disturbances result from the social situations that blindness creates and not from the sensory privation in itself (p. 122).

> ... The seeing members of society and the self-regarding attitudes they induce in the blind are entirely responsible for the emotional disturbances found in the blind as a group (p. 124–25).

This evaluation provides some clues as to strategies for resolution of the blind student's adjustment problems.

The blind population in the United States is a very small minority and many, if not most, of the sighted have never known a blind person. But sighted people do have preconceived notions, possibly due to the folklore and stereotype of the word "blind." These preconceptions, plus a fairly strong dose of pity, make most first encounters between a sighted and a blind person awkward at best. Unfortunately, it is often the blind person who has to attempt to put the sighted person at ease in the encounter. He not only has to deal with emotional strain from awkward social meetings, but also with the outright rudeness of such acts as oversolicitous, unnecessary offers of help.

The blind have other unique problems of adjustment, including those related to physical mobility. They must be formally instructed in travel techniques in order to move about freely and independently in their environment, where this is a very natural and incidental part of the sighted child's existence and is learned informally at an early age. Independent movement is sometimes considered the prime problem of adult blind which determines to a large extent how well he solves his economic and other problems (Chevigny and Braverman, 1950, p. 3).

Independent travel for the blind is a skill which requires ability to judge depth, space, and distance (Chevigny and Braverman, 1950, pp. 236–49). This knowledge is gained mainly through the sense of hearing. It must be learned, as must all skills, through training.

The components of orientation and mobility may be defined as mental orientation to the environment and physical movement. Mental orientation for the blind student is forming a mental map between himself and his surroundings. Physical locomotion is the simple walking or movement from place to place. Adolescents should be given opportunity to learn to use the cane, dog, or human guide by a qualified instructor. The student should be able to select, with the help of his parents and instructor, the mode of travel which will serve him best as an independent travel aid. Orientation and mobility is an important area of the school curriculum because it helps the visually handicapped child meet many of his other needs. (See chapter 8 for a more complete discussion of Orientation and Mobility Training.)

While all children need the respect and understanding of their parents and family, perhaps the blind need it even more. They are too often the victims of overprotective or rejecting parents, because the parents do not understand their capabilities. The blind child also has a need

> to ask the most intimate questions of his parents and other adults who may be comfortable and mature enough to try to help him find answers to questions which may not be fully understood by him. Deprived of visual observation, he will need answers which are real for him (Abel, 1961b, p. 325).

If the blind person is congenitally blinded or blinded during early childhood, his very early experiences in life and with his family are crucial. As with any child, the parents have the most influence in his early life and in the development of his self-concept. It is essential for appropriate professionals to work with the family of the blind child as early as possible. A blind child is unexpected and may be a shock to his parents, who will require a period of adjustment. Assistance to these parents by the social worker or other professional may be of great benefit not only to the parents, but to the adjustment of the child. Early childhood experiences are crucial in later social relationships. Unless children who are visually handicapped enjoy healthy experiences during their early childhood years, they may have adjustment problems throughout life (Harth, 1965, p. 57). They must be allowed to touch, smell, and hear a variety of elements in their surroundings. The child who is constantly told "don't do that" by adults is likely to develop unnecessary inhibitions and anxieties, which in turn may inhibit his learning about his environment.

PARENTS AND CHILD MALADJUSTMENT

Parents bear the main burden for psychosocial development of their children. They may be emotionally healthy, neurotic and insecure, or average parents who are able to withstand a moderate amount of stress. Parents must encourage their visually handicapped child, while at the same time have the ability to set limits. They must try to provide positive experiences. The role of the parent of a blind child must reflect knowledge of the child's peculiar problems, combined with standard good child rearing practices. They need to help the child master his physical and emotional environment and help him to master many practical situations which the sighted child learns incidentally. Their child must remain within the norms of what is socially acceptable, remembering that exploration and independence are vital in the development of the blind child's self-concept. Consequently, it is not surprising that parents are sometimes subject to great emotional stress, which may affect their ability to plan appropriately for themselves and their children unless relief in the form of professional services is available.

> The visually handicapped infant or child who is deprived of personal contacts with warm accepting parents, even more than the child who can react to the visual stimuli around him, may be prone to withdraw into a restricted world of his own in search of substitute satisfactions. (Jones, 1969, p. 4.)

In an attempt to determine to what extent the child's adjustment is related to family environment and parental attitudes, Sommers (1944) devised evaluation scales to appraise those parent-child relationships which have a conditioning effect upon the emotional reactions and social behavior of the blind child. There was a total of twelve scales to evaluate the three broad areas of: (1) physical, cultural, and emotional environment of the home, (2) parental attitudes toward the child, and (3) the child's attitude and reactions.

The findings were that parents of any socioeconomic level may be overprotective and oversolicitous in their attitudes toward their blind children, and this may unfavorably affect the child's own attitude toward his handicap. The conclusion was that when the blind child is emotionally secure and feels accepted by his parents, his adjustment to school, to life, and to his handicap are wholesome and constructive.

Abel, in two studies (1961a; 1961b) has indicated that perhaps the most crucial need of the blind adolescent is to be "respected and understood as a blind adolescent by the family" (Abel, 1961b, p. 325). She goes on to conclude that with the adolescent who has been blind from birth, this understanding of his place in the family should have been realized by adolescence. On the other hand, those who became blind during or immediately preceding adolescence have yet to realize their relationships within the family.

FACTORS AFFECTING SCHOOL ADJUSTMENT

As the blind child enters school, the teachers' actions and attitudes are of paramount importance. Whether it is an integrated or segregated classroom, the teacher's attitude will be quickly transmitted to others. Equality, easy rapport, and self-respect should be nurtured (Langley, 1961). Teachers, like parents, may serve as hero figures which can strengthen ego identification. These children must live in a sighted world and their classroom activities must prepare them for that world. Like the sighted child, the visually handicapped child must be taken from where he is to where he needs to go in his development. The teacher must realize that the way the child feels about himself will significantly affect his functioning and outlook. Therefore, the teacher must be able to look objectively at problems relating to blindness in order to seek help when needed.

The adverse reactions that a blind child meets can be a retarding influence on his psychosocial development. There is continuing widespread belief that there is a link between intellectual and visual impairment (Lairy, 1969, p. 37), which, of course, is untrue, but persistent. When a visually impaired child is functionally retarded, it may in fact be due to an enforced lack of freedom in his movements.

Often people with whom blind come in contact are poorly informed and have unconsciously subscribed to the notion that the blind live in a world of darkness and are only to be pitied. Thus, public opinion often has to be appropriately changed to minimize its detrimental effect on blind individuals. It is not enough to work toward the proper psychosocial development of a blind individual if his next-door neighbor will never be able to do more than tell him how sorry he feels for him, or if no employer will consider giving him an opportunity to try out on the job.

In addition to an atmosphere of acceptance and understanding, the blind person needs to be able to adequately function independently in his environment. The visually handicapped child must be taught that behavior patterns that are offensive to other individuals can be changed. Any additional training needed in such areas as hygiene, posture, control, establishing sound social relationships, overcoming personal problems, orientation, mobility, eating, or any other skills should be provided by parents, counselors, teachers, or other appropriate persons.

ADOLESCENCE AND SCHOOL ADJUSTMENT

Adolescence presents special problems for many young people, both handicapped and nonhandicapped. In what specific areas would adjustment be more difficult for the blind adolescent when compared with his sighted counterpart? What part does lack of vision play in any maladjustment? Some investigators of blindness have taken special note of the adjustment of blind adolescents in the areas of sex behavior, dating, mobility, and their outlook on the future. Recognition of the differences in the intensity of concern in these areas by adolescents who are newly blinded and those whose visual loss is congenital has also been noted.

Sex Behavior and Dating

Two areas in which visual experiences play a dominant role during adolescence are sex curiosity and dating (Lowenfeld, 1959, p. 312–13). The lack of sight creates special problems in our culture in these areas where much of the information on the characteristics of the opposite sex is derived through visual observation. The blind child may use "flash-back" into earlier childhood sexual exploration to satisfy sexual curiosity, but Lowenfeld points out that since "this knowledge is no longer active knowledge, it is repressed and he [the adolescent] is again driven by the urge to know and find out." (1959, p. 312.)

Dating, in contrast to sex curiosity, implies direct social contact. Some of the handicaps the blind child has in dating relationships are the lack of freedom in choosing and approaching a partner, the absence of the strong visual element in flirtation, and customs requiring male roles of initiative and aggressiveness. This aggressive role of boys, requiring boys to approach girls, may be the reason most blind boys meet seeing girls while only the exceptional blind girls meet seeing boys (Lowenfeld, 1959, p. 313–14).

Mobility

An aspect of mobility which is of keen interest to practically all adolescent boys and which may be a source of frustration for the blind boy is the autonomy and mobility provided by the automobile. The new feeling of independence which the automobile affords sighted adolescents is akin to that presented to blind boys when they can travel without assistance on foot and with public transportation. However, the blind boy may also share an interest in the automobile with his seeing peers. This is frequently a topic of conversation among adolescent boys, and it would be strange indeed if the blind boy would not cultivate an interest as a result of these contacts. The blind adolescent will soon recognize that although he can share this interest in conversation and even manipulate certain mechanical parts of the car, he will never be able to drive. While this interest should not be discouraged, it is important to encourage this boy to discover and develop talents or assets he may possess in order to withstand this disappointment as well as other frustrations which lack of vision may present (Abel, 1961b).

Outlook Toward the Future

With all of the physical and social complications of adolescence, plus the added task of functioning without sight, it would appear that the blind adolescent would be rather pessimistic about his future. This is not entirely true.

Although older blind adolescents have anxieties in their contacts with the opposite sex, some negative attitudes toward themselves concerning vocational prospects, and anxiety in other areas, research indicates their outlook is not substantially different from that of sighted peers. The blind adolescent of today is in a better position in some respects than his counterpart of the last generation. "It is obvious to one who has an opportunity to compare blind adolescents of today with those of, say, 30 years ago, that the former have an entirely different and infinitely more positive outlook and attitude toward their future economic life." (Lowenfeld, 1959, p. 315).

Newly Blinded Adolescents

Several writers on blindness have discussed the birth of a new personality when an individual is newly blinded (Carroll, 1961, pp. 11–13; Cholden, 1958, p. 51; Cutsforth, 1951, p. 123). The interpersonal relationships, the self-concept, body image, and other aspects of personality are altered, if not completely changed. The newly blinded adolescent seems to be particularly subject to great personality changes.

Cholden (1958) discussed psychological acceptance of blindness in terms of coordinating an awareness of (1) the need, aims, and difficulties in developing psychological acceptance of the disability, and (2) the values and goals of the counseling effort. This awareness is related to the need of the disabled person to accept his handicap with the help of counseling. The adolescent, with all the problems associated with adolescence, finds it especially difficult to accept blindness. Some of the preoccupations of the adolescent which create particular difficulty in accepting blindness have to do with masculine strength and independence, need for dependence as a result of blindness at a time when he is developing independence, and compulsion to be conspicuous at a time when the adolescent desires anonymity.

Chevigny and Braverman (1950, pp. 233–36), in discussing adjustment to blindness, present another aspect of being newly blinded. Those who are totally blind seem to adjust more quickly to their handicap than do those who have lost their vision only partially, perhaps because hopelessness may contribute to quick adjustment. An individual who retains some vision hopes for eventual increase or complete return of vision. This keeps him in a constant state of waiting before attempting to adjust to "blind ways of doing things."

This same problem is recognized by Cholden (1958). In treating newly blind individuals, he indicates that in order for rehabilitation to take place the blind person must believe he is disabled and learn to live with this disability. Friends and doctors who hold out any hope of recovering sight by giving news of miraculous cures, or delaying informing the blind person that he is permanently blind, are hindering the rehabilitation process. Rather than encourage belief in eventual recovery of sight, friends would be more helpful if they would offer encouragement by showing that the blind individual can live a full life with blindness.

Peer Relationships

Adolescence is a period when it is particularly important to be accepted as a part of the group. Peer approval inspires much activity which is directed toward conformity to peer group demands. The blind adolescent, as has been indicated earlier, has the same social needs as do his sighted peers. Therefore, it would seem important to know something about the reactions of sighted adolescents toward their blind peers to determine what, if any, unmet needs the latter group has as a result of association with sighted peers.

In a study comparing problems perceived by blind adolescents with those of sighted peers, it was found that blind and seeing worried about the same problems, but with a different emphasis. The blind worried

more about problems of employment and financial security, whereas the seeing adolescents worried more about school problems. When these two groups were compared relative to what they wished for most in life, the blind desired security and independence, in contrast to the sighted, whose main concern was a happy marriage and home (Sommers, 1944, p. 25–26).

Under any conditions, the variations among the circumstances of an individual blind person's life make it important to interpret these data with caution. Knowing whether these group differences would be present today would require a more recent study. As Lukoff and Whiteman (1967, p. 23) point out, ". . . the assessment of a blind person's capacities is related to his other characteristics . . . the milieu of one blind person is unlikely to correspond to another's despite the frequent assumption by many . . . that blind persons face an invariant environment."

Aids to Healthy Peer Relations

The adolescent blind needs answers to questions which require visual interpretation. The sighted youngster is in a position to fulfill this need. Much of the information the blind teen-ager receives is from adults, such as teachers and parents. Certainly the answers given by these people are important to the visually handicapped child, but there is also the necessity of supplying information interpreted by peers. In addition to interpreting the visual experiences, it is while with his peers that the blind boy or girl will have opportunity to have day-to-day tactual and other sensory experiences which are more meaningful to him.

The greatest confidence which the adolescent blind can express in his sighted friend is to request an evaluation which requires vision about a person or situation. The sighted person has the obligation, under these circumstances, to supply the visual information as concretely as possible to minimize prejudicing the blind person by his own impressions or reactions (Abel, 1961b, p. 325).

Problems in the area of social relations among teen-age boys and girls who are blind have been identified (Lowenfeld, 1959). The blind adolescent has much less freedom in choosing and approaching a partner at a party or dance. The visual element in flirtation is absent in this group, which tends to hinder closer boy–girl relationships. Some of the lack of vision under these conditions is overcome by verbal communication and physical contact (such as holding hands). The problems involved in a blind boy calling on a girl for a date or visit are difficult, not only because of the inability to observe visually, but also because of the lack of acceptance of a blind boy by the parents of a seeing girl. Parents of the blind youngster also occasionally have difficulty accepting the fact of blindness.

SCHOOL ADJUSTMENT, BLINDNESS,
AND THE TEACHER

Parents of blind children have a variety of emotions associated with their relationship to their blind child (Sommers, 1944, p. 9–14). A majority of the parents have some difficulty in accepting the child and his visual handicap. None of the parents expected to have a seriously handicapped child. With all of the feelings of guilt, injustice, inadequacy, and other emotions, it is not surprising that some of these parents have difficulty meeting needs of their blind child. Under these conditions it would appear appropriate for the special teacher, with his skill and knowledge in dealing with these children, to go beyond the usual scope of the curriculum and meet some of the needs of the blind child in mobility, social graces, and other areas not normally considered part of a school curriculum.

There is evidence that sighted adolescents hold inaccurate perceptions of blind classmates (Gowman, 1957, p. 64–96). This suggests that an effort be made to orient or "educate" the sighted adolescents to the real abilities and aspirations of the blind. The goals of the blind adolescent are similar to those of his sighted peers. This similarity should be communicated to the sighted adolescents, as well as to other people, so that stereotyped attitudes may be modified. The elimination of some of the detrimental attitudes would help to make this handicapped group accepted by those classmates who are sighted. An incidental effect would be to enhance the self-concept of the handicapped individuals involved.

The fact that the blind adolescent is as greatly concerned about his economic future as his sighted peers should be noted and dealt with by parents and the various professionals. The implications of this are more directly the concern of the school vocational counselor than the special teacher, but both can profit by an awareness of this concern. The special teacher can certainly help ease this concern by knowing that it exists, and by being alert for any special vocational interests and talents. The obligation of the vocational counselor is, in part, to give the client an honest, positive outlook on his future economic possibilities after evaluting his vocational assets as well as his liabilities.

The blind child needs the confidence that comes from knowing that he is walking and behaving as much like others as possible. He needs to know that his behavior patterns will not draw negative reactions. He must also be confident in his ability to move from place to place independently and learn the best means of exploiting his remaining potentialities in an effort to achieve satisfactory integration into the sighted world. With proper training and the balanced attitudes of those with whom he comes in contact, the blind individual can become a contributing member of his community because he thinks well of himself and knows that he is a contributing member.

The blind do have problems in adjustment, some uniquely their own. With the help of understanding professionals, families and friends, and (almost of equal importance) the understanding and acceptance of the general public, he can make these adjustments successfully and be a self-respecting member of society. Yet one important fact remains— "Probably the most important fact yet discovered about the psychology of the blind is the relatively small amount of personality disturbance that accompanies it" (Pringle, 1964, p. 136).

ADJUSTMENT AND PEER ASSOCIATIONS

Much of the literature discussing peer association among blind and sighted children in extracurricular activities relates to blind children in residential school settings. Under these circumstances modifications can be made in activity to accommodate blind children. Blind children are not particularly conscious that the extracurricular activity is different or modified in some way. Sports activities can be modified so that each blind child can participate without disadvantage to any other child. Different standards of excellence and competitiveness can be arranged among those participating without being unfair to any child. Problems discussed in student government, fund-raising activities, parties, dances, and club activities can be arranged so that opportunity to participate is possible for each student since visual considerations are minimal. Most of these modifications would not be practical for a blind child in an integrated public school, particularly in high school.

The blind child in a public school should be able to achieve some participation in extracurricular activity with only minor, if any, modification in the conditions of participation. The sighted child would probably not tolerate much modification in some of the extracurricular activities for the sole purpose of including a visually handicapped student. Some insight into the activities a visually handicapped child wants to participate in, and the obstacles he feels must be surmounted, would aid in appraising his participation possibilities.

Some information into the difficulties in peer associations between blind and sighted children can be acquired through literature dealing with the self-concept and abilities of these individuals. There appear to be no differences in the self-concept of blind and sighted adolescents, although the blind tend to be at the extreme of high negative or positive attitudes toward themselves (Jervis, 1959). There is some evidence that with those blinded later in life, some rather substantial difficulties in accepting the handicap are present; they consider blindness to be the worst type of disability (Gowman, 1957, pp. 64–96).

Other difficulties a blind individual may encounter with peer associations are suggested by studies of stereotypical attitudes toward the blind. Gowman (1957) found, in examining stereotyped attitudes of sighted high school students, that there was a consensus on some attitudes. High school boys felt less sure of the capacities of blind than did the girls. Most of the respondents felt the blind should support themselves economically, that everything a blind person does is a real achievement, and that blind have a mystical "sixth sense." There appeared to be little evidence of negative attributes often imputed to the blind, nor did the subjects of this study want to segregate the blind overtly (Gowman, 1957, pp. 64–96). These results suggest that there are some unique attitudes toward blind adolescents as a group, but the effect of these attitudes has not been established.

There has been some discussion among teachers and others concerning the effect of certain mannerisms of blind children. Some common mannerisms are rubbing the eyes, rocking, clapping the hands over the ears, and shaking the head or hands. There appears to be an assumption that these mannerisms are not harmful and will be outgrown by the child if less attention were brought to bear (*The Lookout*, 1963). No evidence seems to be available concerning the effect these behaviors have on peer association during adolescence.

A careful analysis of autobiographies of persons with physical disabilities, which included blind, suggested that the conforming demands of the adolescent can make allowance for physical deviations in many kinds of group situations. There seemed to be little difficulty in finding companions among members of the same sex; however, the adolescent with a physical handicap experienced some trying times in establishing heterosexual adjustments. This study concluded that heterosexual adjustments are difficult for the disabled adolescent, but they are also a problem for the nondisabled (Wright, 1960, pp. 186–95).

References

Abel, G. L. Adolescence: Foothold on the future. *New Outlook for the Blind, 55,* 1961a, 103–6.

Abel, G. L. The blind adolescent and his needs. *Exceptional Children, 27,* 1961b, 309–10, 325–34.

Carroll, T. *Blindness.* Boston, Little, Brown and Company, 1961.

Chevigny, H. and Braverman, S. *The Adjustment of the Blind.* New Haven, Yale University Press, 1950.

Cholden, L. S. *A Psychiatrist Works With Blindness.* New York, American Foundation for the Blind, 1958.

Cutsforth, T. D. *The Blind in School and Society.* New York, American Foundation for the Blind, 1951.

Gowman, A. G. *The War Blind in American Social Structure.* New York, American Foundation for the Blind, 1957.

Harth, R. The emotional problems of people who are blind: A review. *International Journal for the Education of the Blind, 15,* 1965, 52–58.

Jervis, F. M. A comparison of self-concepts of blind and sighted children. *Guidance Programs for Blind Children,* Watertown, Massachusetts, Perkins Publication No. 20, Perkins School for the Blind, 1959.

Jones, J. W. *The Visually Handicapped Child.* Washington D.C., U.S. Government Printing Office, 1969.

Lairy, G. C. Problems in the adjustment of the visually impaired child. *New Outlook for the Blind, 63,* 1969, 33–41.

Langley, E. Self-image: The formative years. *New Outlook for the Blind, 55,* 1961, 80–81.

The Lookout, Evanston, Illinois (edited report of Jerome Cohen research), *XIV,* No. 7, 1963.

Lowenfeld, B. The blind adolescent in a seeing world. *Exceptional Children, 25,* 1959, 310–15.

Lukoff, I. F. and Whiteman, M. *The Social Sources of Adjustment to Blindness,* Research Series 21, New York, American Foundation for the Blind, 1967.

Pringle, M. L. K. The emotional and social adjustment of blind children. *Educational Research, 6,* 1964, 129–38.

Sommers, V. S. *The Influence of Parental Attitudes and Social Environment on the Personality Development of the Adolescent Blind.* New York, American Foundation for the Blind, 1944.

Wright, B. A. *Physical Disability: A Psychological Approach.* New York, Harper & Row, Publishers, 1960.

Zahren, H. A. A study of personality differences between blind and sighted children. *British Journal of Educational Psychology, 35,* 1965, 329–38.

Integration Into Regular Classes

Since 1960, more than one-half of the legally blind children in the United States have been enrolled in local schools (Jones, 1969, p. 27) and practically all children identified as partially seeing are educated with their nonhandicapped peers in public schools (Misbach and Sweeney, 1970, p. v). This shifting of educational responsibility has been of rather recent origin. As late as 1945, 27 percent of all children in residential schools for blind were partially seeing (Lennon, 1948), in spite of rather early general agreement that it is undesirable to use residential placement for these children in schools for blind (Farrell, 1956, p. 70–71; National Society for the Prevention of Blindness, 1952). A majority of blind children continued to receive their elementary and secondary education in residential schools until around 1960, when educational programs for blind became generally available locally.

Some provision has been made for education of blind since 1900, and for partially seeing since 1913. However, local school programs grew slowly until 1953 when the rapid increase in numbers of blind children due to retrolental fibroplasia resulted in new patterns for education of the blind.

RESIDENTIAL SCHOOLS

All states still either maintain residential schools for blind or have made arrangements with neighboring states for this service (Jones, 1969, p.

23). Standard educational programs with curricula similar to those in ordinary public schools are common in these institutions. Besides education, total care, including medical and child care, is provided during the school year for the typical child attending a residential school.

Some residential schools have accepted day school pupils from the vicinity of the school, thus allowing these students to live at home. Other residential schools send visually handicapped students to public high schools as day school pupils while the students reside at the special institution. These programs are primarily for students requiring special subjects not included in the residential school curricula and incidentally provide associations with sighted children (Jones and Collins, 1966, p. 18).

LOCAL SCHOOL ORGANIZATIONAL PLANS

Special Class Plan

Initial provision for education of visually handicapped in local schools resulted in the Special Class Plan in which students were placed full-time with a special teacher during the school day. This plan was originally the only one available and first appeared in the large cities. Separate rooms for blind and partially seeing children were set up with a specially qualified teacher providing all instruction. This plan is also sometimes known as a self-contained or segregated day class. Beginning with these early special classes, other forms of organization for instruction evolved in which regular classroom teachers assumed more of the daily instruction.

Cooperative Plan

The first clearly articulated departure from the Special Class Plan involved participation by visually handicapped students in certain specialized curriculums, such as art and music, in which the regular classroom teachers cooperated in the instruction. Hence the term "cooperative" was used to label this plan. Under a Cooperative Plan, the visually handicapped student continues to be registered with the special teacher and maintains a homeroom with him.

While basic instruction is still typically performed by the special teacher, some programs have substantial instruction completed by regular classroom teachers. Primary responsibility for academic achievement remains with the special teacher and separation from nonhandicapped children for instructional purposes is maintained. In the past it was assumed that appropriate education of those with serious visual impairments required special teachers. Recently it has been found that regular classroom teachers can educate handicapped students in basic subject-matter areas.

At the present, the Cooperative Plan appears a viable educational plan with those visually handicapped who have several handicapping conditions. These multiply-handicapped children require highly individual instruction in very specialized areas. For these children, the Cooperative Plan would seem to continue to be a useful pattern for providing instruction.

Integrated Plan (Resource and Itinerant Programs)

The most recent evolution in organizational patterns for teaching blind and partially seeing children have been the resource teacher and the itinerant teacher programs. The "resource program" has been used synonymously with the "integrated plan" (American Foundation for the Blind, 1957). The resource and itinerant programs are also sometimes called "integrated instructional programs" (Misbach and Sweeney, 1970, p. 17), emphasizing that these two organizational patterns are the ones which most thoroughly integrate visually handicapped children with nonhandicapped students for education purposes. Both the resource and itinerant programs have been developed largely during the 1950s, although some have existed at least since 1938. These two types of programs are by far the most common programs in local schools (Jones and Collins, 1966, p. 7).

The unique feature of these programs is that primary responsibility for education of blind is no longer with the special teacher, but is shifted to the classroom teacher. In each of these programs the handicapped student is enrolled in the regular classroom and uses the services provided by the special teacher only when these cannot be provided by the regular classroom teacher. Advantages attributed to these plans over the self-contained special class include (Jones, 1969, pp. 26–28): (1) emphasis on the handicapped child's abilities and likeness to other children rather than on differences, (2) availability of a wealth of resources by including these children in general school activities, (3) more accessible services of specially prepared teachers, (4) full-time individualized instruction in the areas of greatest specialization, and (5) closer approximation of the social situations the visually handicapped child will encounter in adult life.

The primary difference between the resource and itinerant teacher programs revolves around the fact that the resource teacher is available within a single school building throughout the day. The itinerant teacher will only be available in a single building for a part of a day, since teaching service must be provided in two or more buildings. As a practical matter the itinerant teacher may be available at less than daily intervals, depending on the number of students and the amount of aid required. In either case the typical special instruction is provided in a room separate from the regular classroom. In the case of the resource teacher, the room may be called the resource room. The resource program can provide larger amounts of time per student since no time in travel between schools is necessary. The itinerant program, on the other hand, provides instruction which is more likely to allow the handicapped child to continue with his nonhandicapped peers throughout school as he moves from elementary to junior high school and high school.

Certainly in determining type of program consideration should be given to the amount and kind of special instruction necessary. When intensive regular instruction for several children is necessary in specialized areas, such as beginning braille reading and writing, use of abacus, and typing, the resource program would appear to be most appropriate. Where occasional tutoring or instruction in a new appliance is required, the itinerant program may suffice. These judgments must be made periodically by the school administrator and special teacher as student numbers and progress dictate.

While this discussion relates to resource programs in local schools, the resource room can and does operate in residential schools. One-fourth to one-third of the staff may be used as resource teachers in this context while the remaining staff are elementary or secondary teachers responsible for subject-matter content (Jones and Collins, 1966, p. 34).

Teacher-Consultant

A variation of the itinerant program is the teacher-consultant. In areas with new or developing programs, a low prevalence of visually handicapped children, and limited amounts of special services and instruction, this pattern of organization has evolved (Jones, 1969, p. 28). While the teacher-consultant may perform the same duties as an itinerant teacher, the emphasis is different. More time is spent by the teacher-consultant in talking to classroom teachers and administrators than in the case of an itinerant teacher. However, in the discussion of integrated programs in this chapter, itinerant and teacher-counselor programs will be considered synonymous.

PREPARATION FOR PLACEMENT IN AN INTEGRATED PROGRAM

Planning for initial placement of a visually handicapped child in a regular classroom should include a strategy for creating a climate of acceptance by teacher and students. This may be done by minimizing any uneasiness resulting from uncertainty of how to act toward the handicapped child. Establishing structure for the relationship between the special teacher and classroom teacher, and between the classroom teacher and handicapped student, will facilitate mutual acceptance of an integrated pattern of instruction.

Prior to the first day of school, the student should be oriented to the objects and rooms which will be significant to him during his first days. The special teacher will physically orient the student to his locker, resource room, homeroom, gym, toilet, and other rooms and allow the student to practice in walking between these locations. Special effort should be made to acquire all textbooks, workbooks, and other classroom material in braille, large type, or recorded form. Commonly this material is ordered before summer vacation for receipt by September. If the material does not arrive, interim arrangements for recordings or use of people as readers must be scheduled.

The special teacher should initiate meeting the classroom teacher before the first day to relieve him of any anxieties he may have about having a blind student in class and assure him of support available in the form of special teaching service. The special teacher should use this opportunity to confirm a tentative schedule for the students' period with the special teacher and attempt to acquire any assignments for the first day which need to be brailled or prepared for student use in class. He should attempt to have a brailled or large-type class schedule, menu, and notices available for the visually handicapped students on the first day.

During the first few days of school, the special teacher should establish a pattern of movement within the school for the student which is both efficient and comfortable. It is necessary to insist that the student maintain books and papers in an orderly fashion and at convenient locations, so that he is prepared to work with the other class members and will not disrupt the class by coming in late and searching for materials. The special teacher should determine what specific services the classroom teacher requires and provide for these needs.

SPECIAL TEACHER IN THE ELEMENTARY SCHOOL IN AN INTEGRATED PROGRAM

It is not possible to give an exhaustive list of procedures for the resource teacher. However, in order to give a clearer concept of the function of and rationales used by a resource teacher, a hypothetical day's activities will be discussed, out of which come some generalizations about philosophy and procedures.

One Teacher's School Day

Miss B is in her third year as a resource teacher at Dawes Elementary School. Mr. W is the regular classroom teacher for Albert, who is a blind third-grade pupil receiving some special aid in Miss B's resource room. Miss B has six other visually handicapped students in grades 3 through 6 who receive some special aid while they are enrolled in regular classrooms.

Miss B's day begins one-half hour before any pupils arrive for classes. She must go to the classroom of each elementary teacher who has a visually handicapped student to copy any material off the blackboard. The handicapped students will need this brailled or in large type. While in each room she checks with the teachers to determine whether any worksheets need to be provided in braille or large type, returns braille assignments requiring translation to print, and notes areas of instruction which should be reinforced through additional instruction in the resource room. Problem areas related to student behavior, incomplete work, and special events will be noted for resolution later in the day or over a period of time.

As Miss B enters Mr. W's room, she finds that a new spelling list is written on the blackboard with questions to be answered for the succeeding day concerning today's reading assignment. After writing these on a pad, she gives Mr. W the previous day's spelling words which Albert has completed in braille, with the words written by her in pencil over the braille words exactly as spelled by Albert. Mr. W can now correct and grade them. Mr. W expresses concern for Albert's slow progress in spelling and his apparent inability to quickly assemble his books, papers, and braille writer, which sometimes results in the class having to wait for him to begin quizzes and other classroom activities.

Halloween is two weeks away and the class will present a program for parents with the holiday as the theme. All class members are expected to sing, perform in a skit, or read prose or poetry. Albert has indicated he would like to read a poem but needs help in choosing one. Miss B completes her conversation and leaves Albert's room. She completes similar visits to the rooms of the other visually handicapped students and returns to the resource room before the beginning of classes.

Albert is scheduled to come into the resource room each day for 30 minutes during the morning and 30 minutes in the afternoon. He is an able pupil with occasional lapses in motivation. The two teachers have determined that this is sufficient time for those special instructional activities afforded in the resource room. Albert arrives in the resource room 15 minutes after classes have begun. This is because he has participated in the morning routine of attendance taking, collection of milk money, announcements, flag pledge, and singing of "America" with his class. While Albert is in the resource room, the rest of the class is busy reading in preparation for answering the questions on the blackboard as well as copying the new spelling words. Miss B has two other students in the room during this same time.

Each pupil is quickly assigned work individually, and Miss B moves from one to another while maintaining instruction. It has already been ascertained that Albert needs help in spelling, organizing for study in the classroom, and choosing a Halloween poem. Miss B asks Albert to correct the spelling on his previous spelling test and queries him about his spelling difficulties. In the course of a brief conversation she finds that Albert had not received the braille words from Mr. W in sufficient time to practice adequately. Miss B moves to help one of the other students, then returns to Albert and arranges to meet him during part of his lunch period to help him organize his desk for better accessibility to material. Once again she moves to help another student and returns to Albert with a book with simple poems appropriate for Halloween. After she reads several to him, Albert indicates he likes one of them. Miss B tells Albert the poem will be brailled for him by that afternoon.

Miss B continues working with different visually handicapped students throughout the morning. At lunch, she orients two of the students on how to go through the school cafeteria line. She has previously provided the students with a brailled weekly menu, and the students have been instructed to select the items prior to going into line at the cafeteria so that they can simply ask attendants for appropriate foods. Thus, today it is only necessary to briefly monitor the process. Also during this noon hour she helps Albert to organize his desk while the rest of the class is out of the room.

The afternoon is a series of instructional sessions with individual students, brailling or typing in large type the material required by students on short notice, and hurried resolution of classroom teacher request for material or information. Albert arrives at his scheduled time. Miss B gives him the brailled Halloween poem and reassures him that on Monday of the following week she will orient him to the stage and arrange for a classmate to guide him to and from his place on the stage if necessary. The dismissal bell rings at the end of the day, and Miss B hurries to monitor the departure from school of two of the blind children who tend to loiter at their lockers and risk missing the bus. She collects material which must be brailled for the succeeding day to be completed at home and stops at her mailbox, on her way out, to collect braille papers from classroom teachers for transcribing into print for the next day.

This scenario presents a brief sketch of activities of a special teacher in an integrated program for education of visually handicapped. It suggests some important educational procedures as well as aspects of the relationship of the special teacher to the classroom teacher, including:

1. The special teacher must initiate contact with the classroom teacher in order to monitor student progress in the classroom routine. This contact must occur at least once daily at the elementary level to maintain adequate academic progress.

2. The special teacher must actively seek out student needs in the classroom so that no supporting instructional service is denied a child simply because monitoring was neglected.

3. All educational experiences available to the nonhandicapped should be made available to visually handicapped children insofar as possible. The special teacher should take pains to aid in reproducing classroom experiences as accurately as possible. If classroom experiences are considered important to other children, then they are also important for visually handicapped children.

4. Accurate feedback to the blind student on his progress must be maintained and should include the same system of punishments and rewards which is applied to all other children in the class.

5. Prompt response to both implied and explicit requests for assistance by students and classroom teachers must be completed. The special teacher should not retard student progress because of avoidable delays in providing service to the classroom teacher or student.

6. The visually handicapped should participate in extracurricular as well as curricular school activities as completely and actively as possible. The special teacher should devise the means for overcoming any obstacles.

7. An intensive attempt should be made to schedule resource room assistance for students at times when it interferes minimally with participation in classroom experiences. The student should be impressed with the importance of the classroom as the primary source of instruction.

8. Instruction performed in the resource room should be supplemental to classroom instruction and directed at areas requiring the most immediate attention in order to maintain progress in the major subject or curriculum areas. All instruction in the major curriculum areas should be initiated by the classroom teacher so that the visually handicapped student may participate in problem-solving group interaction.

9. The special teacher must provide instruction and counsel in those areas which involve developing independence in the student. This in-

volves informal activities, such as those involved in self-care, movement (orientation and mobility) in school, and any actions of the handicapped student which convey the erroneous impression to others in school that he requires constant assistance and is therefore grossly different from other students.

10. Good personal and professional relationships between the special and classroom teachers are necessary to the success of an integrated program. Antagonism over trivial issues should be avoided.

Common Responsibilities of Resource or Itinerant Teachers

The generalizations extrapolated from the scenario illustrate some of the significant educational practices and philosophy associated with the role of resource or itinerant teacher. The important point to note is that the special teacher in resource or itinerant programs is an active but *supplementary* teacher who is a specialist in meeting only those instructional needs of visually handicapped children which are caused or accentuated by their ocular disabilities. These responsibilities include (Jones and Collins, 1966, pp. 34–37; Misbach and Sweeney, 1970, pp. 39–40):

1. Member of the committee which determines admission of students into resource or itinerant programs.

2. Determines whether braille, print, or both modes of reading are most appropriate for a child.

3. Develops maximum use of optical aids and residual vision.

4. Teaches braille or print reading and writing.

5. Orients children to new aids and instructs them in the use of a wide variety of aids.

6. Instructs children in effective use of sighted readers, tape and disc recordings, typewriters, and braille writers.

7. Teaches children use of note-taking, braille shorthand, and use of summary and reference material.

8. Gives orientation and early mobility training and prepares the child for independent travel training.

9. Confers periodically with parents on student education progress.

10. Provides counseling and instruction on social competency for adolescents.

11. Teaches eating and grooming skills and use of playground equipment.

12. Aids adolescents in learning to put sighted peers at ease, obtain proper educational aids and materials, and cope with more difficult math and science study.

13. Plans instructional program for individual visually handicapped students with the classroom teacher and acts as a source of

information on the educational implications useful to educational planning.

14. Exchanges information on individual students with other school personnel, such as counselors and nurses, and uses their expertise in assisting the students.

15. Cooperates with ancillary groups and individuals, such as braille transcribers, readers for blind, mobility instructors, and vocational rehabilitation counselors, and uses their assistance efficiently.

This list is not considered exhaustive, and special teachers frequently encounter unique methods of aiding students when required. There is great variation in the amount and kind of assistance which visually handicapped children require. Exhaustive lists of competencies necessary for teachers of blind and partially seeing have been prepared and reported (Mackie and Cohoe, 1956; Mackie and Dunn, 1955). These teacher competencies were ranked for importance by a sample of teachers nationally and reflect in considerable detail teacher responsibilities in the education of visually handicapped children. See appendix A for a more extensive list of competencies required of special teachers of visually handicapped.

THE SPECIAL TEACHER IN A SECONDARY SCHOOL INTEGRATED PROGRAM

There are important differences between elementary and secondary level students which have implications for resource and itinerant programs. Entry into junior high school presumes certain prerequisite skills acquired in the normal elementary school curriculum.

Preparatory Skills for Entrance to High School

Orientation and mobility skills should be highly developed. The student should be able to orient to classrooms and the school building. His stride, gait, and posture should indicate confidence in walking in familiar areas of the building; they are important components in achieving peer acceptance.

A key indicator of academic readiness for junior high school is proper development of reading skills. The student should be able to read braille or print smoothly and with comprehension. Some experience with student readers and the ability to listen to recordings of class material are also essential. Competent use of a braille writer and the ability to use a typewriter properly are of critical importance to the blind student's adequate academic progress in junior high school. Ability to use an abacus and the Nemeth code of braille mathematics should have developed to the point where they can be used proficiently in mathematics. (All of these benchmarks to readiness for secondary school assume that the student does not have substantial handicaps other than vision.)

When visually handicapped students lack the basic preparatory skills to begin a high school program, the resource or itinerant teacher will need to provide instruction in problem areas in order for the student to maintain adequate progress. Particularly in those skills associated with orientation and mobility, it is necessary to have certain minimum competencies in order to progress in the changed school environment. Frequently students have considerable anxiety upon entering high school, and competency in basic skills will go a long way toward minimizing this fear.

Special Teacher Duties in Secondary School

There are several unique features about secondary schools and adolescent students' characteristics which are the basis for some variation in resource and itinerant teacher practices. Although these features appear substantially different, the function of the special teacher requires only minor modifications.

The move from the self-contained classroom of the elementary school to the departmentalized instruction in high school represents some procedural changes for both the visually handicapped student and the teachers who will be involved in his education. The resource or itinerant teacher will certainly find it more difficult to contact classroom teachers personally each day and will need to develop a new communication method. Some combination of personal contact initiated by the special teacher, written notes placed in faculty mailboxes, and messages relayed by the student will need to be used. The complexity of maintaining contact with each classroom teacher becomes apparent when one notes that six visually handicapped students with five courses per student equals thirty courses, with a good probability that most of these thirty courses have different classroom teachers. Fortunately this is mitigated to some extent by the greater independence of the student and his experience in functioning in the normal classroom for at least several years prior to secondary school attendance.

The high school curriculum provides for a greater degree of specialization in coursework, resulting in a need for more specialized material and equipment, adaptations to new classroom instructional procedures, and methods of rapid assimilation of a greater volume of reading material. The blind student will need to make regular use of recorded material and reader service if material is unavailable in braille. Early appraisal of the special equipment needed in order for a visually handicapped student to participate in classes which have lab components will be necessary. The classroom teachers must be advised of methods of instructing visually handicapped; new methods of instruction may need to be developed jointly by the special teacher and the classroom teacher.

The departmentalized nature of high school instruction requires that students frequently move from one room to another throughout the day, rather than remaining in one room for most of each day as is true in the typical elementary school. Intensive orientation to the building must be completed as soon as possible so that the student can promptly arrive in each class. This may necessitate arranging a sighted classmate to be a guide during the first few days of the first year in a building.

The high school student who is visually handicapped must organize his material and movements with much greater efficiency than was necessary in the elementary school. Since a blind student cannot carry sufficient numbers of bulky braille books for all classes during each half of a school day, he must rely on organizing the location of the appropriate volumes of textbooks for quick pick-up between classes. This may require certain volumes of a braille text to be placed in classrooms as well as the resource room so that the student does not need to leave a classroom while class is in session in order to obtain a book.

One advantage of the organization of a high school is that it is possible to schedule resource room periods more flexibly without interfering with the students' classroom attendance. The typical high school curriculum provides for study periods which may be regularly scheduled in a specific room or during a part of the class period. In either case, these periods may be used to provide assistance by the resource or itinerant teacher.

There is, of course, a greater variety of extracurricular activities available in the high school. These should be considered as important to visually handicapped as they are to nonhandicapped students. The special teacher can help the student to select appropriate activities and provide assistance in the initiation into these experiences by interpreting the students' abilities to the sponsoring faculty member as well as providing aid in acquisition of necessary material and equipment.

Much of the work of a special teacher for visually handicapped in high school will continue to be additional instruction (tutoring) in classroom work which has already been presented in class. This should typically take the form of facilitating student completion of an assignment made by the classroom teacher. It is not a function of the special teacher to initiate instruction in new subject-matter areas unless he is competent in those areas. More appropriately, the special teacher will help the student seek competent assistance in learning material in subject-matter areas if the student is unable to acquire aid. Usually the blind student can be helped on an assignment by the resource teacher who can locate braille references, describe and interpret diagrams, provide special equipment, or explain problem format.

REGULAR CLASSROOM TEACHER IN AN INTEGRATED PROGRAM

Occasionally classroom teachers are anxious about enrolling a blind or partially seeing student in their class. Recollections of folklore about the inadequacies of the blind and the horrors of blindness may make the classroom teacher skeptical of how much he can contribute to the education of a blind child. It remains primarily for the special teacher to provide orientation information which will relieve apprehension about a blind child attending the regular class with his normally sighted peers. This is accomplished through assurances of assistance for the classroom teacher in those areas of instruction in which he feels inadequate or in which he must spend a disproportionate amount of time. Most of the instruction of the visually handicapped child will be done by the classroom teacher. There are some suggested procedures which will aid him in providing the best possible education for all children in his room (Affleck, Lehning, and Brow, 1973).

Knowledge of the Characteristics of Visually Handicapped Children

The classroom teacher must recognize that the blind child has abilities, interests, and needs which are for the most part the same as those of all children. There are, however, a few needs which are unique to those who are blind. For example, the sighted child will be able to examine the physical school environment visually and arrive at some conclusions. The blind child will need to examine the environment through the other senses (primarily tactual and auditory) or accept a verbal report from another person to conclude something about that environment. The two types of data may result in somewhat different conclusions about the composition of the environment. The visually handicapped child will be experiencing and reacting to some interpersonal relationships which are different. The typical sighted adult or child will respond differently to a blind child than to one who is sighted, when the only variable is visual acuity.

A general guideline to the appropriateness of an educational program for visually handicapped is that he be provided with the same basic curriculum which is provided all children. Adaptations and curriculum additions occur mainly by the use of special equipment, textbooks, and development of certain specialized skills which facilitate progress in the general school curriculum. These adaptations are the responsibility of the special teacher. The classroom teacher does have an important function in making the visually handicapped child feel comfortable in ambiguous or anxiety-producing situations. The result should be a student who has the strength and confidence that makes it possible for him to refuse assistance when it isn't needed as well as to request assistance when it is needed.

Unique Classroom Behavior Management Activities
There are some unique requirements of visually handicapped children which are not directly related to subject-matter instruction, but which are necessary for efficient classroom functioning. These suggestions should aid the classroom teacher as well as the visually handicapped child.

The blind or partially seeing child should be required to care for his own material. He should learn to organize his papers and books for easy access and should be held responsible for prompt completion of classroom assignments.

> These children should grow in their responsibility for efficient use and care of their equipment and should be expected to manage all of their books in the classroom without requiring too much help from their teachers or disturbing the other children in the room unless there is a valid reason. (Abel, 1958, p. 317).

It is accepted procedure to insist that blind children also care for personal items, such as clothing, gym shoes, canes, or other equipment used by them in school.

Using a classmate to act as a guide can be a useful technique for minimizing anxiety for the student as well as providing instant assistance. This buddy system can be used to assist the blind child in learning motions to accompany songs, games, in leaving the building during fire and disaster drills, and in taking field trips. It may require the resource or itinerant teacher to provide instruction in the proper guidance technique if the student is blind or has only very limited vision. The buddy system has also been found useful in high school lab classes and gym activities. Discretion must be used in the selection of a student guide to avoid assignment of a guide who is reluctant or resentful. Unnecessary help by classmates should be discouraged.

The classroom teacher should expect the same standards of behavior from the visually handicapped child as from his sighted classmates. Any type of disruptive behavior by the blind or partially seeing child should be resolved immediately. The same rewards and punishments should be applied to these handicapped students as to any child. To allow misbehavior to go uncurbed with the blind child is to invite resentment by the other children because of the obvious injustice.

The blind child should be afforded opportunity for informal conversation with nonhandicapped classmates. This may be during recess, lunch, or immediately preceeding or following classes. This is perhaps more important for blind than sighted students since it stimulates more meaningful interpretation of comments by sighted friends and provides an enriched experience not probable in the exclusive company of blind. Opportunities for informal conversation are also present through participation in extracurricular activities and should be encouraged by the teacher.

The blind or partially seeing child should not be allowed to simply sit while classmates are engaged in an activity. If an activity cannot be adapted, then the teacher should assign another appropriate activity for the visually handicapped child. When these periods occur regularly, they may be used as scheduled periods in the resource room.

The teacher should make the visually handicapped child feel that he is a contributing member of the class by assigning special tasks available in every classroom. These tasks may be distributing and collecting papers and material, watering plants, or delivering messages to other rooms. When calling on children to respond alternately, the teacher should not skip the blind child. He can usually follow the verbal discussion and, with occasional prompting, can determine his turn to respond.

UNIQUE FEATURES OF CLASSROOM INSTRUCTION

Successful instruction of visually handicapped in the classroom requires the use of approximately the same methods as are useful with all children. The few exceptions which are necessary pertain to the methods of exploiting the remaining senses to achieve classroom instructional objectives.

All printed material necessary in the classroom can be brailled and should be available to the blind child if it is considered necessary for sighted classmates. The special teacher is responsible for acquiring this material in braille through the many sources at his disposal. This includes not only textbook and workbook material, but also bulletin board notices, flash cards, and classroom worksheets. It is possible to have some printed material dictated by a sighted classmate to the blind student for brailling. However, discretion must be used so that this activity does not deprive the two students of other necessary classroom experiences.

Visually handicapped children are typically given typing instruction beginning in the elementary grades. Therefore, children who can type should complete classroom written assignments in typed form, with the papers appropriately labeled. Assignments completed by students unable to type may be turned in to the classroom teacher in braille, who in turn has the special teacher transcribe them into print for grading by the classroom teacher. Exams should be completed in braille so that the student may examine his responses after completion of the exam.

Provision should be made to allow visually handicapped children to tactually explore objects displayed in classrooms. Pictures, diagrams, or charts may be described if they convey information which is useful when presented verbally. Occasionally pictures are of ornamental value and only a brief statement of the subject of the picture is necessary. Visually oriented material can sometimes be made tactually interesting through the use of textured material or prominent outlining with dark heavy lines or embossed lines. This may be done with an embossing wheel, stitching, or other means. Blind children comprehend objects which they can hold in their hands better than those objects too large to hold. Opportunities for tactual exploration of objects for the blind child should be provided on field trips as well as in the classroom.

The teacher may describe classroom activities to a blind child, particularly when the child needs to express a preference for an activity. Choices among games, discussion groups, art activities, or other events will require some verbal description in order for the student to make an appropriate choice. With young children, a running conversation by the teacher will benefit the blind child when he is involved in sandbox and other play activity. This provides information about the experiences of the other children which can be enjoyed by the visually handicapped child.

When oral reading is necessary, the visually handicapped child should follow the material read in class in his book. There should be opportunity for the blind child to read aloud also. Participation in contributing to group discussion should be encouraged, perhaps by asking the handicapped student whether he has had similar experiences or how he feels about a particular event or episode. During reading in a primary grade reading circle, a table or place where the blind child may place his book should be available. This is necessary because of the bulk of the book, as well as for reading convenience. Occasionally a sighted student who volunteers may read aloud material that is not available in braille or recorded form, so that a blind child may take notes. This must be done with discretion to avoid situations where the blind child is deprived of participation in other important classroom activities.

The classroom teacher should encourage visually handicapped students to participate in all curricular areas, including physical education, art, industrial arts, and laboratory sciences. The special teacher can provide procedures for necessary adaptations of methods and material. The blind child should not be permitted to simply sit through curricular activities. In those rare occasions when adaptations are not possible, the blind child should be provided some constructive activity to perform.

These suggestions are only a guide to more meaningful integration of the visually handicapped child. There are a myriad of adaptations classroom teachers have made which have enhanced student progress in the milieu of the regular classroom, and no doubt teachers will continue to develop specific adaptations of method and material as idiosyncratic needs of students are recognized.

References

Abel, G. L. The education of blind children. In Cruickshank, W. M. and Johnson, G. O. (eds.). *Education of Exceptional Children.* Englewood Cliffs, New Jersey, Prentice-Hall, Inc., 1958, 295–338.

Affleck, J. Q., Lehning, T. W., and Brow, K. D. Expanding the resource concept: The resource school. *Exceptional Childen, 39,* 1973, 446–55.

American Foundation for the Blind. *The Pine Brook Report.* New York, 1957.

Farrell, G. *The Story of Blindness.* Cambridge, Harvard University Press, 1956.

Jones, J. W. *The Visually Handicapped Child.* Washington, D.C., U.S. Government Printing Office, 1969.

Jones, J. W. and Collins, A. P. *Educational Programs for Visually Handicapped Children.* Washington, D.C., U.S. Government Printing Office, 1966.

Lennon, E. The partially seeing child in a school for the blind. *New Outlook for the Blind, 42,* 1948, 40–45.

Mackie, R. P. and Cohoe, E. *Teachers of Children Who are Partially Seeing.* Washington, D.C., U.S. Government Printing Office, 1956.

Mackie, R. P. and Dunn, L. M. *Teachers of Children Who Are Blind.* Washington, D.C., U.S. Government Printing Office, 1955.

Misbach, D. L. and Sweeney, J. *Education of the Visually Handicapped in California Public Schools.* Sacramento, California Department of Education, 1970.

National Society for the Prevention of Blindness, *Report of the Committee on Education of Partially Seeing Children.* Publication 149. New York, 1952.

4

Use of Severely Limited Vision

One group of visually handicapped students who exhibit unique needs are the partially sighted children. These children have visual deficiency severe enough that they cannot profit completely from educational opportunities provided for the normally seeing. Several wordings of a definition have been used in defining the partially sighted child. Medically and legally, the partially sighted child is defined as those children whose vision falls between 20/70 and 20/200 (on the Snellen Test) in the best eye, with optimal correction. Experience, however, has established that some children with visual acuity which is poorer than 20/200 can see well enough to profit from education by using vision with some specialized equipment and methods provided for the partially sighted child. Likewise, some children whose vision is better than 20/200 have serious visual difficulties that prohibit them from learning through visual media. Therefore, it has become necessary for educational purposes to define the partially sighted child as one who "can use enlarged ink print or limited amounts of regular print under special conditions as media of learning" (Ashcroft, 1963, p. 371). It is therefore essential that the child with limited visual acuity be considered in light of his own needs. That is, he must be carefully screened, diagnosed, and placed in an educational situation in which he will receive the optimal benefit from any specialized instruction.

The techniques, methods, and media used in educating the partially sighted child are very new. As late as 1955, partially sighted children were placed in classes designated as "Sight-Conservation." Up until that time, some educators still believed that use of the eyes by people with limited visual acuity would aggravate existing eye pathologies, thus endangering the remaining vision. Although the first classes for the partially sighted occurred in the United States as early as 1913 (Hathaway, 1959, p. 7), 1955 marked the more general transition toward optimal use of limited vision for partially sighted children. It was noted at that time that:

> Educators became dissatisfied with the visual acuity cut-off points on which many had relied so extensively in the past. They began to seek new criteria for defining, classifying, and placing children (Ashcroft, 1963, p. 372).

Research that followed brought about the advent of new procedures, media, and optical aids to further the abilities of low vision children to use their eyes as a principle mode of instruction.

The primary concern historically has been with the visual acuity of children in determining useful vision. The necessity for a rigorous definition for legal-medical purposes resulted in the widespread use of a measure of acuity relying on the Snellen distance vision chart as the sole measure of useful vision for educational placement purposes. During the last several decades, increased interest has been shown in the factors which influence visual acuity (Westheimer, 1965) and in those variables which can enhance ability to discriminate in spite of poor visual acuity (Barraga, 1964; Cohen, 1962; Institute for Development of Educational Activities, 1969). These factors, together with practices developed by educators, eye specialists, and psychologists, are the basis for this chapter.

It is interesting that in the past less attention was paid to the partially seeing than to the blind, even though those with some remaining vision were and are far more numerous. Statistics indicate that those with sufficiently severe limitations in visual acuity to be classified as partially seeing may number as many as one out of 500 of the school age population (Hathaway, 1959, p. 16). However, initial programs for partially seeing were developed more than fifty years later than for blind. While the first school for blind in the United States was begun in 1832, it was not until 1913 that separate and distinct educational provisions were made for partially seeing children. In many instances children who had some remaining vision, but required braille as a reading mode, were recognized as requiring some special education, although prior to the middle of this century this often involved placement in residential schools for blind. This, however, did not necessarily result in appropriate education for this group of children, in spite of the efforts of such pioneers in education as Winifred Hathaway, who pointed out the inappropriateness of educating partially seeing with blind in residential schools (Hathaway, 1959, pp. 6–7). Eventually practices changed; it is relatively rare today to find a child with sufficient vision for print reading in a residential school for blind.

LOW VISION AIDS

The recognition that use of the eyes in visual discrimination activities does no harm is the basis for the strategy of using vision as much as possible. This is necessary because of the slower reading rates of braille, the alternative method. In attempts to use the remaining vision more efficiently, low vision aids and clinics to teach use of these aids have been developed throughout the United States. The purpose of the clinics is to fit and instruct clients in the use of refractive optical aids, such as magnifiers. The development of low vision aids clinics has been accompanied by the recognition that many children who previously would have functioned as braille readers can now read print as well as use vision in other educational contexts, such as scanning diagrams, charts,

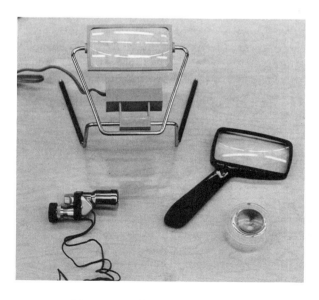

Figure 1. Low Vision Aids

and pictures. These aids are also valued in making independent travel possible; distance refractive lenses can make reading of street names, house numbers, and room numbers possible.

Perhaps some type of distance glass, magnifier, high-plus reading spectacles, or other lenses should be attempted with most of the common eye pathologies. One list of twenty-four common eye pathologies suggests the possibility of using an appropriate lens in almost all of the twenty-four cases (New York Lighthouse for the Blind, 1969). It would appear that some degree of myopia accompanies many other eye pathologies, although by no means all.

EDUCATIONAL SIGNIFICANCE
OF PARTIAL SIGHTEDNESS

The admission of a child into a special education program for the partially seeing depends on (1) having visual acuity between 20/70 and 20/200 in the better eye after all medical and usual optical aid has been provided, and (2) being unable to function with normally seeing peers in regular class (Hathaway, 1959, p. 17). Although grouping of these children has been done according to the specifications above, partially seeing children are basically sighted children; and education should orient them to operate as much as possible as seeing children. Children who are born blind learn to see by interpreting the physical and psychological world without the use of vision. Those with severely limited vision learn to use the minimal vision available, and the disability has a modifying influence on the development of the child and on the method used in education. It must be kept in mind that the child may be otherwise normal, a complete and physical whole, organized to function on his own level of achievement with the sensory equipment at his disposal.

It has been estimated that 80 percent of the work a child does in school is built around close visual activity. Defective vision can influence a child's personality, behavior, and health if it interferes with his participation in routine classroom activities and thus prevents him from attaining a satisfactory level of achievement (Pelone, 1957, p. 13).

The extent to which a partially seeing child can adjust and achieve in a regular class is an individual matter and dependent upon useable residual vision, interests, and capacities. Research has not always shown a perfect positive correlation between severity of physical disability and severity of resultant educational, vocational, and social problems (Siegal, 1969, p. 5).

ORGANIZATIONAL PLANS FOR
EDUCATION OF PARTIALLY SEEING

Beginning with the first class for partially seeing children in 1913, these children have been placed in one of several types of school programs. These are: (1) residential schools for the blind which have a department for the partially seeing, (2) special schools for all handicaps where "sight-saving" classes make up an integral part of the school organization, (3) special classes in local public schools where activities are confined to a single class of partially seeing, and (4) integrated programs using a resource, itinerant, or teacher-counselor as a supporting teacher for the regular classroom teacher. The primary difference between the resource room program, on the one hand, and itinerant or teacher-counselor, on the other, is that the resource teacher is available to provide supporting help in a building during the entire day, whereas the itinerant teacher or teacher-counselor is responsible for several buildings and hence is available for shorter periods of time per building (Pelone, 1957, pp. 3–4).

The shift from full-time special classes prevalent in local school programs prior to 1946 to the more fully integrated resource and itinerant teacher patterns show that children with poor visual acuity can function in regular classes. Prior to 1946, 70 percent of the programs for visually handicapped had units which provided special instruction and other services to the partially seeing exclusively, rather than servicing both blind and partially seeing in the same program (Jones and Collins, 1966, pp. 14–15).

METHODS FOR EFFICIENT USE OF VISION
BY PARTIALLY SEEING CHILDREN

The movement to change teaching procedures for the partially sighted from sight-saving to specialized methods using vision led to the emergence of many studies about teaching the partially sighted. Evolving from these studies were several new procedures, including instruction methods, material, and special physical room arrangements. Of contemporary interest are methods of efficient use of vision.

Among the more prominent studies in use of vision as it relates to partially seeing children is one by Natalie Barraga in 1963. The study resulted in the development of a procedure for systematically instructing visually handicapped children to learn to discriminate visually. The hypothesis which was tested and confirmed was: "That a short period of experimental teaching would enhance the visual behavior of blind children with remaining vision to the extent that there would be a significant increase in Visual Discrimination Test Scores." (Barraga, 1964, p. 32.) The children used in the study had very little residual vision. Residual vision was defined as

"... any degree of vision which, though not describable in numerical terms, could be clinically described as light perception, object perception, or counts fingers, and was sufficient to enable the individual to discriminate and recognize visually suitable materials within his low vision range." (Barraga, 1964, p. 4.)

The ages of the children were between six and thirteen years, with tested intelligence in the normal range and no other physical impairments.

For purposes of the study, a visual discrimination test and a series of daily lesson plans were developed which were used for a period of eight weeks in the program. (See sample lesson in appendix B.) Results of the study indicated that blind children with remaining vision can improve their visual discrimination ability useful in education if given appropriate instruction. While there is no improvement in visual acuity, the study concluded that visual efficiency can be improved. There are a number of variables determining visual efficiency. These include: (1) attention in order to bring the stimuli within visual range, (2) awareness and recognition of visual form, which involves cortical and emotional factors, (3) response as an indication that learning is occurring, (4) satisfaction, an emotional component, which determines the success or failure of the learning process, and (5) repetition, the means by which learning patterns are fully established (Barraga, 1964, p. 14). It was concluded that if one of the variables is missing, visual efficiency may not reach maximum level of development. The results of the study indicated that children with limited vision can be helped substantially by specialized methods and through visual means of instruction. This investigation led to the publishing of instructional material by the American Printing House for the Blind which would improve the visual discrimination ability of visually handicapped. It also led to several regional workshops for teachers.

The regional workshops initiated in 1971 to develop and use material similar to those in the Barraga study also resulted in a *Visual Efficiency Scale.* This scale contains forty-eight separate items in eighteen separate areas of visual discrimination. (See appendix D for a list of visual training areas.) When the scale is administered to a child, a graph profile of his visual skills is developed. This in turn aids in isolating areas of instruction in the development of visual discrimination skills (U.S. Office of Education/Michigan State University, 1971).

Much thought and care must be used in selecting the specialized physical equipment necessary in the classroom for the partially sighted child. Classroom environment is important to the educational achievement of partially seeing children (Hathaway, 1959). Besides adequacy of working space, partially seeing children require extra storage space and unique equipment. While natural light is desirable for classroom purposes, adequate artificial illumination should be provided as an alternative to allow for variation in amount or intensity of light. There are children with pathologies such as albinism which require less intensity of light, and others which require more than normal intensity. While specific needs must be determined by individual classroom situations, a minimum of thirty footcandles is recommended for regular classrooms, with fifty footcandles for the partially sighted child (Hathaway, 1959, p. 92). (A footcandle is the amount of light received from a standard candle on a surface one foot from the light source in any direction.) The color of the walls and ceiling in a classroom also deserve consideration, and color adds significantly to classroom efficiency (Hathaway, 1959, p. 97). Recommendations for room colors have commonly resulted in rooms painted in pastel colors with white ceilings to reflect the light. The paint should be a flat variety to reduce glare. Desks and chairs may be of a fairly light neutral color in a dull finish. Desks should be adjustable for height and angle of work and positioned so that the work can be brought close to the eyes while preventing poor posture. There are several types of desks which have tops which tilt.

For written work, unglazed cream manila paper that is slightly rough is recommended. Lined paper should allow three-fourths to one inch between the lines in the primary grades. Students may use soft lead pencils, grease pencils, or felt-tip marking pencils for ease in writing and reading. Large-size soft white chalk is used for chalkboard work on either the green or black chalkboards. Typewriters are essential in the classroom of the partially sighted child, preferably with large type size.

INSTRUCTIONAL METHODS AND MATERIALS

There are a number of methods and materials unique to the education of partially sighted children. In addition to some specialized reading material which will be discussed later, materials for optimal use of vision have been developed. The visually impaired child learns through his visual and, to a lesser extent, tactual senses. Therefore, maps and diagrammatic information must be enlarged and printed in large clear black lines with relatively little detail for easy discrimination. Globes and maps which are embossed or raised to conform to topographic features are also available. It may be desirable for the teacher to outline significant features of a graph, chart, or diagram with a black marking pencil or felt-tip marker for ease of visual discrimination. Occasionally students may construct details of surface features on maps with clay or plasticine to aid recognition.

Many other media of instruction are used in teaching the partially sighted child. Among these are slides which are projected on a screen. The teacher should include slides which are relatively free of large amounts of background material. Simplicity is of great importance, with clear, legible, and contrasting lettering with wide margins. Marking pencils or felt-tip markers to outline on paper the significant aspects should be available to the student. Movies and television are also excellent media of instruction. Television in particular is appropriate because the student can sit and view it from close range without obscuring the picture. In any viewing, the teacher should make provision for rest periods, since fatigue is common.

There are also several types of audio aids available from the American Printing House in the catalog *Recorded Educational Aids to Learning* as well as from other sources. These enrich and supplement the classroom instruction and include a wide range of subject matter presented in dramatized style in many cases. Certainly other audio devices such as tape recorders, record players, and talking books should be considered also. The teacher must use discretion in the use of these aids, however, to avoid use of these to the exclusion of reading. Practice in reading is necessary to constantly improve reading rate and comprehension.

LARGE PRINT BOOKS

One of the more effective media in the teaching of the partially sighted child is enlarged print. This can be done for any reading material by various firms, which provide estimates of cost on request.

The first effort at enlarging print was made by Dr. Robert Irwin in Cleveland. Irwin did extensive research on type size and directed the production of books which were printed in 36-point clearface type which had been designed by the American Type Founders Company. When reception by teachers proved unenthusiastic, Irwin continued his research and seven years later published the Century Schoolbook and Caslon Bold types in 24-point clearface type. While many details of this study are unclear, the results of his work influenced the development of large type print (Eakin and McFarland, 1960, pp. 3–4). No further research on type size was done for twenty-three years, when Ethel Fortner, of the Oregon State School for the Blind published a study which compared the ease of reading material in 18- and 24-point type under standardized conditions. The 18-point type size approximates typewriter letter in "bulletin" or "primary" size type. The results did not demonstrate significant differences between use of the two sizes of type. Subsequently, a study conducted by Evelyn M. Carpenter (Eakin and McFarland, 1960, p. 7) with the aid of Mergenthaler Lithograph Corporation resulted in the formation of Stanwix House as a publisher of large-type books. The year 1946 saw the first publication by offset lithography, enabling books to be photographed in larger sizes without resetting type. Stanwix House adopted the use of height of ascender above body line for measuring type size, and this standard of measurement is used today for large-type edition publications for the partially sighted. The most recent study of large type was conducted by Nolan (1959) in three residential schools in Ohio, Illinois, and Kentucky. This research studied the two factors of type size and type style. Type size studies compared the ease of reading 18 point and 24 point. Type style research compared the effect of sans-serif type (Metromedium Style) with a serif face (Antique Old Style). Major findings of this study were that: (1) visually handicapped were able to read serif typeface faster than sans-serif type; (2) children with visual acuity 20/70 read more rapidly then those with visual acuity 20/200; and (3) there was not sufficient evidence to prove there is a difference in reading speed between 18- and 24-point type. The historical development of large type for the partially sighted saw the evolution of four major studies on print enlargement: the Cleveland study by Irwin, the Fortner study, the Stanwix studies, and the study by Nolan (Eakin, Pratt, and McFarland, 1961).

There are today several producers of large-type print (See appendix C). These include the American Printing House (APH) as well as com-

18' Futura Medium
18' Century Schoolbook
24' Futura Medium
24' Century Schoolbook

Figure 2.   Type Samples

mercial publishers. When large-type books were first produced, publishers were reluctant to offer many titles, as it was believed there would
be little demand. However, the number of people in need of large-type
material has been greater than originally anticipated, and a number of
commercial publishers have entered this phase of publishing. Some
commercial microfilm companies will supply single or multiple copies
of books in a wide variety of print sizes. Whatever method of reproduction and selection of reading materials is used, the main consideration
should be that each child should read the smallest type he can with
minimum inconvenience and discomfort.

Teachers of the partially sighted children have available to them a
multitude of resources. A wide variety of materials are produced for the
education of the partially sighted child. The Instructional Materials
Reference Center for the Visually Handicapped at the American Printing House for the Blind (APH) has a complete listing of all available
materials in large type, as well as other sources of large-type material.
APH is the largest single available source of textbooks and other material for visually handicapped children in elementary and secondary
schools, as well as of tests of achievement, intelligence, and aptitude.

The teacher of the partially sighted child needs to remember that the
child is an individual and should strive to provide activities that are
self-directing and independent, a goal that can be achieved with the
many aids to teaching which are available to visually handicapped
children from both specialized and nonspecialized sources. Of particular
significance with reference to print size are the preprimers, primers,
phonics flashcards, word recognition cards, math flashcards, and the
many readers which have larger than typical print and are available
from normal education publishers. It is therefore possible for a teacher
of the partially sighted to obtain teaching material in his own school
library as well as to order from specialized publishers of large-type
material.

OPTICAL AIDS

The trend to use the residual vision of partially sighted children has
resulted in greater use of optical aids. The use of optical aids helps the
visually handicapped child to develop and use his vision to the greatest
possible degree. To facilitate this purpose, optical aids or low vision aid
clinics have been established.

The optical aids clinic is typically staffed with a team of professionals
which includes a resident ophthalmologist, a consultant ophthalmologist, an optometrist, and a social worker. In the clinic, patients are

examined, fitted, and trained to use various optical aids that will help them achieve the maximum use of their remaining vision. There are several advantages to being treated in a clinic rather than in a physician's office. First, the patient receives the help of several professionals, all of them experts in their fields. In addition, two or three extended visits are required, which may be more than would be possible in a physician's office. The social worker is often helpful in understanding a patient's limitations, dealing with motivations and fears, and interpreting background social information involved in using optical aids. The clinic also provides for professional evaluation of data along with a therapeutic approach to help counteract negative attitudes and help establish positive rapport with the patients. The selection, fitting, and training in the use of optical aids is a slow process that requires a great deal of time and patience. The clinic provides a visually handicapped child with the facilities and personnel to provide the best possible aid.

The many professional examinations made by planning teams must be properly evaluated before an optical aid can be prescribed. Primary criteria in determining whether a patient needs, and can use, an aid is a distance acuity measure determined by a cycloplegic refraction. This is an examination to determine refractive errors of the eye and correction by optical aids. It provides an index by which success or failure of optical aids will be achieved. Secondly, it is important to note how recently the person has lost his vision. Newly blinded persons are more difficult to fit than those with a congenital problem. Age also is an important factor in evaluating need, as children are more adaptable than adults. In addition to these factors, the patient's needs must be considered. It is important to know whether the patient will need help in school, at work, or solely for pleasure. Each factor must be carefully considered (Gordon, Silberman, Mintz, and Gaynes, 1964).

One of the variables in selecting an aid is the degree of magnification. The power of a magnifying device can be estimated by the following formula (Gettes, 1958, p. 81):

$$\text{Suggested power in diopters} = \frac{\text{Denominator of Snellen Fraction}}{10}$$

$$\text{Example:} \quad \text{Visual acuity} = 20/400$$
$$\text{Lens power} = 400/10 = 40 \text{ diopters}$$

The magnification, or power, of a magnifying device, or lens, is found by dividing ten by the focal length of the lens. The focal length of the lens and the working distance (i.e., the distance between the lens and the object when the image is sharply defined) are essentially synonymous. Hence, a lens with a focal length of four inches is a 2.5X or 2.5 power lens. Four diopters is equivalent to one unit of magnification or power (Gordon and Ritter, 1955, p. 705).

Magnifying lenses are always convex. Concave lenses have the power to diverge parallel rays of light and are used to correct refractive errors in myopia or near-sightedness. These lenses are also known as diverging lenses or minus lenses. Convex lenses have the power to converge parallel rays of light and to bring them into focus and are used to correct refractive errors in hyperopia as well as to provide magnification in low vision aids. These lenses are also known as converging lenses or plus lenses. There is a third type of lens used merely to change the direction of light rays, a prismatic lens. The eye specialist determines the kind and strength of magnification needed by the patient.

A distinction is made between lenses used for correcting refractive errors and magnification. Any magnification resulting from correcting a refractive error with a plus (hyperopia) lens is incidental to the primary function of aiding accommodation for seeing print within normal reading distances. Additional magnification beyond normal correction of refractive errors involves either telescopic or microscopic magnification (Gordon and Ritter, 1955, p. 704).

There are many kinds of optical aids available to assist those with visual limitations. The most common are the high plus lenses. These can be of great magnification, beginning at 5:00 diopters and extending up to and beyond 20 diopters. The patient's needs determine the specific type of optical aid. A variation in the type of lens which has proven particularly useful is the contact lens. This has been useful to patients with high myopia, astigmatism, keratoconus, corneal scarring, and certain other pathologies. The fitting of contact lenses is an exact and tedious process with the low vision patient and can take six to eight weeks to accomplish. Other optical aids which have proven useful are (1) *the loupe,* an ordinary convex lens used as a hand reading glass which has some limited use; (2) *spectacle magnifiers,* ordinary glasses fitted to give one or both eyes a closer focus; (3) *telescopic aids,* an appliance that can clip over the lens of an ordinary eye glass; (4) *triple aplanats,* a double-convex lens of crown glass between two negative lenses of flint, which is inserted completely through the lens and positioned so as to correspond to the patient's usual reading level; and (5) *projection enlargers,* used in the classroom in the magnification of opaque material by projection.

There are many misconceptions and controversies regarding the use of the eyes. These can often be overcome during visits to a low vision aids clinic. Some of these misconceptions about the use of the eyes are: (1) It is harmful to the eyes to hold print too close. The fact is that holding material closer for reading gives added magnification. (2) Strong glasses harm eyes. This has no physiological basis. (3) Using the eyes causes deterioration of pathological conditions present. This would be true in only rare cases which would be clearly stated by the physician.

Once a patient has been examined and an optical aid prescribed, it is important that proper training in its use be given. A great deal of patience is required if the person is to be successful in using an optical aid. Often clinics will let a person try a loupe or other optical aid before prescribing one specific one. It may be necessary for the visually handicapped person to return to the clinic several times to complete proper fitting of an aid.

The process of acquiring low vision aids may be quite expensive. Fortunately, expenses involved in this circumstance are borne by social and public health agencies in cases where family income prevents private acquisition of the service. It is important to contact the state agency responsible for services to blind in cases where financial hardship prevents children from receiving these or other services.

EDUCATION OF PARTIALLY SIGHTED CHILDREN

During the past few years there has been an increased movement away from the segregated self-contained room for blind and partially seeing children. Instead, educators have recognized that the visually impaired are more like than unlike their sighted peers, and integrated programs for education have developed (Jones and Collins, 1966, pp. 9–10). There has also been concern for the detrimental effects of limiting interaction to only other visually handicapped children. These children are now given the opportunity to participate in social and other activities with both normally sighted and visually handicapped children. This is desirable both for the visually handicapped child and his normally seeing peer. The sighted classmate will learn early what the true nature of blindness is in terms of functioning. The handicapped child learns how to relate to those children who are sighted, to their mutual benefit.

The amount of time that the typical teacher will spend with these children depends on the number and characteristics of the visually handicapped population and the type of education program organized in the local school. In rural areas or small towns, where the number of visually handicapped students is small, the child may have to attend a residential school for some portion of his education because the facilities at the local public school are inadequate. Partially seeing children should rarely, if ever, require residential placement. Those children who are visually impaired as well as having other handicaps may require placement in a residential school, and with increasing frequency this is the type of child who is admitted to the residential school. Some schools may employ an itinerant teacher who travels from school to school and supplements the instruction provided by the regular classroom teacher. Administrators tend to favor this plan since the number of visually handicapped children is sparse and scattered in the typical community. In larger communities, the visually handicapped may receive service from a special teacher at scheduled times during the school day. Jones (1969) refers to this as the resource room plan.

Increasingly the practice is for visually handicapped children to start school as early as possible. This usually means that they can start as soon as they are toilet trained. Initially the instruction may be presented in the home, but prior to kindergarten the child may enter a program in a classroom. For the first few years in school, the child may spend much of his day with non-visually handicapped children. The early beginning is valuable in allowing the visually handicapped child more time to acquire the social and motor skills which other children acquire incidentally. Particular emphasis is placed on reading, writing, and arithmetic (as is the case with non-handicapped children). If the child has no other impairments than vision, he will learn to write either in braille or print. As the student becomes more proficient in these special areas, he will spend more of his time in regular classes where skill in these areas continues to be developed.

When visually handicapped children are included in the regular class-room, there are procedures the classroom teacher can follow which will facilitate the instruction of these children. The regular classroom teacher may have the child for substantial parts of the day and has an important part to play in the education process. Recognizing this responsibility, the teacher will want to be prepared to do the most that he can for his handicapped students. Consultation with the school nurse will determine any medication or treatment underway, if a special teacher is not available. The special teacher (itinerant or resource) can describe the educational functioning, degree of vision, and resources available. The classroom teacher may also use the services of the school counselor concerning the visually handicapped student's scholastic achievements and social adjustment, as he would with any student in the classroom.

Depending upon the age of the children in the regular classroom, and their exposure to visual handicaps, it may be helpful to discuss the new student and his handicap with the class. In this process the teacher may uncover stereotyped attitudes which may prove detrimental to the handicapped child's school functioning.

The teacher's attitude toward the child is very important. If he caters to him or is oversolicitous toward him, the handicapped child and other members of his class have been treated unfairly, which may cause resentment. To avoid this, the teacher should evaluate the child on the basis of his behavior and achievement. "There are signs of a potential renaissance and a new era in the education of visually impaired children. The focus of attention is on re-examining the educationally significant attributes of visual impairment." (Ashcroft, 1963, p. 371.) The child should share equally in any classroom work to demonstrate to the class and to the visually handicapped child that he is a useful, functioning member. Sometimes inventiveness on the part of the teacher is required for meaningful experiences in collaboration with other class members, but this should be true of the teacher's relationships with all children.

Once the child becomes a member of the class, there are some physical provisions to be arranged. Preferential seating for the partially seeing child will only be necessary if the visual loss is minimal and the child can comfortably see the chalkboard and other charts, demonstrations, bulletin boards, and chalkboard from his seat, or be permitted to walk up to these displays without feelings of inhibition (Hathaway, 1959, p. 100–2). The teacher should also avoid having the child work on highly polished surfaces, because the glare may create visual discomfort. Glossy pictures or plastic-covered pictures and charts may cause the same discomfort. The diagrams and pictures and other visual displays presented to the partially seeing child should be clear and relatively uncluttered by much background detail.

Aids to reading become increasingly important to the partially seeing child as the volume of reading increases. The teacher needs to be aware of the availability of reading stands and easels specially designed for use with books. Desks should be arranged so that natural light may be used. Care should be taken to seat the child so that shadows do not develop on the working area, unless the child prefers light dimmer than normal room lighting for some work.

When completing written work, the teacher should allow rest periods because of fatigue resulting from intensive visual concentration. This involves planning a variety of activities to take advantage of the rest periods. Oral drills can be used with spelling and arithmetic as is true with students in a normal classroom. Students can also use the chalkboard for working problems. Most students enjoy working at the chalkboard periodically. Recreational activities may also provide relief from intensive visual activity.

Writing for these children should be large and clear when handwritten or when typed. When these children work at the chalkboard, they may use soft white chalk which is somewhat larger than the standard chalk. When writing at a desk, children may use soft black lead pencils or felt-tip markers which provide a broader line. Oversize crayons are also available for artwork and other activities (Pelone, 1957, pp. 34–46).

Most visually handicapped children begin learning to type with a typewriter soon after the primary grades. This is a valuable asset for transcribing classroom materials into more legible form. The student, whether he is partially seeing or blind, will find the typewriter useful in completing homework assignments as well as for personal writing chores. Sometimes these children find it more convenient to take exams on the typewriter, and this option should be available to them.

The school program should build the child's confidence. There will, of course, be certain types of activity where the child's vision handicap will limit the extent to which he can function and his performance level will not be commensurate with that of his peers. The child must be helped to accept this difference and realize that each individual differs in his abilities. Realistic knowledge of one's abilities, and a positive concept of self, leave an individual free to pursue courses of action appropriate to the fulfillment of goals which have been planned in education.

References

Ashcroft, S. C. A new era in education and a paradox in research for the visually limited. *Exceptional Children, 29,* 1963, 371–76.

Barraga, N. *Increased Visual Behavior in Low Vision Children.* New York, American Foundation for the Blind, Research series #13, 1964.

Cohen, A. S. A dynamic theory of vision. *Journal of Developmental Reading, VI,* 1962, 15–25.

Eakin, W. M. and McFarland, T. L. *Type, Printing, and the Partially Seeing Child.* Pittsburgh, Stanwix House, 1960.

Eakin, W. M., Pratt, R. J., and McFarland, T. L. *Type Size Research for the Partially Seeing Child.* Pittsburgh, Stanwix House, 1961.

Gettes, B. C. Optical aids for low vision. *Sight-Saving Review, 28,* 1958, 81–83.

Gordon, A. H., Silberman, C., Mintz, M. J., and Gaynes, E. Why a low vision clinic? *New Outlook for the Blind, 58,* 1964, 54–57.

Gordon, D. M. and Ritter, C. Magnification. *A.M.A. Archives of Ophthalmology, 54,* 1955, 704–16.

Hathaway, W. *Education and Health of the Partially Seeing Child.* (Revised by F. M. Foote, Dorothy Bryan, and Helen Gibbons.) New York, Columbia University Press, 1959.

Institute for Development of Educational Activities, Inc. *Report of an International Seminar: The Role of the Ophthalmologist in Dyslexia.* Melbourne, Florida, 1969.

Jones, J. W. *The Visually Handicapped Child.* Washington, D.C., U.S. Government Printing Office, 1969.

Jones, J. W. and Collins, A. *Educational Programs for Visually Handicapped Children.* Washington, D.C., U.S. Government Printing Office, 1966.

New York Lighthouse for the Blind. *A Worker's Guide to Characteristics of Partial Sight.* New York, 1969.

Nolan, C. Y. Readability of large types: A study of type sizes and type styles. *International Journal for the Education of the Blind, 9,* 1959, 41–44.

Pelone, A. J. *Helping the Visually Handicapped Child in a Regular Class.* New York, Columbia University, 1957.

Siegal, E. *Special Education in the Regular Classroom.* New York, The John Day Company, Inc., 1969.

U.S. Office of Education/Michigan State University, Regional Instructional Materials Center for Handicapped Children and Youth. *Workshop Coordinators Guide.* East Lansing, Michigan, 1971.

Westheimer, G. Visual acuity. In *Annual Review of Psychology.* P. R. Farnsworth, (ed.) Palo Alto, California, Annual Reviews Inc., *XVI,* 1965, 359–80.

5

Reading Instruction

Reading is a complex process, whether it is accomplished visually or tactually. Many of the concepts and generalizations that have been applied to the teaching of reading to sighted children apply equally to the teaching of reading to blind children. Before beginning reading instruction, both blind and sighted children must have achieved a certain level in intellectual, physical, and emotional development in order to profit. Some differences in learning to read by blind arise because of certain reading readiness factors. Emphasis on auditory and tactual discrimination, in contrast to visual and auditory discrimination in the seeing child, appears to create slower language development and a smaller breadth of experiences with blind children (Nolan and Kederis, 1969, p. 43). Basic growth in certain areas of experience may still be under way in the upper elementary grades for blind, while these achievements are practically complete for their seeing peers. Skills may be retarded and reading may be fairly mechanical even at upper elementary levels. The teacher's task then is one of exploiting the basic maturational processes to allow the child to make more rapid growth in reading skills.

PRESCHOOL READINESS FOR READING

Lack of vision creates a hurdle in terms of language development. Opportunities for experiences necessary to language development and the related progress toward independence and emotional stability are a major burden of the parents, but one which can be shared with the teacher once the child enters school. From the time the infant first notices sounds and objects around him until he begins to form concepts, the parents will need to facilitate his language development. This development begins with listening in such areas as the infant's ability to distinguish praise, love, disapproval, questioning, and the voices of those around him. It is vital for the development of language in the blind child that he be afforded verbal contact while still an infant. Parents and others should remember that unless verbal contact with the child is maintained continuously, his opportunity for communication will be severely restricted. Constant physical contact with the blind infant may be impractical, and often unnecessary from the language development point of view, so a desirable alternative is to maintain verbal contact. Even while in another room, an infant can benefit greatly if he can hear the parent humming, singing, or talking to himself.

As the blind child grows older and can understand what others are saying, the importance of verbal contact increases. Verbal communication develops in a child as comprehension increases. Often when parents are doing chores around the house, working on hobbies, or even reading the paper, they forget that the blind preschooler will not be aware of what the parent is doing unless he is told. There are many tasks and experiences that seeing children learn and participate in through visual observation that must be deliberately explained or demonstrated to blind children.

The blind preschooler has two primary avenues by which he gathers information and develops mentally and emotionally: sound and touch. Norms establishing the degree to which a preschool blind child discriminates auditorially have not been determined. Therefore, teachers will need to develop informal evaluation methods in order to know where to begin instruction. Auditory discrimination begins with and parallels language development. The blind child must be capable of discrimination between sounds in terms of information and physical and emotional reactions. He must learn when to be careful, happy, afraid, exhibit love, and when to respond with a question. Every sound elicits some reaction, either passive or active. When a blind child hears a car traveling by his house, he must be able to conclude "That is a car, it is not a freight train, not an airplane, not a whistle, not my mother's voice—it's a car."

If a child learns to recognize these differences in sound during pre-school years, he will be ready for greater discrimination in school. He will be able to hear initial and final sounds within words and detect subtle sound differences between words as formal instruction begins with the teacher.

Tactual discrimination contributes little to growth until the child is actually able to discriminate differences in texture, form, or shape (Lowenfeld, Abel, and Hatlen, 1969, p. 128). When he picks up a favorite stuffed animal, he must be able to internalize: "This is my favorite stuffed animal. I can tell by its feel. It is not my mother's hand. It is not a spoon. It is not the leg of a table. It is my favorite stuffed animal."

The ability of a blind child to move from place to place within his environment, whether it be bedroom, entire house, back yard, the block on which he lives, or the entire community, will affect in many ways his language growth and development. There are examples of blind babies who at five or six years have never been allowed outside their playpens or cribs. Under these circumstances of limited experiences with the environment, it is doubtful whether these children would be ready for school at the usual school entrance age. It is widely recognized that "the ability of the child to move within his environment, to explore things, to become familiar with objects, to be motivated toward sounds and objects is basic to both language development and auditory and tactual discrimination." (Lowenfeld, Abel, and Hatlen, 1969, p. 129.)

The seeing child can explore his environment visually long before he can walk. The blind child, who must touch objects in order to observe them, must be able to move about in order to explore. He should be encouraged. However, any child must have reason to move and the movement must result in some satisfaction. The satisfaction may be nothing more than retrieval of a lost toy, finding a lost brother or sister, or location of a lost pet. Whatever the reason, there must be some reward in moving so that motivation for future movement grows. The child may also be required to move in the home to gain the satisfaction of fulfilling a family obligation. The young blind child, as well as the seeing child, should be given duties at home that benefit the entire family, which will enhance his self-image as a contributing member of the family. This will aid his emotional and mental development so that he will be able to comprehend and establish relationships between objects and experiences. During this process of establishing new contacts in the environment, and the concomitant verbal interaction, the child acquires an ever-increasing ability to use language which is meaningful to him.

Intelligence and ability to read are highly correlated in all children. However, symptoms of low intelligence and developmental retardation are very similar. Neither the child with low intellectual ability nor the blind child who is developmentally retarded will be ready to read when children are generally expected to perform this task. The teacher of blind children should reserve opinions on the intellectual level of the child with whom he is working until he has exhausted every possibility that the child is not developmentally retarded (Lowenfeld, Abel, and Hatlen, 1969, p. 134).

Blind children, long before they are of school age, should be made aware of braille. Sighted children have many experiences with print before they enter school—TV, billboards, books, labels, newspapers, magazines. Anything with printed words affects his motivation, curiosity, and readiness to read. The blind child, in contrast, regardless of his readiness in other respects, will not have braille presented in the incidental fashion in which print is presented. As a matter of fact, the typical blind child is presented the braille character for the first time following entrance to school.

There is no reason why many of the books a parent reads to his blind preschooler should not be available in braille and placed in the hands of the child. (These can be obtained from a variety of sources listed in appendix C.) He does not need to learn to read at this point, but he is learning that there are tactual forms of words that have meaning—word meaning, story meaning, and experience meaning. This can also be done by writing the words over the symbols in any braille book—a task which can be done by volunteer braillists, friends, a teacher of braille, or others—so that it can be read to the child by anyone at any time.

Blind children should have labels on important things in their environment, particularly those things that are of functional value to them. Pasting a label on a toy box or record shelf with the appropriate braille word creates motivation to read. There is no reason why he should not find in braille those words which sighted children find in their environment. Toys, household objects, articles of clothing, and other items can be labelled for color. This is not teaching reading; it is simply exposing a blind child to the medium he will soon be reading. He will begin to understand that objects in his environment have names which cannot only be verbalized but which can also be written. This only makes up in part for the casual opportunities seeing children have to meet printed letters and words.

SCHOOL READING READINESS

In school, readiness for reading may need to be determined without formal evaluation methods. The teacher must use informal methods for determining when a blind child is ready to read. Commonly by the time a blind child enters school, his verbal skills should be at a level in which he can speak clearly enough to be understood, ask pertinent questions with more than one-word answers, and communicate information such as his name, address, and the names of his siblings. He should be able to follow directions, take turns, assume responsibility for certain positions in a game, move from one place to another, and observe either auditorially or tactually in a careful sequential manner. All these have an influence on his development and all have a bearing on his readiness for school, as do familiarity with playground equipment and ability to use basic play equipment such as a tricycle, wagon, roller skates, and play equipment which requires less activity, such as beads, pegboards, scissors, and clay. An interest in stories and the ability to relate play to experiences is also important.

Interacting with others in a group requires experience, and it is perhaps true that there is no more difficult adjustment for the kindergarten blind child than to attempt to work and play as a member of a larger group if he has not had prior experience with at least a few other children. The ability to work and play, to give and take, to know when to respond and when not to, is difficult for seeing children and may be even more difficult for blind children. It is not unusual for a blind child in kindergarten to speak out in class, move about freely, and demonstrate a general lack of recognition that he is one of many within the group. This may mean he has never had the experience of having to share the attentions of an adult or be responsible to a larger group of children. For the blind child who has had the undivided and unshared attention of doting parents, the problems presented by sharing one teacher with many other children can be difficult. For the blind child who has become accustomed to getting what he wants when he wants it, the formal school situation can be almost unbearable. This is not necessarily the exclusive problem of blind children, but the emotional environment in which the blind child grows may cause additional stress.

The reading readiness program in school generally considers the continued growth of the factors basic to reading readiness: auditory and tactual discrimination, language development, and general experiences. Obstacles to development in these areas may result in slower reading progress.

AUDITORY PERCEPTION IN READING READINESS

The blind child must be able to do more than listen and comprehend spoken language. He must be able to make discriminations, to hear that different words sound alike, or that they begin or end with the same sound. He must recognize phrasing in sentences and rhythm of words. There are many games and activities that can strengthen auditory perception and discrimination and may be used either with blind children alone or with both blind and sighted children. Below is a list of activities to enhance sound discrimination and perception. These may be used from time to time with sighted children blindfolded for these games.

1. Good morning game. One child stands in front of the room, while the rest change their seats. Another child is touched by the leader, and says "good morning" to the child in front, who then guesses who spoke.

2. Find the hidden music box. A music box is placed in the room and the first child to locate it is the winner.

3. The students respond to loud and soft tones; high, medium, and low pitch; and various rhythms.

4. The teacher plays sound effect records and the students identify the sounds.

5. The teacher plays tape-recorded sounds which suggest a story and asks the children to tell a story around the sounds.

6. Rhyming exercises. The teacher says, "What will I do if I spill the ink?" and child must answer with a statement that rhymes, such as, "Wash your clothes out in the sink."

7. The teacher asks students to identify a word, such as "story," whenever it occurs in a narrative over a period of time. Each time the teacher uses the word, the first child who raises his hand gets a point.

8. The teacher shows a tray with ten objects that make a noise. He demonstrates each item, asking the children to try to remember all of them. Then he sees how many they can remember by sound.

9. The teacher can read stories that draw attention to the value of listening to sounds, words, letters or sentences, and stories with plots which depict a breakdown in communication due to faulty listening.

10. The children can make up stories, but instead of telling them with words, they can tell them with sounds.

11. To sharpen sensitivity to listening, the pupils make lists of "What Interfered with Our Listening Today?" such as a lawnmower outside during class or people interrupting.

12. The teacher makes up poems and stories with obvious ending words missing, with children offering any logical rhyming word.

An example would be "Once there was a little mouse. He lived in a little _____."

13. The children clap at every word which rhymes with a predetermined word. Words that rhyme with "bat" in the book *The Cat in the Hat* by Dr. Seuss would be an illustration.

14. Gossip. One child whispers a sentence to next child, who whispers to the next, etc. The last child tells what he heard and the first child tells what he said. The children compare to see how well they whisper and listen.

15. The teacher can play some beautiful recorded music such as the "Nutcracker Suite" and have children paint or model clay while listening.

16. Round Robin story. One child tells the first sentence of a story, the second creates the next, and so on until the last child or the teacher ends it.

17. The class can listen to recordings and dramatize ideas suggested by the music.

18. The teacher reads a poem such as *The Sugar Plum Tree* by Eugene Field, and the children imitate as many objects as they can remember.

19. Children can listen to and reproduce their favorite TV commercials and then change them to suit themselves.

20. The pupils interpret music with rhythm instruments.

21. Courtesies in society. The children dramatize social courtesies, such as introducing a man to a man or a child to an adult and answering the phone properly.

22. The teacher can scramble oral sentences and have children arrange the words in the correct order.

23. The teacher reads a short paragraph containing several words that have the same or similar meanings. The children pick out these words. An example would be "Soon the *little* man came to a *small* dining room."

24. Children can listen to special types of sounds on their way to school and make a list. These might be building noises, play noises, or beautiful noises.

25. The teacher can read poems that require responses.

26. The child can talk into a toy telephone as though he were talking with his mother (or someone else) and have others try to guess what the other person is saying by listening to the one-sided conversation.

27. The class can play a verbal tennis game in which the children face each other in rows. The teacher gives a word like "head." The first child rhymes it with "dead," the child across thinks of another word that rhymes, and so on, until one child can't think of additional words. Points are allotted to show which side has the greatest number of words.

Auditory perception skills should be practiced throughout elementary school. Games that blind children who can write in braille can play include:

1. The students rhyme words and note similarities and differences of initial beginning sounds. The children can write the names of objects on 3 X 5 inch cards. Each child receives ten cards. A beginning letter is called, and all the words with that beginning sound are placed in a pile. This is repeated a prespecified number of times.

2. Shopping at the supermarket. The children write the names of supermarket items on cards and spread these on their desks. The desks are make-believe counters behind which each child is the clerk. One child is chosen to be the shopper. He takes the shopping bag and goes from desk to desk, shopping for an item that begins with a particular sound. If the shopper does not take all the cards on a particular desk that begin with the sound, he must give up the shopping bag to the child at that desk.

3. A child makes a chart with his own name at the top and lists all the words that he can find that begin with the same sound as his name.

4. The children categorize sounds on a chart. They set up columns for words that end alike, words that start alike, words that have the same middle, and names that sound alike.

5. Barnyard Frolic. The teacher assembles two sets of word cards with the name of an animal commonly found on a farm on each. Print the word "barnyard" on one of the cards. The leader keeps a complete set of the cards for himself and distributes the other set one card to each player. When the leader reads the card with, for example, the word "dog" on it, the child who holds the matching card must bark. When the leader reads the "barnyard" card, each child responds with the sound made by the animal on his card.

6. The children each take a card with the word of an object and attempt to make the noise of the object so that the class can guess what it is.

7. Children can reproduce sound effects from stories in their readers while others guess the stories.

8. Each child can keep a diary over a period of time listing all the sounds heard.

9. Each child divides a sheet of paper in half lengthwise. The teacher then asks where certain sounds are heard. The teacher might ask for the "t" sound and pronounce words such as "report," "tinkle," "tank," and "part." If the child hears this sound in the first part of the word he writes it on the left side of the paper, and if the sound is found in the last part he writes it on the right side of the paper. He then adds all the words he can think of to fill in both columns on the page.

10. The children make a list of how many sounds they hear in a two-minute period.

11. The children can list the sounds that were not here when Columbus discovered America.

TACTUAL PERCEPTION IN READING READINESS

The development of tactual discrimination continues to fourth grade, with great variability among young blind children in their abilities to recognize common household objects by touch (Nolan and Kederis, 1969, p. 43). In the preschool and primary years, it is important to stress tactual perception development. Gross examination of real objects, which can actually be part of vocabulary development exercises, and two- and three-dimensional studies of texture and form should be a part of the reading readiness program. As training continues, introduction of finer discriminations can include categorizing materials according to a variety of attributes such as size, shape, and texture. At the end of this process, training may begin in the perception of punctographic forms (raised dots). The braille dots may be examined by the child and discussion begun on the physical relationship of the dots or the patterns formed by the dots. At this level of experience, no literal meaning need be attached to the characters (Nolan and Kederis, 1969, pp. 49–50). There will be, of course, blind children who will be prepared to read braille immediately. The General Catalog of Tangible Apparatus of the American Printing House for the Blind lists a number of items that may be of use in teaching tactual discrimination. Some of these are listed below.

1. Aluminum diagramming sheets used for drawing diagrams.
2. Constructo set, which includes a large number of pieces of hardwood with wooden bolts to be used as an erector set.
3. Plastic or wooden pegboard and pegs.

4. Squares of cardboard perforated for sewing.

5. Roughness Discrimination Test used to predict braille reading readiness. This consists of cards with pieces of various textures of sandpaper mounted on cardboard.

6. Form board with removable hand imprints.

7. *Touch and Tell,* a reading readiness book designed for blind children.

8. Shoelace aid to teach lacing and tying.

9. Giant textured beads used to introduce solids of different shapes, sizes, and textures. Bead stringing on an easily manageable level can be useful in developing muscular coordination.

10. Shape Board consisting of a tray with pegs on which are hung five different shapes in three sizes for the purpose of sorting.

11. Swail Dot Inverter for hand embossing of line drawings.

There are other items which can be acquired commercially from various companies producing educational material. Teachers themselves may devise useful aids to teaching tactual discrimination.

The Science Curriculum Improvement Study has developed a teacher guide with the objective of teaching children to recognize material objects in their own environment. This can easily be adapted for use by blind children. Familiar objects in the classroom, home, and playground are used to introduce the concepts of object and property. These new concepts are then applied to other objects, plants, and to animals and their parts. Collections of buttons and wooden blocks that can be sorted according to a number of properties, such as shape, texture, and size, are also available. This guide provides for the child's comparison of similarly shaped pieces of aluminum, brass, pine, walnut, vinyl, and polystyrene and leads to the introduction of the concept of material. This concept is then applied in further work with other metals and various kinds of wood, as well as with rocks, liquids, and gases. Provision is made for experiments with various materials, and these experiments can be adapted for use with blind children (Huckins, 1970). While this guide is primarily designed for the study of science, it does provide suggestions for tactual perception activities.

Haupt (1959), from observation of school-age blind children, suggests another method for development of tactual perception through the use of clay modeling. From her observations she concludes that intelligence and academic standing do not necessarily predict ability to manipulate objects. Those children who came from homes where they were free to explore at their own pace could manipulate objects well. Children with limited opportunity to explore at home and those who had been continually coerced to explore no longer appeared to have the desire to explore. They were not only inadequate in the use of their hands but demonstrated greater dependency in orientation and mobility training. Some children who were intelligent and superior in academic work did not know the shape or form of many common objects in their daily surroundings. These children knew verbal facts about the objects but had only primitive tactile concepts concerning the forms or shapes because they had rarely examined them by touch. They had little or no concept of the character of a fish, a bottle, or an arch. One child thought a rabbit's ears were like a human's; another thought a tree was as big as he was because he had been told the biggest part of a tree was its trunk.

Imparting knowledge which is based on the sensory reality of all common objects is one of the first and continuing responsibilities of teachers of blind children. Learning to read is learning to convey experiences from one person, place, and time to another. When the objects are not available each teacher should try to provide an accurate model of them in some form. There is a reason for the shape of things; and if the reason as it is related to function is explained to the child, he can more easily remember the form. Each child may be taught how to handle substances such as clay so that he may copy the object and, while doing so, form a mental image of it. Repetition will be necessary in this process just as "we who see do not learn all about an object the first time we see it." (Haupt, 1959, p. 67.)

Pittam (1965), in a discussion of reading readiness skills, suggests that teaching these skills should be part of the entire day's school program. While teaching tactual discrimination skills, various abstract concepts are taught. In teaching concepts of size, such as big, little, long, short, or tall, some activities which may be useful for the teacher include:

1. Let the children handle buttons, clothes pins, dolls, toy airplanes, and cars.

2. Provide a set of cans that fit inside of each other.

3. Use commercial games that provide concepts of size, including toys involving nesting, blocks, and pyramids of rings.

4. Have the children sort objects such as long and short straws, sticks, strips of paper, and pipe cleaners.

5. Demonstrate the concepts of "alike" and "different" and teach discrimination of common shapes, such as triangles, circles, and squares. The teacher can use cut-outs from cardboard, felt, foam rubber, or flocked paper with instructions for the child to match similar shapes which have been mounted on paper.

6. Use a vacuum-forming machine (Thermoform) to reproduce raised shapes, perhaps using four shapes with one different from

the other three. The machine can also reproduce familiar objects such as scissors which are open or closed, wooden spoons, and buttons.

7. Teach discrimination of texture and consistency, using sandpaper with various degrees of coarseness, velvet or other cloth, dough, and papier-maché. Also compare soapy water with clear water.

8. Place a different puzzle on the corner of the bulletin board each day with instructions for the children to find the shape which is different.

9. Make available collections of books with stick-on shapes which illustrate concepts of size, top and bottom of a page, and left and right. Each page can introduce new concepts. For example, one page can denote top and bottom if the teacher places squares along the top and circles along the bottom edge. The next page may show a large triangle on the left edge of a brailled vertical line and a small triangle on the right.

Some of the concepts illustrated here are frequently learned incidentally to common daily activities performed by the sighted child. This is not the case with the blind child. These concepts must be deliberately taught to him in order to facilitate his readiness for reading braille.

BRAILLE READING AND THE BRAILLE CODE

The system of touch reading most commonly used by blind is called braille. The entire system is derived from arranging combinations of a maximum of six embossed dots to represent the alphabet, numbers, scientific and mathematical notation, and musical notation. To aid in identification of the dot positions, Louis Braille, the developer of the braille code, numbered the six dot positions (as shown in Figure 3). Sixty-three different dot patterns can be formed by arranging the dots in different positions and combinations. Some combination of these six dots together with appropriate spacing and use of contracted forms makes up every braille symbol necessary in reading literary English, mathematics, science, and music.

Braille derived his system from a 12-dot cell developed by a French army officer, Charles Barbier, for use in night communication on the battlefield (Farrell, 1956, pp. 96–100). When Louis Braille introduced the first version of his system in the Paris School for Young Blind in 1834, the writing system for blind in existence was "line-type" (contrasted to the present "point-type") or the embossing of letters of the Roman alphabet. This was extremely difficult to read and was reluc-

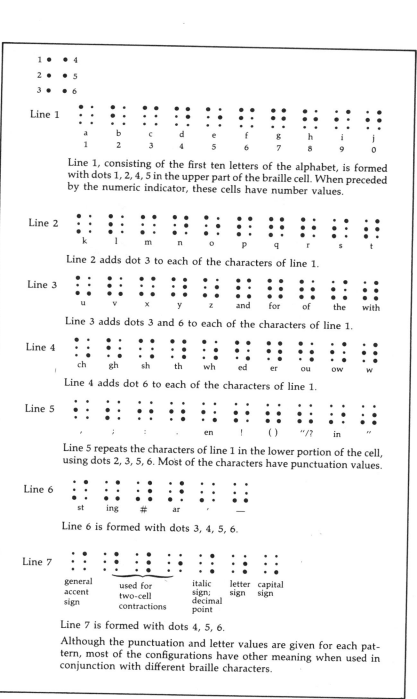

1 ● ● 4
2 ● ● 5
3 ● ● 6

Line 1

 a   b   c   d   e   f   g   h   i   j
 1   2   3   4   5   6   7   8   9   0

Line 1, consisting of the first ten letters of the alphabet, is formed with dots 1, 2, 4, 5 in the upper part of the braille cell. When preceded by the numeric indicator, these cells have number values.

Line 2

 k   l   m   n   o   p   q   r   s   t

Line 2 adds dot 3 to each of the characters of line 1.

Line 3

 u   v   x   y   z   and   for   of   the   with

Line 3 adds dots 3 and 6 to each of the characters of line 1.

Line 4

 ch   gh   sh   th   wh   ed   er   ou   ow   w

Line 4 adds dot 6 to each of the characters of line 1.

Line 5

 ,   ;   :   .   en   !   ( )   "/?   in   "

Line 5 repeats the characters of line 1 in the lower portion of the cell, using dots 2, 3, 5, 6. Most of the characters have punctuation values.

Line 6

 st   ing   #   ar   ,   —

Line 6 is formed with dots 3, 4, 5, 6.

Line 7

 general   used for   italic   letter   capital
 accent   two-cell   sign;   sign   sign
 sign   contractions   decimal
                          point

Line 7 is formed with dots 4, 5, 6.

Although the punctuation and letter values are given for each pattern, most of the configurations have other meaning when used in conjunction with different braille characters.

Figure 3. The Braille Code

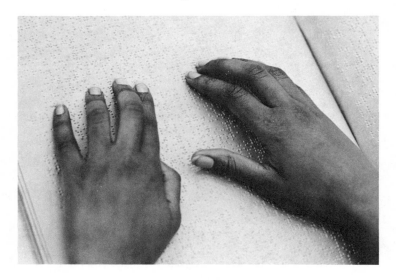

Figure 4.   Reading Braille

tantly read by the blind students. Braille's system simplified tactual reading for blind and was immediately accepted by the pupils, although the teachers suppressed it because its configurations were so different from the print alphabet. Therefore, it was not until 1854 that official recognition of the braille system occurred.

The first acceptance of braille in the United States occurred at the Missouri School for the Blind in the late 1850s. Up to that time, American schools for blind had been teaching various forms of raised-line characters, not too different from embossed Roman alphabet letters. Dissatisfaction with the impracticability of line-type as a means of reading and writing for blind had been growing; however, even after the Missouri School's adoption of braille, other schools were slow to follow their example. William Bell Wait published a system of raised dots known as New York Point in 1868 which gained some popularity. Ten years later, Joel W. Smith introduced a raised-dot system based on Louis Braille's six-dot cell. This system took into account the frequency of recurring letters in English with the most frequently occurring letters receiving the least number of dots. This modified braille, or American Braille, achieved some popularity and rivaled New York Point. The issue of standard braille was resolved in the United States in 1917 with the official adoption of Grade 1½ braille (Farrell, 1956, pp. 105–18).

The version presently used is called English braille, American edition 1959, revised 1962. It consists of sixty-three characters used singly and in combinations to represent letters of the alphabet, words, punctuation signs, and numbers. The characters are arranged in cells containing a maximum of two rows of three dots. This arrangement was determined in the early 1900s to be the most favorable configuration for simultaneous touch perception. The highest unbroken dot which can be embossed today has a height of .017 inches. Experiments have shown that differences of .005 inches in dot height can always be tactually detected, although some blind people can detect smaller differences. Zichel and Hooper (1957, p. 82) concluded that for pleasurable reading, uniform height of the embossed dot is more important than whether the dot is embossed above or below the standard height. They suggested this was probably because the finger always feels only the top rather than the whole dot. It was also found that the interdot and between-line spacing presently in use results in the best readability for children and adults. Children can read better if intercell spacing is close, while adults need wider intercell spacing for optimal reading rate and comprehension.

SOME COMPLEXITIES OF BRAILLE IN READING INSTRUCTION

Learning to read may be conceived of as a relatively short stage during which the child learns that spoken words can be represented by tactual forms, followed by a relatively longer stage where he learns to use the code for reading and develops skill. There appears to be no evidence of one best method for teaching reading to all blind children.

The differences between touch and visual reading should be considered before a decision is made concerning the best way to begin teaching blind children. The results of two comprehensive studies dwell on these differences (Lowenfeld, Abel, and Hatlen, 1969; Nolan and Kederis, 1969). The conclusion of one of the studies was "the results of the studies reported in this monograph make explicit the greater complexity of the braille reading process as compared to print and suggest its greater difficulty." (Nolan and Kederis, 1969, p. 47.) Some of the special problems encountered in the reading of braille are (Lowenfeld, Abel, and Hatlen, 1969, pp. 160–71):

1. Braille characters differ widely in the ease of recognition and are affected by such factors as number of dots, configuration of dots, amount of open space within a character, the frequency with which the character appears in print, and the frequency with which each dot position occurs in braille reading.

2. Contractions (there are 189 of them) and the multipurpose use of the same embossed character forms represent ambiguities beyond those found in the print system.

3. In visual reading it is possible to read more than one word simultaneously and to interpret sentences almost at a glance. A child can perceive a sentence of several words with a few pauses of the eye, while an adult can see a whole line with a single pause. There is no comparable phenomenon in braille—the finger reads by many consecutive, not simultaneous, stimulations. "To the blind child, the strain of remembering a long succession of small touch impressions is much greater, for an equal number of words, than it is for the seeing child to remember a succession of synthesized wholes." (Lowenfeld, Abel, and Hatlen, 1969, p. 18.)

4. Seeing children rarely have trouble with punctuation marks, as these are so different from letters, which is not true in braille.

5. Seeing children experience letter reversals, but braille permits even more. In fact the braille system almost encourages reversal.

6. Spelling presents some problem in braille due to the use of contractions.

7. Certain mechanics of reading pose special problems for blind children, including finding the top of the page, page numbers, the first line on a page, and the beginning of each line. Finger use in reading can also be a problem.

8. For the purposes of scanning, outlining, and note taking, the tactual discrimination span does not even approach the effectiveness of the visual discrimination span.

The problems inherent in the recognition of braille characters become very important if one considers that "whole word reading is not characteristic of the braille readers studied, and that the perceptual unit in word recognition is the braille cell." (Nolan and Kederis, 1969, p. 36.) This conclusion appears paradoxical when one notes that "in general, it appears that most teachers of braille reading consider the whole word as the unit of recognition, and that the word is perceived on the basis of its over-all shape or form." (Nolan and Kederis, 1969, p. 18.) However, this is consistent with the Lowenfeld, Abel, and Hatlen study (1969), in which a survey of the present status of braille reading instruction was obtained from questionnaires completed by 520 teachers at local and residential schools. Results indicated that most teachers today teach the whole words and/or meaningful sentences, although it takes longer to recognize a whole word in braille than it does to recognize each character in that word. This contrasts with findings in print reading, where whole word recognition is faster. In the light of this evidence one might question whether, as the unit of recognition, the letter rather than word should be taught in braille reading. Perhaps those who teach the whole word or sentence method have demonstrated that the blind child proceeds quickly from letter to letter in moving his reading fingers, and the letters combine so rapidly that the child appears to recognize words. Teachers in the Lowenfeld, Abel, and Hatlen study who stated they taught whole words also stated that they used a basic reading series. Nolan and Kederis (1969, p. 20) noted that basal reading series combine a variety of methods, so "letter" and "word" methods are commonly combined in any reading instruction using a basic reading series.

The rate of development of braille reading lags behind that for print reading, a result primarily attributed to retarded development in readiness. Mechanical aspects of reading (character recognition and knowledge of the braille code) continue as problem areas in upper elementary grades (Nolan and Kederis, 1969, pp. 43–44). However, training is effective in improving braille character recognition, which is accompanied by an increase in the efficiency of the total reading process.

BRAILLE READING INSTRUCTION

Grade 1 braille consists of no contractions; grade II braille includes all of the 189 braille contractions. It is generally accepted today that teaching contracted braille, beginning with initial instruction, is the most acceptable method. There is some evidence to support this contention (Loomis, 1948, p. 41). Hooper (1946, p. 20) found that 144 of the 189 braille contractions are in the vocabulary of first grade children and that most of the braille signs occur often enough in written literature to be of practical use. But braille contractions cause problems in reading instruction. They are neither logical nor do they consider phonetic or structural elements. Contractions prevent auditory analysis and contribute to problems in syllabication. They make use of the phonics methods of teaching reading difficult and retard spelling instruction.

WORD RECOGNITION

There are a number of characteristics affecting word recognition other than the braille characters. These include the context of words, experience with the probabilities with which letters and letter groups follow one another in print, and knowledge of the grammatical properties of language. Grammar and morphology of words should receive added stress in the upper grades together with practice in the anticipation of word endings and word sequences.

Another strong influence upon word recognition is word familiarity. This emphasizes the desirability of stressing concept utilization and vocabulary development. It is desirable to begin in preschool years with emphasis on spoken vocabulary development based on experiences real to the blind child and should continue with emphasis on both spoken and reading vocabulary development. Emphasis can shift with cumulated experiences from concrete to abstract experiences.

The following methods of word recognition taught to seeing children have a counterpart in the reading instruction of blind children:

1. Identification of the word by sight.
2. Recognition of word by configuration.
3. Context clues such as words preceding and following the word to be recognized.
4. Phonetic analysis of word to be recognized.
5. Structural analysis of word.

Some educators feel that for sighted children a combination of all these methods is best, while others (Chall, 1967) argue that the preponderance of research evidence leads to the conclusion that a method of stressing alphabet and phonics at the beginning of reading instruction has better results than the whole-word or sentence reading-for-meaning method. Some contend that when the child learns to recognize in print the words he knows from previous experience, reading by meaning can be introduced. This would appear to be a particularly useful method in braille reading instruction, since the Nolan and Kederis evidence (1969) indicates the perceptual unit in braille reading is the individual braille character.

The typical braille spelling book has each word written first in contracted form and then in grade I (noncontracted) braille. But if students are kept aware of the letters represented by each contraction, they should have no difficulty when spelling a word letter by letter, with the occasional exception of whole-word contractions. Errors may be minimized by referring to each contraction by letter, rather than dot number, when spelling. If contractions are spelled out consistently during spelling instruction, there need not be excessive spelling difficulty. The early use of the typewriter will aid the child in recognizing the importance of spelling words out letter by letter. Spelling difficulties are common among children, and there appears to be no conclusive evidence of greater incidence of spelling difficulty among blind children.

REVERSALS

There are methods of avoiding reversal problems in reading and writing braille. Those symbols which stand for different letters when reversed (i–e, h–j, d–f, o–ow, or n–ed) should not be introduced together. Introduction of a letter should be delayed until the letter commonly confused with it is established in the child's memory. This will not eliminate those reversal problems which are caused by the individual's uniqueness. Reversals also occur when learning the use of the slate and stylus. Writing must be done from right to left to produce braille readable from left to right. The teacher must stress that only the direction is reversed. Reversal of direction may need to be practiced for a considerable length of time by having the children write only dots without referring to any letters: e.g., writing a complete row of dots, 1–4, 2–5, or 3–6. When reversal of direction has been established, letters can be introduced. If the teacher prepares children using these general writing directions, slate and stylus writing will not include any special reversal problems (Lowenfeld, Abel, and Hatlen, 1969, pp. 164–66).

METHODS USED BY
TEACHERS OF BRAILLE READING

Lowenfeld, Abel, and Hatlen (1969) tested braille reading ability of blind students in the fourth and eighth grades. The results show some of the characteristics of a good braille reader and suggest some useful teaching practices in braille reading instruction.

The findings of this study supported the notion that both-hand readers are superior to single-hand readers. The trend indicated that both-hand readers may be slightly more efficient, with a higher reading rate and better comprehension. The handedness of both-hand readers did not appear significant, although those who read ahead with one hand while the other finished the preceding line tended to read more rapidly. Students who use both hands in reading and more fingers than the index finger tend to be superior in both comprehension and reading rate. Those fourth grade braille readers who "rub" braille letters frequently read less efficiently, suggesting that this is both a cause and effect of poorer reading ability. The results of repeated rubbing of the braille symbols are consistent with the additional finding that braille readers who read using an even movement are superior in comprehension and reading rate. An indication of a poor reader in the study was one who loses his place frequently.

Gross behaviors such as student mannerisms while reading were also investigated. Students with superior reading ability did not tend to accompany their reading with silent speech, nor did they have as many overt mannerisms as the poorer reader. Braille readers who were relaxed when reading tended to be superior in comprehension, but not different in reading rate. Students who frequently read outside of the classroom were superior in both comprehension and reading rate.

These findings suggest that the braille reading teacher should attempt to encourage students to use both hands in reading, with the book held parallel to forearms and with "rubbing" of braille discouraged. Fingers in addition to the index fingers should be used. The hands should move at a smooth, even rate. It would also appear desirable to eliminate any student tenseness before reading and to help the child minimize or eliminate physical mannerisms. There is certainly evidence from this study for motivating students to do extensive leisure-time reading.

The study also reported data on the procedures the teachers use. The typical braille teacher begins braille reading instruction during the first semester of the first grade, using the braille alphabet with whole words. The overwhelming number of teachers begin reading instruction with grade II braille, and pupils are permitted to use whichever hand they wish as the dominant reading hand, although they are encouraged to use both hands. Reading books, including preprimers, are introduced at the beginning of braille reading instruction or after words or sentences are read by blind children. Instruction is conducted primarily through a combination of oral and silent reading by the student. While double-spaced material is commonly used at the beginning of reading instruction, few teachers use enlarged braille cell material in the process of teaching reading.

Most reading teachers of sighted children use some basal reading series in the initial teaching of beginning reading (Austin and Morrison, 1963). This is also true of blind reading teachers. *Ginn Basic Readers* and the *New Basic Readers* (Scott-Foresman) are the most popular with teachers of blind (Lowenfeld, Abel, and Hatlen, 1969, p. 55), although extensive use is made of supplementary material in the form of workbooks and teacher-made material. In spite of the many methods of reading available, such as the initial teaching alphabet, phonic methods, and linguistic methods, basic readers apparently continue to be the most popular with teachers of blind.

Comparing methods of first grade reading instruction, the Bond and Dykstra (1967) study did not find any method clearly superior as used with sighted children. They concluded: "No one approach is so distinctly better in all situations and respects than the others that it should be considered the one best method and the one to be used exclusively." (Bond and Dykstra, 1967, p. 211.) Hence, use of any one method to the exclusion of others may be disadvantageous to students learning to read. Fortunately for those teachers wishing to use a basic reading series, the most recent catalog of braille publications from the American Printing House for the Blind lists several basic reading series. Also, volunteer braillists produce series not published nationally by APH but used by local schools who have blind children integrated with their sighted classmates for reading and other instruction. There should be no serious problem in obtaining appropriate basic readers.

Perhaps the reason for the popularity of the basic readers is the detailed, graded, and systematic instructions included for use of each reading series. Another reason for the popularity of basal reading programs is that they typically include some components considered important by all reading teachers. These include (1) systematic introduction of new words, (2) guidance for silent reading by the student, (3) guidance for oral reading and discussion, (4) phonics and word analysis, and (5) enrichment activities.

SUPPLEMENTING AND ENRICHING READING INSTRUCTION

Alert teachers have continued to discover additional methods of supplementing and enriching reading instruction to both enhance reading rate and comprehension and create more interest in the reading process. Kenmore (1957) describes methods of enriching the primary reading program in integrated programs. Braille books can have print written above the braille words to help the regular teacher and sighted peers. Braille reading books should duplicate print readers, word for word, line by line, and page by page when used in the first grade. Much of the enjoyment a sighted child gets is from pictures through which he interprets parts of stories. The blind child may quickly lose interest and make slower progress if he is merely reading words; but if he can enjoy the thoughts conveyed by pictures, his appetite for stories may be whetted. The teacher can make stories come alive in a number of ways: using real props, acting out situations, turning chairs into cars or wagons, having the child make items such as wooden sailboats, clay cats and dogs, a paper house, or a miniature farm. A character in a basic reader may be funny because he powders pets in the story, so a powder puff with powder brought to school and used in acting out situations may help clarify it. Stories such as one about children falling out of a wagon onto the grass can be acted out. Other similar activities may be a partial substitute for lack of pictures.

Experience charts may be constructed to develop reading skill and interest. Developing stories a child dictates in class about his interests and thoughts is a good source for reading experience, although he may memorize the stories without fully recognizing all of the words. When a child is ill, sending home stories about him will continue his interest. When a child finishes a preprimer, he might write a book using the same vocabulary and his name and the names of people he knows. The sighted child has incidental reading experiences. To compensate for lack of casual reading opportunities for the blind, riddles or short poems may be placed on his desk, exhibits may be labeled, directions for the use of a brailler or typewriter may be placed at convenient locations, school announcements may be placed on bulletin boards in braille, and the names of family members may be brailled on Christmas tags. All contribute to additional reading practice. Some teachers ask that names on all students' lunch tickets appear in braille and print so that the blind students in an integrated class can take turns passing them out. Signs that may be seen along the way on a field trip may be brailled. Brailled surprises and other reactions may be placed on corrected papers, such as "good work," "neat and accurate," or "must work on items _____."

Children may write stories using words that contain contractions under consideration. An example might be: "Stella stopped sticking stones in the stove and started sticking sticky stamps on the stairs." A phonics game can be developed out of lists of friends in which the names are spelled phonetically: "Sharel," "Sheral," "Sheraril," "Shairl," "Sharyll." Discretion would need to be used to avoid compounding spelling problems with certain words in this phonetics game.

Books for blind children can be made attractive using different sizes, shapes, and textured covers. A story about a rooster could have a feather glued on the front or one about a rabbit could have a ball of fur. "The House That Jack Built" can be written on pages of differing lengths so that as the story increases, the size of the pages does also. Other size and shape differences may be used to emphasize characters or events in a story.

A compilation of a series of games that teach vocabulary recognition, improvement of phonetic skills, and recognition of braille contractions is available. All materials are written in braille and print so blind can play with sighted children (Schmidt, 1958).

RESIDUAL VISION AND READING INSTRUCTION

So far in this chapter the assumption has been that the blind child has been determined to be blind for educational purposes and that braille is the appropriate reading medium. As a matter of fact, only a minority of those who are legally blind would have no useable residual vision. Most children who are visually handicapped should read print rather than braille. Every effort should be made to determine as early as possible whether a child can read print. Hence, periodic rescreening is necessary to identify those children who may have some remaining useful vision. This can be done by the teacher informally by observing the day-to-day functioning of the child. When evidence appears that a child is using vision in an attempt to see small objects, letters, or classroom paraphenalia, the teacher may encourage the child to use vision to identify objects in the room as well as print letters and words. If a more formal and systematic method is desired, the teacher may adapt material developed for visual discrimination purposes (Frostig and Horne, 1964; Kephart, 1960), although focus in these is on vision perception development. Visual discrimination training materials for blind children who have some residual vision have also been developed (Barraga, 1964). The objective of these materials is to help the child observe characteristics of the symbols and objects to facilitate subsequent visual identification of similar objects or symbols.

Evidence seems to point to the conclusion that many of those children who have sufficient vision to read enlarged print (partially seeing) regularly require special placement and teachers because of problems other than limited visual acuity (Peabody and Birch, 1967; Kirk, 1965). This is significant since these children have been reported as apparently acquiring improved visual acuity over time (Hathaway, 1959, p. 108) and functioning adequately in regular classes with only minor modification in material and teaching procedures. Whether the child receives special placement for visual acuity limitations or for a special learning difficulty not attributable to poor vision is significant if the child is removed from substantial contact with his peers. It is inappropriate to place partially seeing children routinely in segregated classrooms for most or all of each day, since the methods used for instruction for partially seeing are substantially the same as for normally seeing children. These children function basically as seeing children. There are, however, some modifications of materials and teaching methods which can facilitate the reading instruction of children who have sufficient vision to see enlarged print or have the ability to read regular print with magnifiers.

Use of vision should typically be encouraged. Only in those rare instances when a specific prohibition against the use of eyes is made by a medical eye specialist is it necessary to restrict use of visual material. Use of print provides the child with a great advantage over braille in speed of reading, use of pictures and diagrams, and accessibility to reading material. (However, it is possible in a very limited number of cases that a particular child cannot read print except with great sacrifice of reading speed, in which case braille may be an acceptable alternative. This child could continue to use print symbols in instances where manipulation of numbers on paper is required, enlarged diagrams or graphs need to be used to summarize information, or when parts of pictures can be perceived.)

Conventional modifications to instructions for reading print by children with severely restricted vision or those who are partially seeing have included primarily material and equipment to make seeing print efficient (Hathaway, 1959). Proper lighting, including a minimum level of 50 footcandles, a room reflection factor of 50 percent or higher, and glare on work eliminated, is important. This is a requirement for all classrooms, so it should not present an additional problem. Since tolerance for brightness may vary depending on the eye pathology (for example children with albinism are frequently sensitive to light), it would be advisable for the teacher to allow the child to find the place in the room where he feels most comfortable in reading and other work.

Other recommended modifications include choice of reading material for the partially seeing child in which consideration is given to spacing, contrast, size and kind of type, illustrations, and quality of paper (Hathaway, 1959, p. 108). The National Society for Prevention of Blindness (1965) suggests that the distance between lines of type be approximately equivalent to the height of the tallest letter in the line. The optimal type size for partially seeing may vary between twelve and twenty-four printer's points (Peabody and Birch, 1967, p. 92). There is some evidence that 18-point type may be the best single type size (Eakin, Pratt, and McFarland, 1961, p. 18). While the McFarland study suggests that 24-point may be superior if only letter discrimination is considered, it becomes less advantageous than smaller type when the book and page dimensions and speed of reading are considered. Hathaway (1959, p. 108) reports on the British Association for the Advancement of Science recommendations that children under seven years of age should begin with 24-point and progress to successively smaller type sizes as they become older, with 10-point type recommended at twelve years of age and over as a rule. The style of type (serif or sans-serif) may aid children in discriminating letters, so it may be worth the teacher's effort to observe whether type style seems to make a difference in ability to discriminate letters and words.

Illustrations, figure and ground contrasts, and quality of paper are other considerations in the development of print reading material for visually handicapped. Suggestions for illustrations include figures or pictures which do not have a background cluttered with many detailed objects in mildly contrasting shades of color. Lack of prominence of foreground may be aided by outlining prominent features of pictures in dark outline and providing sharply contrasting colors. Standard textbooks which have had print enlarged by photographic processes have had colored pictures reproduced in varying shades of gray. Some books are now appearing where color has been added to the pictures to make them more enjoyable and useful for the visually handicapped child.

Teachers can point to certain features of a picture or diagram by covering nonrelevant parts of a picture or simply pointing out the significant features. To eliminate glare, paper which is buff or off-white has been used in the preparation of reading material.

There is equipment which makes the task of reading printed material more pleasant and more efficient. The use of various magnifiers to aid low vision has been developed through low vision aids clinics. Selecting and fitting optical aids and orienting children to the use of appropriate optical aids can improve their ability to see print dramatically. This may replace the use of large print for some children or may provide supplemental reading aid. One of the recent additions to low vision aids has been the "television reader" or "electronic magnifier," an adaptation of a television camera and monitor which a student may use to project from a standard book any desired size print on a television receiver screen. It is possible to vary the print-background contrast with this equipment. A less sophisticated, but still very useful device for the visually handicapped, is the book stand. Many of the books with enlarged print are heavy, and students need to have the printed page close for viewing. An appropriate book stand will hold the book where it is most comfortable for the student, thus allowing longer periods of reading as well as more rapid reading.

Braille and print reading are important to visually handicapped. However, other methods of acquisition of information are also available to them. Other chapters of this book explore listening, writing, and other skills which exploit use of other senses.

References

Austin, M. C. and Morrison, C. *The First R: The Harvard Report on Reading in Elementary Schools.* New York, Macmillan, 1963.

Barraga, N. *Increased Visual Behavior in Low Vision Children.* New York, American Foundation for the Blind, Research series No. 13, 1964.

Bond, G. L. and Dykstra, R. *Coordinating Center for First Grade Reading Instruction Programs.* Minneapolis, U.S. Office of Education, Dept. of HEW, Project #X-001, University of Minnesota, 1967.

Chall, J. S. *Learning to Read: The Great Debate.* New York, McGraw-Hill Book Company, 1967.

Eakin, W. M., Pratt, R. J. A., and McFarland, T. L. *Type Size Research for the Partially Seeing Child.* Pittsburgh, Stanwix House, Inc., 1961.

Farrell, G. *The Story of Blindness.* Cambridge, Harvard University Press, 1956.

Frostig, M. and Horne, D. *The Frostig Program for the Development of Visual Perception.* Chicago, Follett Publishing Company, 1964.

Hathaway, W. *Education and Health of the Partially Seeing Child.* 4th ed. New York, Columbia University Press, 1959.

Haupt, C. Clay modelling—A means and an end. *Concerning the Education of Blind Children.* Georgie Lee Abel (Ed.) New York, American Foundation for the Blind, 1959.

Hooper, M. S. *Braille Contractions and Children's Reading Vocabularies: A Statistical Study.* In 38th Convention of the American Association of Instructors for the Blind, 1946, 18–41.

Huckins, R. L. Current applied research science curriculum improvement study kits adapted for visually handicapped. Association for Education of the Visually Handicapped, *Selected Conference Papers,* 50th Biennial Conference, 1970, 173–77.

Kenmore, J. R. Enrichment of the primary reading program. *New Outlook for the Blind, 51,* 1957, 56–64.

Kephart, N. C. *The Slow Learner in the Classroom.* Columbus, Ohio, Charles E. Merrill Publishing Company, 1960.

Kirk, E. The Detroit program for partially seeing children. *Sight-Saving Review, 35,* 1965, 220–24.

Loomis, M. S. *Which Grade of Braille Should Be Taught First?* New York, Columbia, 1948.

Lowenfeld, B., Abel, G. L., and Hatlen, P. H. *Blind Children Learn to Read.* Springfield, Ill., Charles C Thomas, Publisher, 1969.

The National Society for Prevention of Blindness, Inc. *Guidelines for the Production of Material in Large Type.* New York, 1965.

Nolan, C. Y. and Kederis, C. J. "Perceptual Factors in Braille Word Recognition." New York, American Foundation for the Blind, Research series, No. 20, 1969.

Peabody, R. L. and Birch, J. W. Educational implications of partial vision—New findings from a national study. *Sight-Saving Review, 37,* 1967, 92–96.

Pittam, V. Reading readiness. *New Outlook for the Blind, 59,* 1965, 322–24.

Schmidt, E. H. Teaching reading by use of word games. *International Journal for the Education of the Blind, 8,* 1958, 46–59.

Zickel, V. and Hooper, M. S. The program of braille research: A progress report. *International Journal for the Education of the Blind, 6,* 1957, 79–86.

Writing and Spelling

Admittedly, separating writing and spelling from reading instruction is somewhat artificial. However, the distinction is being made here for convenience in discussing instructional procedures. The teacher of the visually handicapped is at one time or another concerned with writing and spelling in the form of four basic writing modes: (1) the braille writer, (2) the slate and stylus, (3) typewriting, and (4) handwriting. Each of these has ramifications associated with the child's needs and his competencies.

THE BRAILLE WRITER

The child who is blind for educational purposes will need to be evaluated for all four modes (listed above) at various periods in his education. Practically all teachers of blind in the United States initiate writing instruction with the braille writer at the same time that reading is initiated in the first grade. Only a tiny minority (less than 1 percent) of teachers begin writing instruction with the slate and stylus (Lowenfeld, Abel, and Hatlen, 1969, pp. 52–54). It is not difficult to see why the braille writer is popular compared to the slate and stylus.

The Perkins Brailler is a modification of the original Hall Braillewriter and is the most popular braille writer in use today. It consists of only six keys which, when depressed, emboss the braille code on paper. These six keys correspond to the six dots of the braille cell and depressing the appropriate keys simultaneously embosses the desired combination of the six dots. This method of embossing braille is far simpler and more rapid than writing with the slate and stylus.

The relative bulk of the Perkins Brailler is one of its chief disadvantages. There is a braille writer (Lavendar) which is less bulky, but is also less durable, partly due to its plastic construction.

The writing of braille typically parallels beginning reading. Words which are used in reading are the basis for braille writing instruction. Instruction in reading is typically begun by using whole words and meaningful sentences, with only a minority of teachers initiating reading instruction by teaching the letters of the alphabet (Lowenfeld, Abel, and Hatlen, 1969, p. 46). Most teachers of braille initiate writing by practicing whole words as they are learned in the basic readers, followed by introduction to writing meaningful sentences as the students acquire a sufficient vocabulary.

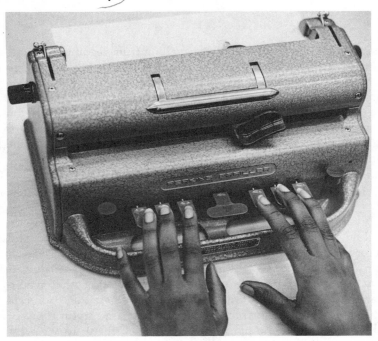

Figure 5.   The Perkins Brailler

Experience stories drawn from each child's daily life are suggested as a supplemental means of motivating writing. The teacher paraphrases experiences as told by a child into sentences that the students can read. All of this writing instruction should be done in grade II (contracted) braille, as is reading instruction.

THE SLATE AND STYLUS

The slate is a metal or plastic plate hinged to another plate so that a sheet of paper can be inserted between the plates. The top plate contains small openings or "windows" with notches along the sides of each window corresponding to the dots in a braille cell. In one of the more popular slates there are twenty-seven rows of windows in four columns. The bottom plate contains slight indentations or pits arranged in the pattern of the braille cell, and these pits, together with the notches in the top plate, act as guides to the dots as they are embossed with the stylus. The embossing of the dots occurs when the stylus is pressed downward against the paper placed between the plates. The stylus must be pressed for each dot. Although it is slow and laborious, compared to the Perkins Brailler, it serves as a convenient writing device for many blind.

Figure 6.   Slate and Stylus

A factor which sometimes presents an obstacle in writing with the slate and stylus is the reversal of the order of the dots when writing (as compared to the reading order of the braille cell). The reason for this is that each dot is pushed toward the bottom plate when the stylus is pressed on the paper. This means that in order to get the proper reading order of the dots within the cells, the embossing must be done from right to left, with the dot pattern a mirror image of the braille as it is read. In spite of this, the blind user of the slate and stylus can, with practice, acquire sufficient speed and accuracy to make it a useful writing device.

REVERSAL PROBLEMS

The reversal problems associated with mirror writing may be minimized by stressing to the child that only the direction is reversed in writing with the slate and stylus. Sometimes this reversal of direction needs to be practiced by having the children write only dots without reference to letters. One suggestion (Lowenfeld, Abel, and Hatlen, 1969, p. 165) is that children may write complete lines of pairs of dots, the top, middle, or bottom two dots across in the braille cell. This may be followed with drill in writing the first dot in the upper pair of dots and alternately writing the first and then the second middle dots and the first and second of the bottom dots. This is done without reference to letters. When the student has established reversal of direction, then letters may be introduced. The first letters to be introduced in slate and stylus writing are *a, c, b, g, f, h* (in that order) to avoid confronting reversal problems until some success is established.

There appears to be little urgency to teach slate and stylus to children until later elementary school because of the greater efficiency of the braille writers. However, as the student feels the need for a less bulky writing device, the slate and stylus becomes an appealing supplementary writing device. Its use is particularly necessary when the student wants a device for note-taking in high school and college, although some blind students do not feel that it is as necessary now that compact sound recording devices are so readily available.

BRAILLE SPELLING INSTRUCTION

The desirability of using grade II braille presents a special problem in spelling instruction. Sooner or later a teacher of blind in elementary grades is faced with making a decision as to whether to have a child write out words for spelling instruction purposes in grade I (uncontracted) or grade II (contracted) form. Some teachers have their students write words in grade I followed by the contracted form for each word, when the words are presented in a practice list. This allows the student to refer to the words during practice and verify the letters used in unfamiliar braille contractions. Another method, which probably saves time, is for the teacher to write the words in contracted form and orally spell out unfamiliar braille contractions. The assumption is that new braille contractions are introduced sufficiently slowly to allow a student to assimilate all contractions introduced previously. Also, students are routinely asked to spell out each word orally to the teacher.

Other problems related to spelling involve the slower reading rate of braille, lack of convenient brailled references which will facilitate students' finding correct spellings independently, and the necessity of eventually typing school work, including spelling. The laborious braille letter-by-letter tactual examination each time a word must be read, and the resultant time consumed in the process, discourages braille reading, particularly when the reading consists of lists of words. Words in a composition which require verification of spelling require considerably more effort in braille than in print because of the relative inaccessibility of reference sources, such as dictionaries, which a blind student may use independently. Braille dictionaries, even in the most abridged forms, contain volumes which must be unshelved, the word located, and then the book reshelved because the volumes are too bulky and numerous to leave on a desk or work table. Some aid is available through recorded dictionaries. A more ideal solution would be a person who is available during certain critical periods to give correct spelling as needed until the blind student becomes sufficiently proficient in spelling. Once proficiency has been achieved, so that spelling references are only needed for relatively few words, use of braille dictionaries becomes practical.

As the student progresses to later elementary grades and beyond, he must learn to type work assignments for sighted teachers, except in a minority of cases where the teacher himself is visually handicapped. When the student types his work, it must be proofread by a seeing person so that corrections can be made in punctuation and format as well as spelling.

TYPING INSTRUCTION

All visually handicapped students should be presented with the opportunity of learning typing in an elementary school. Since all typing is taught by the touch method, the typewriter is a natural for blind students. Partially sighted and blind students learn to type as efficiently and rapidly as their seeing counterparts with only a few minor adaptations.

This skill is frequently begun as soon as possible after a child leaves the primary grades and has acquired good patterns of correct spelling as well as good braille reading and writing skills. There are several of the typewriter manufacturers who modify type size on typewriters at a modest additional cost for those who have some remaining vision. Blind students may use any standard typewriter with no modification of the machines necessary.

Typing instruction for blind and partially seeing beginners is much the same as for normally seeing beginners. Learning to insert the paper, the names of the machine parts and their operation, and other operational functions are taught by verbal instruction followed by tactual examination. The teaching of each key location is also done orally, but drills for developing proficiency are copied by the students from typing books and made available in braille or in large type.

There have been special typing manuals available for teaching visually handicapped; however, more commonly typing instruction is accomplished by using a standard typing manual with minor adaptations by the teacher to meet some unique needs of the child. Instructions brailled by the teacher for drill in typing and made available to the blind student will allow him to progress independently in this skill.

The materials used for partially sighted children will depend upon the degree of vision of the individual child. Some partially sighted students read regular print while others need the large-type print. Book holders or book stands are essential in teaching students with some vision. Children who read print at close range require a book stand which fits over the top of the typewriter, although other types may also be used.

Those visually handicapped who have some remaining vision should use a typewriter equipped with large type. The "bulletin type" machine is commonly eighteen points, or six characters to an inch. These typewriters are particularly valuable for personal use of the partially sighted who are able to read print.

Learning to type proficiently allows the child to complete written class assignments and turn them in directly to a sighted teacher who does not read braille. Furthermore, the visually handicapped child finds that with acquisition of skill in typing he can communicate in writing directly with his friends and family, use the mails for communication with sighted people, and maintain the same privacy that the seeing individuals around him enjoy. Unless the child has other disabilities in addition to visual, he should progress at a rate sufficient to maintain interest in this activity.

While the typewriter is basically a touch instrument, it is helpful at times to make a few additions to the machine for use with blind children. There are several ways of adapting the typewriter to the needs of blind children. One of the simplest is through the use of a heavy adhesive tape, such as masking tape, for marking the location of the paper guide and for marking a guide on the back of the machine so the student will know when he is nearing the end of the page. Determining the end of the page can be done in other ways, but using the tape as a marker has worked well in practice. With some students the setting of margins is difficult, and a piece of tape can be used to mark the place where the margins should be set. After a period of time, all such markings may be eliminated as the student learns these steps by touch.

Visually handicapped students are usually responsive to learning to use a typewriter. Typing to them is an interesting and useful skill to be learned, and they usually approach it with few or no inhibitions. They accept instruction in typing as a routine procedure; and other factors being equal, the teacher may expect the quality of their work to quickly make typing of functional value.

Typing Skills, Methods, and Objectives

The learner should be given a clear understanding of what he is to do and exactly how he is to do it. This includes not only a general idea of how each movement must be made, but a definite idea of the movements as a whole and the kinesthetic impression of how it feels to make the movement. Emphasis should be placed on the sensations of muscular movement as each key is struck as well as on the contact sensations. The teacher should strive to have the student's body, arms, hands, and fingers where they should be when the student is asked to note sensations that accompany a movement. An understanding of how the movement is to be made should include not only a visual impression but also the tactile kinesthetic impression in the normally seeing typist. The visual impression is not critical and retards the blind typist little, if any, in learning to type.

Every voluntary muscular action in typing has an accompanying mental process which includes not only the process that initiated action, but also those processes following completion of the action. The speed of these mental processes largely governs speed in typing. The beginner observes a letter, recognizes it, and makes the proper finger movement toward a letter key, the space bar, or other component. The speed of writing at this stage is governed by the sum total of the time required for all these processes. The finger movement itself usually requires little time, so for the average student the problem of how to increase speed is usually associated with increasing the speed of the mental processes in typing.

Acquiring skill in typing is a matter of forming, improving, and fixing certain habits that enable learners to control their fingers and hands in accurately locating each key to be struck. Many habits are formed and fixed as skill is acquired; since improvement requires some change in habit, this is more difficult than the initial learning. It is easier for the student and teacher to learn proper typing habits at the beginning than change habits later. Certain habits should be prevented just as certain habits should be formed. The teacher must be constantly alert to detect habits of incorrect method before they become fixed, as well as to aid the student in establishing those habits that make for correct technique.

Skill in operating the typewriter depends on the technique developed, and this means careful supervision of detail at each stage of learning. Each student presents a different problem requiring adjustment of instruction by the teacher, as is required in other types of instruction. Some teachers misinterpret the importance of supervision in typing instruction. It is not guard duty, but rather a consciousness of what the students are doing, anticipating difficulties and making oneself available when help is needed. The teacher's concern should be with facilitating progress in typing rather than drill for drill's sake.

Sometimes teachers are guilty of using strictly authoritarian or coercive techniques to assure attention to the task of typing, rather than analyzing why a student's performance is poor. Factors of motivation are important. Children like to type; and if they know what they are to do, how they should proceed, and the goal toward which they are striving, they will typically apply themselves to the task at hand without having to be prodded. If they are confident that the teacher is aware of their progress, they will make greater effort to top previous achievement.

The physical classroom environment must be conducive to concentration—light, temperature, furniture, suitability and condition of equipment, distractions, interruptions, and the general behavior of other students in the room are all important. Unless the surroundings are relatively tranquil, concentration on a task becomes difficult. It is single-minded concentration that makes it possible to coordinate finger movements with perception of symbols to be typed. The first efforts in concentration may not be successful; but as is true with learning other motor tasks, practice in typing will bring ability to concentrate in spite of some distractions.

As new letters on the keyboard are learned, followed by carefully planned drills and exercises, they should be incorporated in phrases and sentences which are the best evidence to the child of his growing typing skill. The child will lose interest in typing if most of his time is spent on drills which have little or no meaning to him, especially during the early stages of instruction. Some repetition is desirable, but it should not cover more than part of each instructional period.

Typing instruction can be correlated with the student's other school work. Spelling words may be used for portions of the drill work. Typing the words repeatedly (singly and in sentences) provides the student with much aid in learning to spell and stimulates accuracy. Some repetition is pleasant, making typing drill and practice exercises more effective.

The typewriter provides clear images of words. The pupils can more readily discover errors in their spelling and correct them. Typing helps provide youngsters with "sentence sense." They become more proficient in recognizing words and word groups. New words may be spelled, defined, and understood.

Typing also enables a partially sighted student to gain effective practice in reading—simply because he wants to read what he has typed.

The objectives of typing are to develop a manipulative skill that facilitates the communication process. Because of the potential personal use of this skill, the instruction can be given as early as the fourth grade.

While instruction in typing has many secondary objectives, the central ones are:

1. To develop keyboard mastery;
2. To develop correct techniques of handling the machine and stroking the keys;
3. To develop copying and composing skills;
4. To develop basic understanding of centering, tabulating, and spacing copy;
5. To develop proficiency in proofreading and error correction;
6. To correlate spelling, punctuation, and other basic English essentials with typing;
7. To develop skill in outlines and correspondence.

These objectives are arranged generally in the order in which they should be achieved, although there is some overlap. Regular periods of instruction and testing, combined with systematic progress toward fulfilling these objectives, will produce a typist, even in the elementary grades, who will have this skill developed to a functional level when he enters junior high school.

The degree of success that is to be attained in this specialized area will depend on the careful planning of work, understanding of the individual and his needs, and the willingness of the students to learn. Much of the ultimate learning success lies with the teacher—for the student's attitude toward his work will be a direct reflection of the teacher's attitude toward him.

INSTRUCTION IN HANDWRITING SKILLS AND HAND SKETCHES

Development of handwriting skills becomes progressively more important as the visual acuity increases. There is no perfect substitute for the ability to write with a pen or pencil for visually handicapped; however, some minimal ability in this area is a practical necessity.

The visually handicapped child with sufficient residual vision to see handwriting should be taught using the same procedures as those with normal vision. The adaptations necessary because of his visual limitations are of two types: (1) modification in the size of the lettering used, and (2) use of pencils or pens which produce a broader line.

Changes in the size of lettering may only require paper which has bold lines which are one-half to one inch apart as guides. There is little reason to modify the teaching methods used with normally seeing children in teaching handwriting. The normal progression is to teach printing in the primary grades and later progress to cursive writing. The printing initially uses only the upper case letters and then, depending on the student's progress, the lower case letters are introduced. If the visually handicapped child's visual acuity is very low, the teacher may find that progress is too slow and difficult and may choose to use only upper case letters. This may be desirable, particularly where the child will begin typing instruction in elementary grade four and use typing as the primary writing mode in school.

With decreasing amounts of residual vision a child may require embossed lines on paper which are one-half to one inch apart to guide handwriting. Time spent in instruction of handwriting may become exorbitant unless it is limited to upper case print letters or a modified cursive form which can be written without use of diagonal lines or curves. This form requires all letters to be formed block style, with all connecting lines at the top of the space between lines or at the bottom. Again, teacher discretion must be used in determining how much time to use in developing this skill after considering such variables as student interest, the priority of this skill relative to the other skills a student must acquire, and value to the student. The teacher should keep in mind that if the student acquires typing skill in elementary school, he has an acceptable writing medium for written class assignments as well as for his less formal writing needs.

Those visually handicapped children with vision approaching total blindness probably require only minimal handwriting skills. Perhaps the functional value of handwriting should be limited to acquiring the ability to record telephone or other numbers and simple messages. The level of skill to be obtained may be determined by the degree of interest in learning handwriting by the individual blind child. The child who perceives handwriting as important after discussing it with the teacher, parents, or counselor, should receive instruction insofar as school time permits. The blind child may use embossed lined paper or use one of several writing guides. The bold line paper, embossed line paper, and writing guides may be obtained from several sources, but most notably from the American Printing House for the Blind and American Foundation for the Blind. It would seem that the absolute minimum handwriting skill necessary is to be able to sign one's name on letters, bank checks, and legal documents.

A special problem related to handwriting occurs when visually handicapped students have some vision, but it is difficult for the teacher to determine whether there is sufficient vision for use with sketches, mathematics notations, diagrams, pictures, or graphs. The general rule that print should be used with visually handicapped as the reading mode whenever possible, even though the print may need to be modified in size, applies in these cases. Some of these children are able to use greatly enlarged print with low vision aids or teacher printing. Similarly, instructing children to use felt-tip or other broad-print marking pens in drawing their own tables, graphs, and diagrams may be useful. In these instances mathematics problems, diagrams, maps, pictures, and graphs may still be viewed with low vision aids, or placed on the blackboard or paper in enlarged size to make visual scanning possible, so that they may be resketched by the student for future reference.

The possibility of enlarging the size of any print symbol or diagram for reading and for monitoring writing has recently been enhanced by the marketing of projection enlargers of printed material. One type of equipment enlarges any image which is on paper on a television monitor by placing the image under a camera connected to the monitor. This equipment allows the student to observe his own writing. The image may be enlarged up to forty times and contrast may be varied. One successful model, developed at the Schiffman Eye Clinic in Detroit by Dr. Morris Mintz and associates, is portable, although somewhat bulky and expensive compared to, for example, existing low vision aids.

For writing without the use of magnification devices, such as the projection devices, only a minor modification in the pen or pencil used is necessary. Both broad-tip pens and pencils are available from both specialized and nonspecialized sources of supply. Pencils with broad soft points, similar to pencils used by carpenters and some other tradesmen, may be used where erasure may be necessary. Grease pencils perform the same task with a darker lettering; however, no erasure is possible. Common felt-tip markers are in general use now and are both inexpensive and easily obtainable. These markers have the disadvantage of smearing unless care is exercised.

The visually handicapped child with some residual vision should have the opportunity to learn to use the chalkboard. While broad tip chalk is available, it is probably unnecessary because of the broadness of the common stick of chalk. Use of the chalkboard is of particular value where it is difficult to predict space needed in writing, as in working mathematical problems or developing original literary material.

The ability to write has historically been the mark of a literate man. Modern technology has produced equipment which provides visual recording in the form of photography and video tapes, as well as audio recording equipment which is practically available to all. In addition to this, there is the mechanical writing equipment, such as the typewriter. All of this equipment makes it possible for man to function with very little handwriting. However, the little handwriting which is necessary (signing one's name) is of such importance in our commercial and legal world that the lack of this ability leaves an undesirable first impression of general illiteracy and dependency which may be detrimental to the visually handicapped person.

Instructional books and teacher references for teaching handwriting are available from Zaner-Bloser Company. This publishing company has detailed instructions on manuscript and cursive writing as well as methods of transition from one to the other. Special education materials presently available are useful for visually handicapped when minor adaptions are utilized. Other material on handwriting available from this firm include suggestions for motivating students, pictures of students in proper position for writing, and film strips on writing instruction.

References

Lowenfeld, B., Abel, G. L., and Hatlen, P. H. *Blind Children Learn to Read.* Springfield, Illinois, Charles C Thomas, Publisher, 1969.

7

Listening

THE NATURE OF LISTENING

It seems evident that an individual must be able to hear speech before he can comprehend it, and hearing is critically important in the process of learning to speak and read. It is also true that children must have normal hearing acuity and discriminatory abilities if they are to listen well, but research indicates that hearing acuity and the ability to discriminate among speech sounds does not necessarily assure listening comprehension. Ainsworth and High (1954) administered a listening comprehension test, the *Seashore Measures of Musical Talent,* the *Templin Speech Sound Discrimination Test,* and the digit-auditory memory span test portion of the *Wechsler-Bellevue Scale* to 273 subjects. Results indicated that specific and separate auditory abilities are not related to listening ability as measured by immediate recall.

It is generally accepted that listening is more than hearing. Barbe and Myers (1971) define it as "the process of reacting to, interpreting, and relating the spoken language in terms of past experiences and future courses of study." Johnson (1957) states that listening is the ability to understand and respond effectively to oral communication. Brown (1954) coined the word "auding" as a substitute for listening and defined this new term as "the process of hearing, listening to, recognizing, and interpreting the spoken language." The important point is that the ability to hear and the ability to listen are not necessarily synonymous. A factor sometimes considered necessary and sufficient for listening to occur has been attention. Detractors of training in listening have sometimes asserted that listening is simply attending. "Set" is a psychological component of attention. "Anticipatory set" has been defined as the ability to say to oneself as he listens ". . . imagine what the speaker is trying to say. . . ." This anticipation and comparison of expectation with outcome may cause the listener to pay attention in order to see if he is right. In attempting to determine the significance of set, two groups of college students were given the *Princeton Listening Test*, with an experimental group receiving preparatory remarks before each section of the test in an attempt to produce an expectation or set. The control group received no advance remarks. The result was that the experimental group scored higher, suggesting that set does play an important part in listening (Keller, 1960, pp. 36–37).

THE SIGNIFICANCE OF LISTENING

One method of determining the significance of listening in communication is to measure the amount of time spent in this activity. One of the first major treatments of the subject of listening (Rankin, 1926) found that 42 percent of adult communication time is spent in listening. Two decades later Markgraf (1966) found that high school students are expected to listen more than one-half of the total time they spend in the teaching-learning classroom situation. Interestingly, he found these students listened to their teachers three times as much as they did to their fellow students. The finding that teachers talked two-thirds of the total time in class suggests that teachers assume that dissemination of classroom knowledge occurs primarily through listening.

Wilt (1949) studied 530 elementary school children and found that listening is a major activity in school and that more than one-half of school time was devoted to listening. She found, in addition, that teachers may not be fully aware of the role which listening plays in pupils' learning experiences. When teachers were asked to estimate the amount of time children devote to listening, they underestimated the amount by almost 50 percent. In all probability far more of the instruction which goes on in the classroom comes through listening than most teachers suspect. The evidence certainly suggests that methods should be developed for exploiting listening to the best advantage of children. When the visual mode is not available, as is the case with blind children, listening efficiently and accurately becomes urgent.

MEASUREMENT OF LISTENING ABILITY

The assumption is sometimes made that listening is a complex of skills clearly separable from reading and that these skills cannot be reliably measured by applying a reading test. If reading skills and listening skills are of a common nature, a test of one should make possible predictions about the other. Brown and Carlsen (1953) found only low correlations between their test of listening comprehension and tests of reading comprehension. Blewett (1952), in investigating listening ability with college students, concluded that reading and listening involve different factors. These results certainly have implications for the braille reader who must be content to read at considerably slower rates than the typical sighted reader, while retaining substantially the same listening rates. No studies of preference for braille reading over listening seem to have been made for children, perhaps because of the observation that listening is overwhelmingly preferred over braille reading for information.

Some researchers have made comparisons of the relative efficiency of listening and reading by the normally sighted. Witty and Sizemore (1959) published an extensive review of this research in which the findings were that listening comprehension is superior to reading comprehension for children in the elementary grades with low mental ages, while reading comprehension is superior to listening comprehension in the secondary grades with students with higher mental ages. Analysis of the results of these studies by the authors indicates that the relative superiority of listening over normal reading may be contingent upon reading rate. That is, when listening rates exceed reading rates, listening results in superior comprehension. However, when reading rates exceed listening rates, then reading results in superior comprehension.

While there are many published tests designed to test reading ability, development of listening tests lagged until the past two decades. This is partly due to the relatively recent interest in the teaching of listening skills. Whatever the reason for lack of tests, listening cannot be successfully taught as a skill without adequate measures of progress. Fortunately a number of listening tests have been developed.

The first test specifically designed to test listening ability was an unpublished test by Rankin (1926). It was not until several years later that the first test specifically designed to test listening ability (the *Dur-*

rell-Sullivan Reading Capacity Test) was published. This test is still used, although it was first published in 1937. It is designed for use in the second through sixth grades. The *Brown-Carlsen Listening Comprehension Test* (1953) was published and has been widely used in research (Keller, 1960, p. 32). It is designed for the secondary school level as well as for the first year of college, but has been found useful at all levels in college and in the business and industrial world as well.

The *Sequential Test of Educational Progress,* commonly known as the STEP Tests (1957), published by the Educational Testing Service of Princeton, N.J., contains a section on listening. It is on four levels and is recommended by the publisher for use in grades four through fourteen. It has also been used extensively in the past (Keller, 1960, p. 32). Other listening tests have also been used to determine listening ability (Stromer, 1955; McClendon, 1956; Haberland, 1956; Blewett, 1952). Of intelligence, scholastic aptitude, and reading ability, intelligence shows the highest positive correlation with listening ability. These findings support the thesis that many listening test items are the same type as items used to test intelligence and that listening tests may more nearly measure intelligence rather than listening. Of particular interest to teachers are the findings which show little correlation between listening comprehension and scholastic aptitude, at least as measured by grades earned (Blewett, 1952) and academic ratings (Haberland, 1956).

VISUAL VERSUS AUDITORY PRESENTATION

Visual cues such as observation of a speaker have been suggested as an important component of listening. This would seem to have relevance to blind listeners in determining the amount of disadvantage, if any, they have in being unable to observe the speaker. There have been a number of studies on listening comprehension when the speaker is visually observed compared to when the speaker is only heard, but the results were inconclusive. Casambre (1962) reported on a comparison of listeners' levels of comprehension of live and taped presentations in which he found no significant differences. However, the addition of visual clues to oral speech was found to aid comprehension both on immediate and delayed recall. In another study, Arnold (1965) presented a TV lecture to 611 college freshmen and sophomores under three conditions: with sound only, with and without printed objectives, and with both sound and video. No significant differences resulted from the presence or absence of the video, suggesting no advantage to listening comprehension from viewing the speaker. In a direct comparison of visual reading and listening, Hampleman (1955) found listening comprehension in intermediate grades superior to reading comprehension. This was inconsistent with the results of eleventh grade pupils who gained more information from reading than from listening. However, this was modified when after seven-weeks scores on a delayed recall test showed no significant difference between the two media in respect to the amount of learning. This study would seem to indicate that there may be a change in listening ability as children grow older.

Direct comparison of sighted and blind in listening comprehension has been of interest to investigators for many years. Studies since about 1920 have been rather consistent in that no significant differences in listening comprehension have been found when the two groups are controlled for the variables of age, sex, and intelligence (Seashore and Ling, 1918; Kwalwasser, 1932; Hayes, 1933; Cotzin and Dallenbach, 1950). More recently Hartlage (1963), using fifty blind and fifty sighted high school students matched on age, sex, and intelligence, recorded a reading selection with presumed high interest to both groups and then gave a test to measure comprehension. No differences were found between the sighted and blind groups. However, high correlations were reported between intelligence and listening comprehension.

Day and Beach (1971) surveyed the research literature comparing the visual and auditory presentation of information. They concluded that approximately one-half of the research supports each mode of presentation leading to best comprehension and that any superiority of either the visual or auditory presentation depends on the particular circumstances under which the comparison is made. These investigators derived several implications:

1. A combined visual and auditory presentation of material leads to more efficient comprehension than the presentation of either auditory or visual material alone.

2. Meaningful, familiar material can be more efficiently presented aurally, whereas meaningless and unfamiliar material can be more efficiently presented visually.

3. Visual presentations become relatively more effective as reading ability increases, chronological age increases (best at ages over sixteen), and intelligence increases.

4. When comprehension is tested by an immediate recall of the material, a visual presentation is more effective. If a test of comprehension is made after a considerable delay, an auditory presentation is superior.

5. One of the most significant advantages of a visual presentation system is the relatively greater referability, or immediate opportunity for reviewing the material, that it affords. It has been found

that the less referability afforded by a visual presentation system, the smaller its advantage over an auditory presentation.

6. Organized and related material such as prose or factual information is better understood with an auditory presentation; material such as code that is comparatively discrete and unrelated is more effectively received with a visual presentation.

7. The comprehension of material can be tested either by the ease with which the material is learned or by the amount which is retained after a period of time. As stated above, measures of retention are higher after an auditory presentation, whereas measures of learning favor the visual presentation.

While the implications are that blind may be at a listening disadvantage when visual presentations accompany auditory presentations, this disadvantage may be more apparent than real. If, for example, a braille selection accompanies the auditory presentation, it may approximate the effect of a printed item accompanying an auditory presentation. The tactual presentation, such as a braille presentation, would have much the same advantage that a visual presentation has, the advantage of referability. However, parallels between braille and print must be carefully drawn because of the differences inherent in the two modes.

Perhaps the most significant implication for blind listening comprehension is that organized and related material such as prose and factual information seem to be better understood with the auditory presentation than with the visual. While this does not take into account the disadvantages of lack of cumulated visual experiences of a sighted child, it does suggest that, other things being equal, reading material assimilated by listening is as readily comprehensible as that presented visually. Of course, the slower rate is the crucial factor in listening versus print reading, although evidence seems to indicate that with perfection of "speech compression," accompanied by listening instruction, this difference may be minimal with certain types of material (Foulke, 1966).

RELATIVE EFFICIENCY OF LISTENING AND BRAILLE OR LARGE TYPE READING

For the education of the blind and partially seeing, a special condition should be considered—that of the reading rates of braille and large type material, as compared to listening rates, in determining which method is most efficient. Unfortunately, reading rates for braille and large type are quite slow. Braille students in elementary grades read at rates averaging between fifty and sixty words per minute, while sighted students in elementary grades read at an average rate of about seventy words per minute. The difference in reading rate is not particularly great at the elementary level, but the rate differential has become quite large by junior high school. By high school, the braille student reads at an average rate of about sixty-five to seventy-five words per minute, as compared to two hundred fifty words per minute for sighted students (Nolan, 1963). Consequently, completing an assignment with extensive reading takes much longer for the blind student, and his slow rate in reading is often thought to be responsible for educational retardation at the secondary level. Since braille reading rates are slow, greater use of auditory communication would do much to decrease the time needed to cover assignments requiring extensive reading. Recordings made for the blind at the American Printing House are approximately 175 wpm, which is substantially greater than the average braille reading rate.

Carter (1962) interviewed 366 blind, full-time college students. This study revealed that 75 percent of these students received all their textbook information aurally, although many problems were revealed in the use of recorded materials. For example, quality and condition of discs was frequently poor, there were problems of finding a particular place in a book, and many students reported that they had never received any instruction as to how to study from a recording. A frequent obstacle encountered by many users of recordings was that their minds were prone to wander while listening. When brief lapses in attention occurred, significant loss of information was reported. Approximately two-thirds of the students interviewed admitted that they sometimes became sleepy while listening to recordings and sometimes dozed off. This usually occurred when listening to uninteresting material, but reader style was also mentioned as a cause for drowsiness. (A study of the effects of voice characteristics by Scott (1953) indicated that male low-pitched, male high-pitched, female low-pitched, and female high-pitched voices were preferred in that order.) The most frequently mentioned solutions to the listening problems reported were to take notes (actively engage in study) and to sit rather than lie down. Unfortunately, taking notes was often cumbersome because it takes two hands to operate a brailler, which means that no hands are available to operate recording equipment.

Lowenfeld (1945) compared reading and listening comprehension of blind children in grades three, four, six, and seven and found that braille reading was not only much slower than listening to the same material on talking book records, but also led to less comprehension.

Morris (1966) administered several 2,000 word reading selections in braille, large print, and tape recording. The selections, which dealt with science, social studies, and literature, varied in levels of difficulty. They were given to blind elementary and secondary school pupils. One group read or heard the passages in a single presentation. Another group read or heard the same passage on three successive days. Comprehension tests were administered at the termination of each of two periods. In each case the three-day groups comprehended more than the one-day groups. High school students learned significantly more in social studies and literature by reading than by listening; however, there were no differences apparent in the science learning. Among elementary school pupils there were no significant differences between learning by listening and by reading. Listening was two to three times as efficient as reading when time saving with listening was compared to reading. If time spent was taken into account, listening was a considerably more efficient way of learning.

The Morris study also pointed out that the problem of slow reading rates is of even greater magnitude for the visually handicapped than previously realized. Instead of high school students reading braille at about one-third the rate of their sighted peers as previously believed, it takes them four times the amount of time. The resultant educational handicap is one that grows as a student progresses through the grades and encounters reading assignments increasing in length.

Nolan (1963) studied the listening comprehension of blind students in elementary and secondary grades. The study showed that learning by listening was more efficient than learning by reading braille. A comparison of comprehension of matched groups of subjects was completed in which one group read while the other group listened to a short passage of scientific material. The results were that the comprehension of the listening group did not differ from that of the braille reading group. However, the listeners spent only about 33 percent as much time in practice as the braille readers.

An experiment was conducted in which visually handicapped children were given material in literature, social studies, and science to read in braille and recordings to listen to at 175 wpm (Nolan, 1966). Elementary school pupils learned equally well from each medium. Secondary school pupils learned more with braille; but when the amount of time spent on reading and listening was equalized, the learning was greater from listening.

ACCELERATED SPEECH AND LISTENING COMPREHENSION

The typical rate on a recording of a trained professional reader is about 175 words a minute. One authority (Keller, 1960) stated that the belief prior to 1950 was that increasing rate led to decreasing listening comprehension; but more recent studies have shown that with the refined development of sound equipment, the rate of presenting material can be increased without appreciable loss in comprehension. There was considerable interest in determining to what extent listeners could be trained to increase the rate at which they could listen, and whether the capacity to operate at faster rates would, as was frequently claimed for reading, make it possible for them to listen more efficiently at slower rates. Beginning in the 1950s there was a flurry of research activity initiated with the perfection of speech compression techniques. Rapid speech and its comprehension was of particular interest to educators of blind children, and it was with these children that some of the more definitive research was done.

Blind children listening to talking books or other records have simply accelerated the playback speed. Unfortunately, this has the effect of raising the pitch and producing an unpleasant "Donald Duck" effect, although it can be used to skim recorded information. Foulke (1967) has outlined five different methods of accelerating recorded speech in order to increase the input of information to the listener: (1) Increasing the rate of speaking. This has only limited range and introduces undesirable changes in inflection. (2) Changing the speed of reproduction or playbacks. This leads to distortion, sometimes called the Donald Duck effect, which is disturbing to the listener. The timbre and pitch of the speaker's voice is radically altered and intelligibility falls off rapidly. (3) Selecting by computer. This enables a selection to be made of the portions of speech to be discarded. A dichotic presentation was suggested in which the compressed speech was directed to one ear and the material discarded to the other. In an experiment, this form of presentation was preferred to the presentation of the compressed speech to both ears. Principal disadvantages of computer speech compression are the lack of availability of suitable facilities to most researchers and the high costs involved (Scott, 1966). (4) Using a harmonic compresser, which doubles the speed of speech and has no distortion in vocal pitch. This device has been simulated on a computer but is presently in the process of being developed. (5) Time compression by sampling and discarding. This can now be done by the use of an electromechanical device called a Tempo-Regulater, which is manufactured in Germany. Speech compression is accomplished by periodically discarding a segment of the material to be compressed. The length of the discarded segment is small enough so that no entire speech element is lost. The amount of compression is determined by the frequency with which segments are discarded. The sampling is not selective but occurs at random. The time compression method is the one which has been developed to some extent as a reading aid for blind.

As early as 1956 Iverson demonstrated compressed speech to forty-five high school students at a school for the blind. The students were asked to evaluate after listening to a selection. Thirty-nine thought compressed speech should be used in talking book records, with almost all of them responding that speech compressed 25 percent is comprehensible.

Foulke and his colleagues (1962) reported on a study to determine the feasibility of using speeded speech to present aural material to blind children. Because compression with the Tempo-Regulator can increase the rate of material from 175 wpm to 375 wpm without any distortion, that method of acceleration of speech was chosen. Previous research had established that taped speech could be speeded without distortion by eliminating part of it and that it is possible to retain perfect intelligibility even when the speech had been compressed as much as 50 percent. Using braille readers in grades six through eight, two 2,000 word passages were presented on tape at five rates (175, 225, 275, 325, and 375 wpm). One passage was literary while the other one was scientific. A test consisting of multiple-choice items was used to test comprehension in both cases. There was no significant loss in degree of comprehension through 275 wpm. However, beyond this rate the decline in performance was rapid, although even at 375 wpm there was some comprehension. These investigators noted that losses in comprehension that were statistically significant were not all educationally important because the time saved in presenting the material was so great. As has been noted earlier, the median reading rate differences at the secondary level, for example, are quite large, with the mean braille reading rate of high school students at only 90 wpm. It was the conclusion of the investigators that the usefulness of the speech compression technique was clearly demonstrated. They stated that "we now know that blind school children can be given information at a rate commensurate with that employed by normal children with no loss in comprehension." (Foulke, et al., 1962, p. 140.) When as a result of subsequent research an efficient training program can be specified, blind children should be able to be trained to understand rapid speech. In initial attempts to develop listening aids to facilitate development of efficient training programs for using compressed speech, Orr and Friedman (1967) found that allowing students to study precise key word lists before listening to compressed speech did *not* aid comprehension.

One unexpected finding in investigations with speech compression (Nolan, 1968) is that uncompressed material is not consistently superior to compressed material in comprehension. The reason for this seems to be that the students in this study performed under specific motivated conditions, while in previous research in this area no special effort was made to influence motivation other than the usual plea for cooperation that is implicit in most instructions to subjects in experiments. It was suggested that this practice results in relatively low levels of motivation, and in turn to depressed levels of performance. Nolan observed that there has been very little acceptance of auditory instructional materials by teachers of the blind. It is unlikely that they will be any more receptive to compressed speech materials unless convincing evidence of their value is presented. Perhaps when well articulated methods of teaching listening skills are developed and tested, more interest will be shown by teachers in using these materials in instruction.

LISTENING SKILLS INSTRUCTION

Until the last decade or two little attention was paid to the importance of developing listening skills. It was taken for granted that everyone knew how to listen. As new data on listening were collected, it became apparent that listening skills can be deliberately taught. Many good teachers still exhort their pupils to "listen," implying that to hear is to listen. Early (1954, p. 18) suggests that "It would be just as reasonable

to suppose that because children can talk before they come to school they need no training in how to speak," and it has been pointed out that except in rare instances, virtually the only instruction in listening that children receive in the schools is the quite useless admonition to "pay attention" and to "listen carefully." Duker (1955) concluded that there is no universal acceptance of the idea that listening is a skill which must be taught. A number of studies on normally seeing and blind children have apparently resulted in increasing acceptance that listening as a skill can and must be taught.

One instruction program (Bischoff, 1967) investigated listening with partially sighted children in grades four through nine. Two experimental groups used the *Weekly Reader* and Science Research Associates material for a sequential program of listening instruction, with a control group receiving no instruction. There were two sequences of twenty fifteen-minute lessons, each given at the rate of two per week. The lessons consisted of a presentation and a comprehension test. The lessons were designed to stress main thoughts or ideas, specific word meanings, and general comprehension. The STEP was used as the pre- and post-test. The experimental groups showed a significant gain in scores while the control group showed score loss, suggesting that systematic instruction of listening with visually handicapped causes a substantial improvement in this skill.

Hollingsworth (1964) reported a summary of sixteen studies which support the idea that instruction in listening will improve reading skills, and evidence (Pratt and Greene, 1956) indicates that listening instruction is effective regardless of the level of intelligence. The question remains as to how a teacher programmatically teaches listening skills. It appears that basal language arts texts offer little assistance in listening. Brown (1966) analyzed the speech and listening content of fifty-four basal language arts textbooks for grades three through six that were published between 1959 and 1964. He found the listening content to be extremely sparse.

Many educators suggest that listening can be taught by deliberate instruction, whether through games, recording and playing back reports, speeches, and oral readings, exercises in finding the central ideas of tasks, or outlining. These, however, lack the continuity of instruction to attain predetermined goals carried on systematically from grade to grade throughout the time a child attends school. There is also reason to believe that teacher example contributes to instruction in listening as it does in other areas of instruction. It has been suggested that the teacher who has not learned to listen effectively cannot teach listening. Children seem to learn to listen best in a classroom where the environment stimulates speaking and listening, is flexible and permissive, and gives many opportunities for interaction among pupils and between pupils and teacher (Lewis, 1960).

A specific curriculum for teaching sequential listening skills has been developed for grades one through six (Rathgaber, 1969). This concise curriculum provides specific listening objectives and suggests methods used to achieve these objectives, while integrated with the normal daily activities of the child. More than twenty types of listening are specified, with methods of achieving or improving listening skills in each area. See appendix E for the curriculum outline.

References

Ainsworth, S. and High, C. Auditory functions and abilities in good and poor listeners. *Journal of Communication, 4,* 1954, 84–86.

Arnold, R. L. An investigation of learning from auditory and visual stimuli. *Speech Monographs, 32,* 1965, 333.

Barbe, W. B. and Myers, R. M. Developing listening ability in children. *Teaching Listening in the Elementary School.* S. Duker, (Ed.) Metuchen, New Jersey, Scarecrow Press, 1971, 31–33.

Bischoff, R. W. Improvement of listening comprehension in partially sighted students. *Sight-Saving Review,* Fall, 1967, 161–65.

Blewett, T. T. An experiment in the measuring of listening at the college level. *The Journal of Communication, 1,* 1952, 50–57.

Brown, D. "Auding as the Primary Language Ability." Unpublished doctoral dissertation, Stanford University, 1954.

Brown, J. I. and Carlsen, G. R., *Brown-Carlsen Listening Comprehension Test.* Chicago, World Book Company, 1953.

Brown, K. L. An analysis of the speech and listening content of selected pupil textbooks in the language arts for the elementary schools: grades 3–6. *Speech Monograph, 33,* 1966.

Carter, B. How to use educational recordings effectively: A survey of blind college students. *New Outlook for the Blind, 56,* 1962, 332–34.

Casambre, A. J. "The Effects of Certain Variables in Informative Speaking on Listener Comprehension." Unpublished doctoral dissertation, Ohio State University, 1962.

Cotzin, M. and Dallenbach, K. M. Facial vision: The role of pitch and loudness in the perception of obstacles by the blind. *American Journal of Psychology, 63,* 1950, 485–515.

Day, W. F. and Beach, B. R. Auditory versus visual presentation. *Teaching Listening in the Elementary School.* S. Duker (Ed.). Metuchen, New Jersey, Scarecrow Press, 1971, 401–5.

Duker, S. How listening can be taught. *Instructor, 64,* 1955, 35.

Early, M. J. Suggestions for teaching listening. *Journal of Education, 137,* 1954, 17–20.

Foulke, E. Compressed recorded speech and faster aural reading. Washington, D.C., American Association of Workers for the Blind, *Annual,* 1967.

Foulke, E. A survey of the acceptability of rapid speech. *New Outlook for the Blind, 60,* 1966, 261–65.

Foulke, E. et al. The comprehension of rapid speech by the blind. *Exceptional Children, 29,* 1962, 134–41.

Haberland, J. A. Listening ability in college freshmen. *School and Society, 84,* 1956, 217–18.

Hampleman, R. S. "Comparison of Listening and Reading Comprehension Ability of Fourth and Sixth Grade Pupils." Unpublished doctoral dissertation, Indiana University, 1955.

Hartlage, L. C. Differences in listening comprehension of the blind and the sighted. *International Journal for the Education of the Blind, 13,* 1963.

Hayes, S. P. New experimental data on the old problem of sensory compensation. *Teachers' Forum, 6,* 1933, 22–26.

Hollingsworth, P. M. Can training in listening improve reading? *Reading Teacher, 18,* 1964, 121–23, 127.

Iverson, L. Time compression. *International Journal for the Education of the Blind, 5,* 1956, 78–79.

Johnson, K. O. Problems in military audiometry. *Journal of Speech Disorders, 22,* 1957, 731–33.

Keller, P. W. Major findings in the past ten years. *Journal of Communications, 10,* 1960, 29–38.

Kwalwasser, J. Are the blind superior to seeing in hearing? *Etude, 50,* 1932, 249.

Lewis, M. S. Teaching children to listen. *Education, 80,* 1960, 455–59.

Lowenfeld, B. *Braille and Talking Book Reading: A Comparative Study.* New York, American Foundation for the Blind, 1945.

McClendon, P. I. "An Experimental Study of the Relationship Between Note Taking Practices and Listening Comprehension of College Freshmen." Unpublished doctoral dissertation, University of Iowa, 1956.

Markgraf, B. R. Demands on listening skills of secondary school pupils. *Teaching Listening in the Elementary School.* S. Duker (Ed.). Metuchen, New Jersey, Scarecrow Press, 1966, 90–94.

Morris, J. Relative efficiency of reading and listening for braille and large type readers. Washington, D.C., *48th Biennial Conference Report,* American Association of Instructors of the Blind, 1966, 65–70.

Nolan, C. Y. Audio materials for the blind. *Audiovisual Instruction,* Nov., 1966.

Nolan, C. Y. Reading and listening in learning by the blind. *Exceptional Children, 29,* 1963, 313–16.

Nolan, C. Y. *Reading and Listening in Learning by the Blind.* Terminal Progress Report. Louisville, American Printing House for the Blind, Inc., 1968.

Orr, D. B. and Friedman, H. L. The effect of listening aids on the comprehension of time-compressed speech. *Journal of Communication, 17,* 1967, 223–27.

Pratt, R. J. and Greene, H. C. Training children to listen. *Monograph for Elementary Teachers,* White Plains, New York, Row Peterson, 1956.

Rankin, P. T. "The Measurement of the Ability to Understand Spoken Language." Unpublished doctoral dissertation, University of Michigan, 1926.

Rathgaber, J. M. *Experimental Listening Curriculum.* Dominican College of Blauvelt, Blauvelt, New York, U.S. Office of Education, Project #6-8477, 1969.

Scott, R. J. Computers for speech time compression. University of Louisville, *Proceedings of the Louisville Conference on Time Compressed Speech,* 1966.

Scott, W. G. A Study of the Effects of Voice Characteristics in the Listening Comprehension of Blind School Children. Unpublished master's thesis, University of Oregon, 1953.

Seashore, C. E. and Ling, T. L. The comparative sensitiveness of blind and seeing persons. *Psychological Monographs, 25,* 1918, 148–58.

Stromer, W. F. Listening and personality. *Education, 75,* 1955, 322–26.

Wilt, M. A Study of Teacher Awareness of Listening as a Factor in Elementary Education. Unpublished doctoral dissertation, Pennsylvania State College, 1949.

Witty, P. A. and Sizemore, R. A. Studies in listening. *Elementary English, 36,* 1959, 297–301.

8

Orientation and Mobility Instruction

The typical child lives in a world which he interprets by means of his senses. For this child the world is perceived through vision, the most important of all senses. The environment surrounding him is observed through his visual field before it is examined by the other senses. A child's eyes, therefore, are an instrument for comprehensive examination of surroundings and an orientation to his physical environment. In contrast, the visually handicapped child is partially or totally deprived of the instrument of vision in learning experiences, and must therefore be trained to utilize his other senses in this process. The development of peripatology and the use of orientation and mobility skills have opened up a new avenue of education to help the blind child achieve physical independence and command of his environment.

From the time a newborn blind infant comes home from the hospital, his parents must give him affection, care, and comfort in order to instill confidence and security. He will thus be better able to meet the many challenges he will encounter as he matures and ventures out into new surroundings.

The normal child develops concepts of spatial relationships through visual perceptions. The blind child is unable to develop these concepts until he is mobile. While his motor development is commensurate with that of the sighted child, it is not until he is able to crawl that he is able to perceive such concepts as distance or direction. A blind child, there-fore, needs the opportunity to explore in order to gain experience with his environment. The family attitudes at this point become critical. Some parents tend to overprotect their child, thus inhibiting natural curiosity, while other parents reject the child, thus discouraging investi-gation of surroundings. The basic needs of infancy for the blind child are the same as for the normal child. Sufficient opportunities for explo-ration must be present, since initial orientation begins even before the infant crawls. Parents must become aware of the child's needs, by pro-fessional counseling if necessary, and provide opportunity, guidance, and encouragement to aid the development of normal motor function-ing in their blind child.

Many important physical developments take place in a child as he leaves the stage of infancy and begins to move around in his environ-ment. During these first few years the normal child is no longer totally dependent on his parents. The crawling infant learns to stand and walk, begins to be toilet trained, forms simple concepts of physical reality, and becomes aware of simple social demands.

The systematic training of young blind children in orientation and mobility skills is a relatively new discipline. While peripatology has been practiced with adults since World War II, the increasing interest in this training for children has resulted from several factors: (1) the recognition that blind children have developmental characteristics simi-lar to those of sighted children, (2) the acknowledgement of the impor-tance of physical independence in feelings of self-esteem and social interactions, (3) the recognition of the vital role of independent move-ment in vocational success, and (4) the success of instruction in orienta-tion and mobility with adults.

There is considerable support for the current idea that sighted and blind people have common basic needs and developmental tasks to be satisfied. The difference between the blind and the sighted, however, lies in the manner in which each relates to and gains information about his surroundings and thereby orients himself (Blaha, 1961, p. 14).

ORIENTATION TO ENVIRONMENT AND
TRAINING IN DEVELOPMENTAL TASKS

Basically, the developmental processes of the blind child are the same as for the sighted child, but some difficulties are encountered in the training. One important concept which has evolved in work with blind is that many developmental skills taken for granted with sighted children must be deliberately taught to blind children. This training is part of the orientation and mobility of blind. The development of these skills is therefore an essential part of the training of a blind child. It should begin with preschool instruction by the parents, followed by formal instruction by the special teacher of visually handicapped and the orientation and mobility specialist after the child's entrance to school.

Some parents of blind children assume that their child will develop more slowly than normal children, and that special instruction need not start until the child enters school. However, studies showing the necessity of having a normal home environment and growth-producing family life also show the importance of fulfilling these needs with blind children. The normal child will progress from crawling to standing to walking. The blind child also follows the normal developmental stages, but he often progresses from crawling to walking without getting many valuable exploratory experiences. Parents must encourage this exploration. When a blind child does begin to walk, he must be allowed freedom to move about his home. Every opportunity should be provided for exposure to the many objects in his surroundings. He should not be consistently closed in a bedroom, or some other "safe room," but should be allowed to examine furniture, doors, windows, and common household objects.

Much valuable experience in orientation to environment is derived through experiences obtained during the preschool years. The blind child will develop distance perceptions, motor skills, and coordination in movements (Royster, 1964). Parents should be aware of the variety of clues which aid in this process of orientation. A loudly ticking clock may be used to orient a child to a specific room, such as the bedroom or bathroom. A puppy has been suggested as an excellent training aid as well as playmate for a blind child (Cutsforth, 1951):

> Another device that encourages increased activity and mobility is to provide an active pup as a playmate for the child. The collar of the pup should be equipped with a small sleigh bell so that the animal may be pursued and run from. The dog has its advantage over human playmates, for it possesses no sentimental social values that will permit it to show either quarter or compassion (p. 22).

Insufficient activity during this period may have many detrimental effects on the future mobility of the child. Poor gait, lack of development of concepts in spatial relationships, and poor development of motor skills may all be the result. Encouragement and proper guidance with activities associated with learning to walk will allow more rapid development of skill necessary for more sophisticated future training in orientation and mobility training.

Another preschool task which is sometimes neglected with blind children is how to feed oneself. Some parents of blind children continue to feed them long after the child has the muscular control to feed himself. The blind child can learn to feed himself with guidance, encouragement, and patience to allow practice. As with all developmental tasks, self-feeding usually occurs at the same age level as with the normal child. The abilities to use a spoon, fork, and cup or glass are important steps toward independence.

SELF-CARE SKILLS AND PRESCHOOL SOCIALIZATION

The typical processes of socialization accompanying maturation that take place in a normal child are also present within the blind child. The child must learn the same social demands which are expected of the sighted child. The familial social group has the greatest influence on any developing child. He should be assigned household chores in the same way that he would receive tasks if he were normally sighted. The family system of rewards and punishment should apply to him as much as to other siblings. He must learn there are certain rules of society that he must obey. Failure on the part of the parents to establish rules in the home for the blind child, as well as the sighted children, may contribute to socialization problems in the future.

During this stage, the blind child begins to make progress toward acquiring orientation to his physical environment. This orientation is necessary if he is to progress in future mobility training. Early explorations about the home, toilet training, walking, feeding, and social demands are all important steps toward a child's future adjustment to his environment. These activities should be as much a part of the normal training of visually handicapped as they are of the nonhandicapped.

Another important task a blind child learns during this preschool period is to dress himself. As is true with the normal child, he can learn first to undress himself, to use buttons and zippers, and to take off stockings and shoes. When he is successfully able to perform these tasks, he then can begin to dress himself, learn to discriminate front from back of clothes, and the order of putting on inner and outer garments. Successful accomplishment of these skills is a further step to independence.

The visually handicapped child's first steps toward the development of personal care skills should be basically complete by the end of the preschool years. In addition to learning to dress himself, the child at this age can learn to wash and bathe himself, initially with the help of his mother. The child should be made familiar with names of parts of the sinks and bathtubs, as well as equipment such as soap, wash cloth, towel, and bathmat. Procedure and technique should be carefully explained and demonstrated. A child can learn the common techniques of oral hygiene. Necessary equipment such as brush, toothpaste, and mouthwash should be explained, as well as technique. Toward the end of this time, or when the parents feel the child is ready, he should be introduced to the dentist. Early instruction in the self-care skills for bathing and oral hygiene create less work for parents as well as providing another step toward independence for the child.

The blind preschool child should be exposed to many social contacts outside the home:

> A child, in order to maximize his awareness of and participation in his social and physical environment, must be given as many meaningful experiences as possible. He should go to the zoo, the park, the museum, for example, and should be encouraged to interact with other children (Whitstock, 1960, p. 91).

Social experience in visiting public places is valuable for the blind child. He becomes increasingly aware of his environment and of the social expectations of his society. Prior to this time, all socialization experiences have taken place within the home. Opportunities for playing with children his own age also have a tremendous effect on later adjustment to school and society. Enrollment in a normal nursery school can provide the blind child with numerous experiences that will prove useful in orientation to the environment outside the home, socialization with his peers, and progress in normal developmental tasks.

The socialization experiences outside the home provide the preschool blind child with early training in orientation and mobility skills. Orientation terms can be learned in family excursions, giving the child a better command of his environment. The young child can learn the significance of front, back, right, left, up, and down. Knowledge of these terms is essential if the child is to begin formal orientation and mobility training when he enters school. It will also aid the child in learning behaviors acceptable to his peers. A healthy self-concept is the direct result of contact with peers and others who can tactfully and honestly report unacceptable behavior to him for modification.

INITIAL ORIENTATION TO SCHOOL

When he begins school, the child discovers new demands made upon him in the formal atmosphere. Whereas his prior contacts have been with his family and included some of his peers, he now is faced with a new authority figure, his teacher. He also finds new requirements in a sighted world and must learn to adjust to these. Success in preschool training will be the foundation for a successful adjustment to a formal school education.

Among the many adjustments a child must make when entering school is orientation to his classroom. After being shown the location of his seat, he should be encouraged to find the seat himself. Also, the child should become familiar with the physical arrangement of the room, including the location of the teacher's desk and other significant objects. After becoming mobile around the classroom, he may be oriented to the rest of the school and eventually the grounds outside of the school. The first steps in formal orientation and mobility training take place during this time. He should be introduced to sensory cues such as odors from the cafeteria and kitchen, sounds from the music room, and the change from carpeted to tile floors. Tactile senses are also utilized at this time in discovering the various materials and textures in such features as blackboards, bulletin boards, and windows in the classroom. The child also is introduced to the use of a sighted guide. For the very young child, this may initially be no more than holding hands with the teacher, but as the child progresses in maturity he should be instructed in the proper technique of using a sighted guide. His progress in attaining skills in these orientation and mobility techniques may be slow, depending on the amount of training the child had before entering school.

One of the objectives in instructing a blind child in orientation and mobility techniques which relate to personal management is his achievement of independence and acceptance by society. He must be taught to act in a manner which maximizes his social acceptability. Many social skills should be taught at school if not completed at home. Some of the basic ones are (Whitstock, 1960): (1) a child should be taught to turn toward the person to whom he is speaking, so as not to deviate from socially accepted patterns of our society; (2) he should be taught to use common conversational phrases which imply use of vision such as "Did you watch television last night?" without being self-conscious; (3) when in a darkened room he should turn on a light to avoid startling sighted people who may enter; (4) he should be neat in appearance and use proper etiquette when eating; and (5) he should learn to use appropriate polite expressions such as "please," "thank you," and "excuse me." Mastery of these skills will help a child to better relationships with students, teachers, and others in society.

CLASSROOM ACTIVITIES

Orientation training should be integrated with other classroom activities. However, the activities should be planned to exploit the primary learning activity optimally. While an exhaustive list of activities for young blind children is practically impossible to complete, below are suggested examples of activities which will train a child to orient to his physical surroundings.

To give common words such as "top" and "bottom" meaning to the young child and to develop his kinesthetic sense, construction type toys are invaluable. From these the children can learn to recognize left and right, front and back, long and short, straight and crooked, large and small, above and below, behind and forward, and other comparisons. The children can learn the meaning of flat, edge, round, square, top, bottom, ball, cube, circle, corner, sphere, prism, triangle, and other concepts. It is necessary that the children notice likenesses and differences between, for example, a corner of a room and a corner of a table. Besides learning the word meanings, the children must learn to put these words to their most logical use. For example, when the teacher says, "put your hands on the top of the table," does she mean the edge of the table farthest from the body or does she mean the top surface of the table?

Manipulative Activities

For finger coordination the child can learn to follow the dots on a sewing card, to hold and use a blunt needle, to manipulate a pom-pom card, to cut, to tear, and to knit. These activities provide valuable orientation to manipulating objects as well as training in finger and hand coordination. Furthermore, craft activities provide satisfaction to the child because of their tangible results.

Building with blocks seems outdated, but continues to be one of the best learning situations for the blind child. Young blind children enjoy using blocks, provided some initial guidance is given concerning their manipulation. The use of blocks should continue for some time after the child is in school. They not only provide reality for learning words of position, but may be used to demonstrate geometric concepts, counting facts, and physics laws of support, while providing a medium for learning social skills while playing with other children.

Modeling clay and sand are fine for sensory perception. When using clay as a toy, the child learns some laws of nature while using his hands. He can make a hole in the clay with his fingers and find that the rest of the clay bulges out. A bubble in the clay has air in it, and the smell of the clay is the earth. Water will wash away sand, but sand can make a dam of the water. Clay and sand can both be outlets for creative expression. When the child is able to create objects in clay and sand, the teacher knows that he has reached a high degree of skill in tactual perception and that his earlier training has been successful. Some art teachers suggest that manipulation of art media such as clay aid other sensory perception development. The ultimate perception of art forms is based on mental and kinesthetic impressions. The blind child need not depend on kinesthetic or any other sense alone, but can simultaneously develop several of his perceptual skills. Early training is important in the use of all his intact senses. "Simple shape, clear line, expressive texture, all come from geometric shapes—or early training" (Cook, 1943, p. 41).

Effective methods used with young blind children to teach specific tasks often provide useful incidental learning. That is, there is learning, but the children are not being taught deliberately and systematically and are not conscious that learning is taking place. An illustration of this which can supplement primary instruction is to have each child play with a generous amount of plasticine, clay, or other similar material while sitting around a table so that conversation can be carried on easily. The teacher talks with the children but makes no effort to have the children make any particular object. Some child will ask the teacher to make something for him. When the teacher does so, then the other children may also have things they wish to have made or may suggest something to go with the object already made (such as a carrot for a rabbit). This will also encourage them to make their own objects for their classmates to inspect. The children will generally choose things within their previous experience, which have not been formerly presented to them. In this way the teacher is able to supply some of the experiences which are necessary, but for which time is lacking. This is also a good opportunity to teach speech and language skills.

Sensory Discrimination Activities

Formal sensory discrimination training lessons can be developed using taste and odor. This instruction would be incorporated into other coursework and incidental activity after some specific training in identification of tastes and odors. Fruits and vegetables are subjects for teaching the child to use the senses of taste, touch, and smell. Such things as sugar, flour, salt, and honey can be taste objects, while ginger, vanilla, rubber, pepper, cocoa, tea, medicines, and others are for smelling. Other sense training projects can be the study and making of butter, touch and smell of flowers, leaves, pine, nests, birds, nuts, and a host of other items which are probably foreign to the blind child. It is not enough to show the child an object and talk about it. The teacher should include as many aspects of touching, smelling, and hearing as possible.

Talking Books have helped the teacher with sensory discrimination for blind students, but even these have minimal value to the blind child without multisensory supplementary material. If the call of a bird is heard on a recording, the child should ideally have a bird to hold in his hands, a nest to manipulate, and a bird's egg to touch. Verbal description has a place in a blind child's education, but reality is receiving *direct* sensory impressions from the environment. Relatively little time need be spent on information which will always require interpretation by sighted people. For example, the various calls of different birds are important. The fact that some have long beaks and some short, and that some feathers are water repellent while others are not, are important. But to attempt to teach the different colors of the birds at this point may be unnecessary. Sensory discrimination should cease when its usefulness ceases. Colors do have their place in the blind child's vocabulary and thinking, but only when they are a necessary part of his life. For example, the child should learn that certain clothing color combinations are desirable and so label wearing apparel.

Tactually examining textures of cloth, carpeting, and tile on school floors and walls and the types of windows and doors in the building are all interesting and useful subjects. Terms may be applied to surfaces along with tactual examination to establish the meaning of crooked, straight, level, slanted, painted, sanded, and varnished. Odor and touch may both be used in this orientation process. A painted or varnished surface could use both of these senses, as could freshly cut wood.

Springtime is a time to encourage the visually handicapped to participate in the excitement of the change of seasons. The child should listen to the birds, notice the feeling of warmth in the air, and plant seeds in planters in the schoolroom. He should be taken outdoors and shown that the ground has become moist and soft and that it is warmer than the air. He should learn that the odors of spring come from the wet earth, from the freshness of buds and leaves as they grow, and from the sap in the plants and trees.

Finger painting is an excellent sensory discrimination training activity. Muscles are relaxed and the child enjoys smooth rhythmic movements. At the same time arms and hands and fingers are becoming flexible and coordinated. The child learns something of creative expression with free movement so different from his usual activities, which often carry a feeling of tenseness and restricted movement with them.

Excursions are suggested for blind children and are one of the best means of gaining sensory and perceptual experience. Adequate time should be permitted; perhaps only one trip should be taken per day so that the children can be allowed ample time to examine objects. The children should have some preparation as to what to expect on the trip and should have people with them who are willing to let them touch and handle as many things as possible. Permission to touch should be sought from the businesses, museums, and agencies visited. After the trip is over it should again be discussed and perhaps be a basis for a class. It is perfectly possible that a second trip to a place is necessary to complete information on the facility. The first visit may be thought of as a general orientation to plant, building, or institution while each succeeding visit allows further exploration which is often slow with visually handicapped. Some guidance on what to observe is necessary, since the children may be impressed by one thing which keeps them from noticing other important things. These field trips can include the school yard, grocery, mailboxes, fire station, police station, bakery, dairy, pet store, depot and trains, library, museum, airport, and the many other community facilities most people take for granted.

Environmental Orientation Activities

Constant experience and practice are essential to adequate orientation to physical surroundings. In school the child should have ample opportunity to explore his room and others and to examine the halls and stairways. He must learn to get to and from other rooms by himself regardless of age. He should be assigned and be able to locate his own locker, his place at the table, cupboards in the room, and in general move about confidently. The teacher should practice employing means of hearing, touching, and smelling continually to teach the child what is contained in his environment.

Besides these actual experiences the teacher can devise games to teach the child to be aware of sounds and smells and what they mean to him. The game of "Mother Kitty" employs movement with the sense of hearing. One child is the Mother Kitty and must find the other children who are hiding in the room, making scarcely audible "meow" noises. Other similar games may be devised to teach sound location.

Children sometimes realize they are using their sense of smell when they try to identify some fellow students who use hair oil, perfume, or cosmetics, although as they grow older they become gracious about verbally indicating this is the clue used. It is interesting for them to tell by sound whether hot or cold water is in a pan and to fill up jars with water without putting fingers into them. This is a help when they pour their own milk at the lunch table, for they learn to tell by the tone when the cup is full rather than by putting a thumb into the cup. The teacher can make these lessons simple by pouring the water first himself and having the children say "stop" when they think the vessel is full. When the children try it individually they will recognize a full cup.

In using the sense of taste and smell for foods, the child should have the proper association of the foods with the smells and tastes of them. Some blind children are reluctant to try any new food and grow into adulthood with little or no practice in eating with utensils. This may be because they have at sometime or other been given bitter or sour food without warning. In trying to develop an attitude of willingness to sample new foods, the teacher should always tell the child whether the food is sweet, sour, salty, or bitter, and should offer cautious bites. The children can be told what foods they are being served, or perhaps they can guess from the smell before being told. Manners, however, should not be sacrificed for an opportunity to smell new foods. The children need not put the food directly under their nostrils but can sit erect at the table while trying to concentrate on the individual odors as they reach them.

Any sensory discrimination training should involve repetition, with frequent testing and introduction of new sensory stimuli. The child who cannot discriminate among common stimuli will not only suffer from poor sensory perception, but may also not have appropriate facial expressions, which makes him appear abnormal to sighted people. This may be the result of a child not having enough normal emotional experiences, a possible manifestation of the lack of opportunity to use the senses. If the visual handicapped child has many experiences while he is young, he will presumably have the accompanying feelings of pain, anger, and happiness which bring about the natural movements of the facial muscles and cause the child to form the habits associated with these natural facial expressions.

These are a few suggestions for exploitation of sensory discrimination and orientation training opportunities available in the typical school. Other activities which can be taught in a more structured fashion are listed in appendix F and provide a basis for additional systematic instruction in orientation and mobility.

FORMAL ORIENTATION
AND MOBILITY READINESS

When is a blind person ready for formal orientation training? A somewhat trite, but essentially true response, would be that he is ready for orientation training at birth. Orientation has been defined as "the process of utilizing remaining senses in establishing one's positions and relationships to all other significant objects in one's environment" (Napier and Weishahn, 1970, p. 59). There is no criterion to be met before a blind child can be oriented to his environment. It begins at birth and is a never-ending process. Every new situation requires a period of orientation which may range from moments to weeks or months, depending of course on the complexity of the situation. Because of the all-pervasive character of this definition, readiness will have to be discussed as readiness for formal mobility training, keeping in mind that orientation cannot be separated from mobility and indeed is very much an integral part of it.

Mobility has been defined as "the ability to move safely, effectively and comfortably from one place to another within the environment by utilizing the remaining senses" (Napier and Weishahn, 1970, p. 59). When is the individual ready to undertake formal mobility training? What criteria should be met? Presently there is very little in the form of tests or checklists to aid and determine readiness. One scale for measuring performance which promises to be useful has been developed (Lord, 1969). Success depends on the individual, on the mode of travel he wishes to use, and, equally important, it depends on the mobility instructor and his methods. There are a few basic criteria that should be met before formal instruction in actual travel techniques begins. The instructor should take a history regarding sight, hearing, general health, attitudes, and personality of the blind individual. This information comes from medical personnel, family, social workers, psychologists, and the individual himself. Questions such as the following are important: How much sight does the person have, and how well can he utilize it? At what age did he become blind? What is his diagnosis and prognosis? Hearing is a very important sense in mobility training and should be tested before training begins so that the instructor has accurate information. Mobility training is a vigorous process and the person undertaking it should be in good general health if he is to profit from training and become an independent traveler. Of equal, if not more, importance are the attitudes of the blind individual and his family toward his blindness and toward mobility training. "Independent travel is risk taking: a stable family is more likely to be supportive provided it is not overprotective" (Graham, 1965, p. 159).

The personality of the blind individual will affect his progress in mobility. What is the motivation of the blind individual toward mobility training? Did he ask for mobility training on his own initiative? If not, who or what influenced him? Why does he want to be an independent traveler? Without motivation, the instructor and pupil will progress slowly. This may well be a reason why specialists sometimes wait until the child is in his teens or close to it before beginning mobility training. Most teenagers want to be independent, to be accepted, to move as freely as their sighted peers, and to have the privacy that independent travel affords them. At this age they begin to think of the future and employment. "The more independent a blind person is, the less blind he is and the more accepting of his blindness. . . . The more independent he is, the more accepted he is by his employers, fellow employees, relatives, friends and neighbors" (Curtin, 1962, p. 18). Much of this independence comes as a result of successful mobility training. A primary goal of orientation and mobility training is to make the individual as independent as possible.

BASIC READINESS FACTORS

The mobility specialist wants the child to understand many basic concepts that come relatively easily to a sighted child but must be deliberately taught to the blind child.

> It has been apparent to orientation and mobility specialists that blind children, especially those blind since, or shortly after birth, tend to lack the necessary concrete knowledge of their environment and the necessary basic concepts of distance, direction, and environmental changes (Hapeman, 1967, p. 48).

There seems to be consensus among orientation and mobility specialists that the child must be allowed to move about in the home, yard, and neighborhood. He must be allowed to explore by sound, touch, smell, and taste the many objects in his environment which are denied him visually. He must be allowed to make mistakes, to fall, to get scratches and bruises, to learn through experience as any child does. This is sometimes difficult for parents of blind children to accept. They tend to be overly concerned, overprotective, and unwilling to let the blind child take the lumps and bumps of everyday living that the sighted child takes without parental qualms. The blind child needs these experiences if he is to become a well-adjusted "normal" child without undue fear of the world around him.

The child must conceptualize body image—the parts of his body and "what is connected to what," the right side and the left side, up and down, forward and back, and other terms designating position. The mobility instructor will be using such terms as "shoulder level," "arm forward," "waist high," "head upward," "feet together," and "right" or "left foot"; and it is essential that the child know what these terms mean.

He must also learn that there are things such as fixed objects, those that are always there, whether or not he can hear, feel, or smell them. These can be used as landmarks in his environment, as something he can depend upon. He must also know that some objects are movable and that there will be some changes in his environment from day to day. There are also moving objects. Parents should relate the movement of his toy cars and wagons to the actual movement of cars, trains, boats, and other vehicles, to give the child more meaningful experiences. He should also be exposed to various types of terrain: rough, smooth, curved, straight, incline, and decline. Parents should explain and allow the child to experience objects, sounds, and odors.

To be a successful traveler, he should know the position of objects in space using such concepts as in front of, behind, next to, across from, away from, overhead. Sound localization is also very important to orient the person to direction and location within the physical environment. Sounds should be associated with the devices producing the sounds.

The learning of these concepts should begin very early in the life of the blind child and continue throughout his days in school. The school can help these children by

> early, thorough, and systematic tactile training using objects of various degrees of complexity, systematic body-image training, affording the blind child a better concept of his body, its location relative to objects, its parts, and its left–right dimensions; and a program of mobility education . . . (Cratty, Peterson, Harris, and Schoner, 1968, p. 116).

If the school system is fortunate enough to have a full-time mobility instructor, he will see that these objectives are met before actual travel training begins, by teaching these concepts. If, however, a mobility instructor is not available, the teaching of these very important concepts is left to others.

RATIONALE FOR TEACHING ORIENTATION AND MOBILITY SKILLS

Why is mobility important?

> It is important to recognize that mobility represents the avenue through which a person who is born blind or becomes blind at a later age, reaches out into his social, educational, vocational, and economic environment . . . Independent functioning on the part of the blind person gains the person community acceptance (Wilson, 1967, p. 287).

Mobility is probably the key element in the (economic) success of blind people. If they can overcome the restrictions that visual impairment puts on travel, they can expect to approach national averages on employment and income (Graham, 1965, p. 160).

And finally, one teenager's reaction to being independently mobile:

> I was actually traveling alone. I had found an obstacle by myself, and I hadn't hit it either. And now I knew something else. I didn't have to sit around instead of going where I liked. I didn't have to wait for someone to go with me either. I felt good, and free (Thomas, 1957, p. 65).

Data was collected on 450 legally blind adults in rehabilitation agencies in California to determine if certain individual characteristics might be related to the subjects' success or lack of success in rehabilitation. One-half of these individuals were successful in achieving vocational rehabilitation. The variables assessed were I.Q., age, age blindness occurred, total years of blindness, degree of blindness, vocational classification before rehabilitation and after, total years worked before rehabilitation, years of education, mode of travel, and others. The conclusion of this study was that the most significant variable that differentiates between success and nonsuccess in vocational rehabilitation is the adequacy of orientation and mobility skills (Knowles, 1969).

The Perceptual Motor Learning Laboratory at the University of California, Los Angeles (Cratty, Peterson, Harris, and Schoner, 1968) constructed an orientation and mobility test to determine the variables which contribute to accurate mobility of blind people. The test measured ability to detect gradients and walk a straight line without vision. Subjects in the study included both blind children and adults. Findings suggested that children should be given training early to heighten awareness of body parts. It was determined that laterality, as evidenced by hand use, though well-established by age six in sighted children, is not as well-established in congenitally blind children. This training should begin as early as possible, and children should be made aware of the terms "front" and "back," parts of the face, location, and names of the limbs. They should understand left and right, and should have body image training that includes understanding that the left arm and leg emerge from the left side of the body and so on. Other abilities to acquire included ability to orient oneself relative to various objects while standing and facing these objects, and then turning the back and sides to objects. This training is determined to be imperative for the child who has no opportunity to observe movement visually. An incidental finding in this study was that veering while attempting to walk in a straight line is caused by perceptual distortion which can be corrected with training.

An eight-week training program involving thirty blind children ages seven to fourteen years of age explored the trainability of perceptual judgments. The results were encouraging. There was 42 percent improvement in elimination of veer after training and 50 percent improvement in the facing movement accuracy. The concept of left and right was also enhanced through training. These findings emphasize the importance of systematic orientation training programs in improving basic perceptual adjustments that assist later mobility (Cratty, Peterson, Harris, and Schoner, 1968). Other factors affecting mobility include hearing, balance, kinesthetic memory, touch, smell, orientation, and previous mobility training. Present travel ability needs to be considered. After these data have been collected, the final decision as to whether or not a particular child is "ready" for mobility training is the decision of the mobility specialist, or special teacher if an orientation and mobility specialist is not available.

Residual vision is appropriate for consideration also since most legally blind children have some vision. Development of visual discrimination through use should be stressed. The blind child observes sounds through the sense of hearing, odors are experienced in relation to sources of the stimuli, changes of temperature and air currents can be felt, textural changes on the surface of the ground can be discerned, and the blind child can learn to observe distances by time, movement, and sound. "Any clue that he can obtain is interpreted for the purpose of safe locomotion and . . . orientation" (Lowenfeld, 1971, p. 177).

THE IMPLICATIONS OF PROPER POSTURE

The word "posture" at one time brought to mind a picture of a mother telling her child to "stand up straight and put those shoulders back," which the child did obediently until his mother was no longer watching. However, posture is now not a static concept as it was, but is a concept of dynamism which encompasses the many "postures" of an individual. These postures are all the positions of the body while standing, sitting, walking, running, or during any activity. These body positions are present whether "mother is looking" or not. Every young child has his own posture pattern resulting from influences of his environment and the society in which he lives.

Children with vision often feel they are moving exactly like their ideal characters. They try to duplicate the walk, standing positions, and mannerisms of their favorite people: television stars, movie idols, or other heroes. It is only natural that many children move exactly as one of their parents. Some of this may be hereditary, but much is due to the child's desire to imitate his parents. These acquired patterns of posture are the result of the child's image of his own body and his idea of how he looks or wishes to look to other people. He may change his body image periodically and thus change some of his voluntary movement patterns. For instance, children are often seen limping, swaggering, taking extra long or short steps, or employing various other exaggerated movements. They are merely assuming their ideal posture for the day, but the basic structure remains the same. They will revert to their more normal movement patterns frequently during the course of these parts they are playing (Davies, 1958, pp. 1–5).

What then of the blind child who is unable to emulate because he cannot see the body position and movement of others? He cannot pattern his posture after people he cannot see, and certainly he cannot build up a proper body image for himself through observation. Everyone's movement should be a rhythm between the lower and upper extremities in which postural reflexes are put into action. This movement should be fluid and brought about with the least possible expenditure of energy. If a person is to achieve this cosmetically and functionally desirable condition he must fulfill three conditions:

1. Adequate spatial orientation including a valid concept of the vertical.

2. Well-conditioned postural reflex mechanisms.

3. An appropriate and accurate body awareness against which stance and motion can be patterned.

The blind child is often sadly lacking in these requisites because of his lack of vision. Often the body image and awareness which a blind person uses as his model for posture is erroneous. The expression of posture in the blind is frequently regulated by reflex mechanism which vision guides in the sighted. Especially in the case of the congenitally blind, there is probably a lack of accurate concept of "vertical," which is so necessary for proper orientation (Siegel, 1965).

Another factor often contributing to the poor posture of blind children is their unfortunate lack of physical activity. Many parents who would not dream of encouraging their "normal" children to be inactive will permit, and even encourage, their blind child to be extremely sedentary. After all, they contend, he might hurt himself if he runs or rides a bicycle; and he certainly cannot join the family ball games, because he cannot see the ball. The blind child, in the face of this discouragement, then sits and perhaps grows overweight, adding another dimension to his posture problem. He is not able to gain any of the

self-confidence in the use of his body which he might otherwise have attained if he had been involved in some vigorous activity.

"A young child's posture patterns may lead to an adult's physical handicap" (Davies, 1958, p. vii). The constant bad posture of the blind child may eventually cause discomfort or deformity and cause difficulty in orientation and mobility. Since good mobility is evidently dependent on the best possible posture, it would seem that a wise procedure would be to include problems of posture directly in a mobility program. Special note should be taken of the body-image and vertical-concept needs of the blind. Good posture usually goes hand-in-hand with adequate kinesthetic awareness. Improving this awareness ought to be a part of the total orientation and mobility training of the blind.

While the blind child may establish any of the various bad habits of posture to which the sighted child is also susceptible, there seem to be certain characteristic postures which the blind adopt. The malposture which would probably be most detrimental to good mobility is the practice of toeing out while standing or walking.

There are certain bad posture habits which are best noted in a side view of the individual and which are most likely to produce discomfort and, in extreme cases, deformity. These often manifest themselves in pairs or groups of malposture. The forward head is very common. This problem is easy to detect: an imaginary line from the ear to the middle of the shoulder will obviously not be the straight one that it should be. When the head is thrust forward, there is often an accompanying round swayback, a continuous curving of the upper back. And rounded back is generally found in conjunction with a low chest. The chest has a low, sunken look rather than being held high. Since the rest of the body is thus thrown out of proper position, another deviation found in this group might be the relaxed abdomen. Abdominal protrusion is often quite pronounced and usually is accompanied by a low back curve (Drury, 1961, p. 4). Obviously these poor posture traits could easily lead to actual pain, especially in the spinal area. They would also impede proper balance—something which is particularly important to a blind person.

Too many of these postural deficits are present in the adult blind, but obviously they were not developed overnight. In these instances it can be said that an ounce of prevention is better than a pound of cure, and it would be particularly true in the case of the "blind" posture. Incorrect posture positions are much more difficult to change after they have become a distinct part of a person than if they had been corrected at an early age. Relaxation and poise are conducive to successful performance and avoidance of fatigue (Lowman and Young, 1960, p. 108); but relaxation and poise will not suddenly spring to life as a child approaches his teen years, when the need becomes critical, if he has not been building his posture along the way.

Since the child spends so much of his day in school, this may be the place where prevention or improvement will have to be activated. The ideal situation would involve having the children participate in a program planned and carried out by a physical education specialist. This, however, is not always feasible, and it is often the duty of the elementary teacher to teach and supervise the gym and outdoor activities as well as the classroom subjects. These activities should be planned for the improvement of posture patterns, and they should be designed to help the child overcome his sedentary existence.

While specific exercise training programs may work well for young blind children, with maturity comes preference for more athletic types of activity. As a matter of fact, they will probably find those which include some social aspect more rewarding. Activities which have been found successful with blind youngsters include ice skating, fencing, and skiing.

Ice skating is quite effective for remedying posture faults, developing antigravity muscles, and encouraging balance and coordination. Development in skating seems to be followed closely by improvement in mobility skills. Fencing also has proved to be excellent for perfecting posture and mobility proficiency. The skills learned in fencing give an especially good backgound for the skills needed in long cane travel. The other activity which is both beneficial and could be quite enjoyable for the blind young man or woman is skiing. Skiing provides aid in developing equilibrium and independence in motion (Siegel, 1966).

The earlier a blind child initiates a program of physical activity, the fewer the postural corrections. However, whether the program is one of prevention or cure, whether it is conducted by a physical education teacher, mobility instructor, or classroom teacher, there must be a postural program for blind youngsters so that they will develop good habits of dynamic posture necessary to efficient adult mobility.

IMPLICATIONS OF BLIND MANNERISMS

Some mannerisms that have been observed in blind children which hinder mobility and social acceptibility include those involving the thrusting of fingers into the eyes, nose, or mouth, or manipulating appendages such as ears, nose, lips, or locks of hair. Other mannerisms sometimes noted are body sway, roll or tilt of the head, arm motion, shoulder shrugs, and exaggerated genuflections. There have been many explanations as to the causes of these mannerisms. For example, mannerisms that include such activities as putting fingers in the eyes and holding the head forward may have their origin in ocular irritation; the child may have developed the habit of putting his hands to his eyes when they hurt him, and this behavior may persist as a mannerism after the irritation is cured. Other mannerisms have their beginnings in infancy when the body becomes a source and object of stimulation. Still others may be attempts of the child to achieve neuromuscular coordination (Morse, 1965).

These mannerisms have been generally recognized as being persistent. Various explanations have been offered for the cause and persistence of these behaviors. One interpretation is that the child who is not sufficiently stimulated from the outside world will turn to his own body for stimulation (Lowenfeld, 1971, p. 102; Cutsforth, 1951, p. 6). The stimulation that may be lacking for the blind child may be physical as well as that ascribed to lack of vision. If, in treating mannerisms, adults use the approach of ignoring the act or attempting to stop it by negative acts or commands, the result may be that the symptom and not the cause is being treated. In order to treat the cause (lack of stimulation), numerous activities should be provided. Lowenfeld (1971, p. 102–3) suggests that children will give up many of their mannerisms if they can become active in a variety of ways. This has important implications for development of orientation and mobility skills early in life.

Helping the child to understand his surroundings, teaching him how to handle his body well, and then teaching him good mobility skills are necessary kinds of aids to the elimination of socially unacceptable mannerisms (Baird, 1961). Closely related to mannerisms is good posture, which can aid blind individuals in their quest for more complete orientation and mobility development. Other explanations suggest that socially unacceptable mannerisms may be the result of a lack of physical stimulation which could have been provided by orientation activity.

MEASUREMENT OF PROGRESS

Progress in the acquisition of orientation and mobility skills is determined both through observation by the orientation and mobility specialist or teacher of visually handicapped and, more recently, through tests or scales. A set of scales was developed to measure the performance of orientation and mobility of elementary school age blind children. Lord (1969, p. 77) noted that "The conviction is growing that fundamental knowledge and habits relating to space and movement in space must be established at an early age." This scale measures the behavioral components in orientation and mobility that are relevant for young blind children in: (1) habitual movement in space, (2) self-help skills, (3) use of sensory cues in travel, (4) employment of directions and turns in travel, and (5) formally taught orientation and mobility skills. While continued development of this scale is contemplated, it appears to be a useful measure of performance.

Detroit's Mobility Evaluation Report (Kirk, 1968) was developed by teachers of the visually handicapped in consultation with a mobility specialist and the supervisor of classes for visually handicapped. It has six sections which include: (1) posture and walking, (2) use of senses and avenues to learning, (3) use of basic knowledge and concepts, (4) indoor mobility, (5) outdoor travel, and (6) needs or inadequacies. Ratings used are "S" for satisfactory, "N" needs to improve, and "X" for not expected to accomplish at present. Both the orientation and mobility instructor and the special teacher contribute to this report of evaluation. This is an example of a systematic evaluation of progress which can be reported to parents and others in aiding in the development of the child's skills.

This chapter has reviewed those personal characteristics of blind children and instructional procedures which the classroom teacher of special teacher of visually handicapped needs knowledge about in order to employ it in their work with blind children. Orientation and mobility specialists or "peripatologists" are sufficiently prevalent today that blind children in most parts of the United States will have some, although not necessarily sufficient, access to them. Therefore, it may be necessary for the teacher with little or no training in orientation and mobility to provide initial orientation skills which will complement the instruction provided by the specialist. It is also necessary for teachers of visually handicapped to provide necessary orientation of the child to the school and surrounding area until an orientation and mobility specialist is available to provide guidance and instruction in this process. It is not the intent here to have the teacher replace the orientation and mobility specialist in the school. The teacher should complement the work of the specialist by providing illustrations of techniques and material which will enhance the functioning of blind and other visually handicapped children in school. Appendix F describes specific orientation and mobility techniques for teachers.

References

Baird, B. Mobility, orientation and travel—A one-day workshop. *International Journal for the Education of the Blind, 11,* 1961, 15–18.

Blaha, L. E. Identification of orientation and mobility skills for young blind children. *American Association for Instructors of the Blind,* 1961, 14–19.

Cook, F. Art without sight. *School Arts, 43,* 1943, 40–45.

Cratty, B. J., Peterson, C., Harris, J., and Schoner, R. The development of perceptual-motor abilities in blind children and adolescents. *New Outlook for the Blind, 62,* 1968, 111–17.

Curtin, G. T. Mobility: Social and psychological implications. *New Outlook for the Blind, 56,* 1962, 14–18.

Cutsforth, T. D. *The Blind in School and Society.* New York, American Foundation for the Blind, 1951.

Davies, E. *The Elementary School Child and His Posture Patterns.* New York, Appleton-Century-Crofts, 1958.

Drury, B. J. *Posture and Figure Control Through Physical Education.* Palo Alto, California, The National Press, 1961.

Graham, M. D. Wanted: A readiness test for mobility training. *New Outlook for the Blind, 59,* 1965, 157–62.

Hapeman, L. B. Developmental concepts of blind children between the ages of three and six as they relate to orientation and mobility. *International Journal for the Education of the Blind, 18,* 1967, 41–48.

Kirk, E. C. A mobility evaluation report for parents. *Exceptional Children, 35,* 1968, 57–62.

Knowles, L. Successful and unsuccessful rehabilitation of the legally blind. *New Outlook for the Blind, 63,* 1969, 129–36.

Lord, F. E. Development of scales for the measurement of orientation and mobility of young blind children. *Exceptional Children, 36,* 1969, 77–82.

Lowenfeld, B. *Our Blind Children.* 3rd ed. Springfield, Illinois, Charles C Thomas, Publisher, 1971.

Lowman, C. L. and Young, C. H. *Postural Fitness—Significance and Variances.* Philadelphia, Lea & Febiger, 1960.

Morse, J. L. Mannerisms, not blindisms: Causation and treatment. *International Journal for the Education of the Blind, 15,* 1965, 12–16.

Napier, G. D. and Weishahn, M. W. *Handbook for Teachers of the Visually Handicapped.* Louisville, American Printing House for the Blind, 1970.

Royster, P. M. Peripatology and the development of the blind child. *New Outlook for the Blind, 58,* 1964, 136–38.

Siegel, I. M. The expression of posture in the blind. *International Journal for the Education of the Blind, 15,* 1965, 23–24.

Siegel, I. M. Selected athletics in a posture training program for the blind. *New Outlook for the Blind, 60,* 1966, 248–49.

Thomas, J. The long finger. *International Journal for the Education of the Blind, 6,* 1957, 62–65.

Whitstock, R. H. Orientation and mobility for blind children. *New Outlook for the Blind, 54,* 1960, 90–94.

Wilson, E. L. A developmental approach to psychological factors which may inhibit mobility in the visually handicapped person. *New Outlook for the Blind, 61,* 1967, 283–89.

Physical Education and Recreation

The Perkins Institution was the first school, and for many years the leader, to offer physical education for the blind. Samual Gridley Howe is credited with leadership in initiating this phase of education for the blind in America. As a physician and health advocate, he knew the benefits of exercise and recreation for children. Although there was some physical education at Perkins from 1832 to 1840, the first structured physical education program was not offered until 1840, when the institution was moved from the Perkins mansion to South Boston. Buell (1966, p. 19) recounts that, "In warm weather Dr. Howe swam in the sea with the boys. This was the first physical education program for the blind in America and was far ahead of most of the physical education in the public schools."

The growth of physical education programs for the blind was slow. However, between 1850 and 1860, more emphasis was placed on physical education programs in general, and more physical education classes were offered for the blind. Soon the Philadelphia and Indiana schools for the blind began physical education programs for their students. Other schools followed suit during the recreation movement of the early 1900s (Buell, 1966, p. 20).

Emphasis is presently being placed on play activities and sports, in addition to general exercise. Sir Francis Campbell is credited with pushing play activities for blind youngsters. He has stated, "The education of the blind, whether literary, musical, or technical, will not be crowned with practical success unless based upon a thorough system of physical education" (Buell, 1966, p. 22).

Today the blind are participating in many sports and recreational activities. Residential schools sponsor teams which compete with other schools in activities such as track, wrestling, swimming, and bowling. Leagues and associations at a national level have been organized to arrange and supervise the competition.

THE NEED FOR PHYSICAL EDUCATION

Physical education is an essential part of the education of any handicapped child. The lack of involvement with nonhandicapped as well as handicapped peers in on-going programs has too often led to a self-depreciating attitude on the part of the blind. They have met with so many denials or have been made to feel that they cannot perform in so many activities that they are discouraged in trying and cannot, in fact, perform many simple physical tasks because of lack of opportunity to participate. Because of attitudinal and man-made physical barriers which have excluded them from those physical activities that most people take for granted, many handicapped individuals cannot fulfill what would otherwise be normal aspirations, interests, and abilities (Nugent, 1969). Through a program of physical education, initiated early in the education of the visually handicapped child, the child can develop a realistic concept of himself and his physical abilities. Active involvement is a necessity of the most basic kind.

Understanding of the physical environment by a blind child through use of remaining senses requires systematic instruction in those skills associated with physical education. Modern motion study techniques in improving the efficiency of even experienced sighted workers have demonstrated the superiority of guided over unguided methods as being most effective (Hunter, 1962). Understanding of spatial relationships can be greatly improved with systematic manual exploration and interpretation.

Observation of people with sensory deprivation has shown two common features: (1) an intense desire for external sensory stimuli and (2) a desire for bodily motion (Hunter, 1962). If this finding is accepted, then the commonly observed mannerisms of blind such as rocking and other body or limb movement become understandable. The individual uses the bodily motion to receive external stimuli. In order to maintain equilibrium, external stimulation is needed. The sighted person is, presumably, not forced to utilize conspicuous body motion to the extent required by the blind since he is not as restricted in movement and he can visually survey the appropriateness of some atypical movements.

PHYSICAL DEVELOPMENT PATTERNS OF VISUALLY HANDICAPPED CHILDREN

The physical attributes of elementary school children may be characterized at various ages. In the primary grades (ages 6–8 years) the child feels the need to test his growing strength and skill. He will experiment with anything he can find to throw, to kick, to climb and balance on, or to jump on, from, or over. He wants to measure up to and control his environment. Each new success contributes to his growing sense of independence as well as his emotional stability through the overcoming of fear and frustration. The youngster in the intermediate grades (ages 9–12 years) is at a "golden age" of motor skill. His growth rate slows down; he seems to know himself and what he can do and he plays harder for longer periods. During this time, boys and girls become increasingly independent of adults and increasingly dependent on friends of their own age (Halsey and Porter, 1963). There appears to be no reason to believe that this pattern is not potentially present in the typical blind child.

Physical growth and maturation may be retarded in visually handicapped children who have other disabilities, are born prematurely, or have not had an opportunity to move and stimulate physical development. A sighted child born prematurely or deprived of physical activity would also show retarded development in growth and maturation. Under these circumstances, the visually handicapped are prone to lack physical vitality; they have less strength and agility than normal seeing children of the same age. Their kinesthetic awareness is poor. Their posture development is retarded, but largely because of their inactivity. It should, however, be emphasized that this retardation in physical development is not "caused" by blindness or visual impairment. It is the result of lack of opportunity to engage in physical activity.

To fulfill the need to understand and adjust to the physical environment, spatial orientation training should include all types of body movement through space, such as those used in physical education programs. The necessity for orientation and mobility training is discussed in more detail in chapter 8, but is closely related to physical education.

Evidence suggests that blind children are sometimes discouraged from participating in physical activity, and as a result physical growth and maturation are somewhat retarded. Height and weight have been reported as less than average (Krause, 1955) for certain blind children, suggesting the need for physical activity as well as proper nutrition. Inactivity has been blamed for poor posture, lack of physical vitality, and the lack of strength and agility in blind when compared with sighted children. One reason suggested for this inactivity is overprotective parents and teachers who are reluctant to stimulate participation in physical activity.

Buell (1956) reported on a study attempting to measure gross physical performance of blind and partially seeing children. About 20 percent of all children over ten years old in schools and classes for blind were included as subjects. Measures for physical activity included the 50-yard dash, basketball throw for distance, standing broadjump, and the Iowa Brace Test. The study showed that on all levels of the Iowa Brace Test the mean scores of visually handicapped fell far below those of seeing children. The weaknesses of the children with defective vision seemed to be general in nature; they did not consistently fall below seeing children in any one factor such as body control, static balance, coordination, or agility. The mean scores on track and field events also fell below those of seeing children. Visually handicapped children who lost their vision after six years of age did not have as much difficulty in adjusting to physical activities as did those blind prior to age six. Buell concluded that the physical weaknesses of the visually handicapped are the result of limited physical activity before entering school and that the leading cause is overprotection.

Specific areas of delayed physical development commonly found in blind can be remediated through physical education (Oliver, 1970). Because of the danger of injury in the exploration of environment during preschool years, parents frequently restrain the activity of their visually handicapped child. The result is less desire to explore than sighted children with the result that their physical development may be adversely affected. As was noted earlier (Buell, 1956), blind chldren do develop skills later. Regular participation in physical activity begun early in school can remedy much of the lag in development.

It has been suggested that high levels of physical fitness are more important to the visually impaired than for persons with normal vision because: "Blind persons must expend more energy to perform, achieve, and succeed at the same level as their seeing peers. This is true whether they are crossing the campus, assembling units in a factory, or working in professional positions" (Buell, 1970, p. 41). A conservative estimate is that only about one-third of the blind and partially seeing children attending public schools in the United States are being offered vigorous physical education (Buell, 1967, p. 248). This is not due to a general inability by the visually impaired to perform adequately in these experiences. It is primarily due to the belief of a large number of school administrators, teachers, and parents that many visually handicapped cannot participate in a vigorous program of physical education in school and maintain normal standards of safety. This attitude is maintained in spite of the fact that residential and public day schools have provided vigorous physical activity, without abnormal accident rates, for more than a century (Buell, 1967, p. 249). A further reason for visually handicapped being excluded from public school physical education is the belief that a blind child requires more supervision by the teacher (Buell, 1967, p. 249). There are also those teachers who are simply afraid to try out the visually handicapped in physical activity because they are uncertain whether the activities are appropriate.

The human body, the way it is handled, and the general physical appearance are fundamentally linked to social living, self-concepts, and very possibly the choice of vocation. An individual's conception of his body appears to be closely related to his total self-concept. If he thinks well of himself, he is likely to be tolerant and accepting of his body. If he is self-rejecting, he rejects his body image (McCandless, 1967, p. 376). Thus, the limitations caused by lack of sight may keep the blind child from the fullest possible appreciation of his potential. Participation in recreational activities enjoyed by his peers may be limited by his attitude toward himself and his blindness rather than by any impairment in potential skill which might allow participation in physical activity. The child who experiences achievement and social adjustment through recreation derives good mental as well as physical health.

PHYSICAL EDUCATION ACTIVITIES APPROPRIATE FOR BLIND

There have been several published lists of recreation and physical education activities appropriate for blind and other visually handicapped (Buell, 1953; Williams, 1964; Seelye and Thomas, 1966; Trevena, 1970). One list (Williams, 1964) reports data compiled from a survey of thirty-six schools in the Midwest which have blind and partially seeing children. Virtually every physical education activity available to normally seeing children is listed, although some adaptations are required for use with visually handicapped. Also included within this report are athletic events for blind in interscholastic competition and those activities which are considered inappropriate. Examination of these lists of activities reveals that some generalizations can be made about those physical activities in which blind may profitably participate. Young blind children do not typically run or jump with ease because they fear the insecurity of unfamiliar space and are reluctant to move freely. Early play experiences usually give them enough assurance of their skill to make them want to move, and this assurance helps them develop self-reliance and confidence to overcome the physical insecurity. Activities that encourage the development of the child's physical orientation to space are necessary to improve his skill and enjoyment of movement (Hunt, 1955, pp. 78–79). Thus, blindness in itself is not a reason to excuse blind children from vigorous activity. A note, however, should be made regarding those rare visually handicapped students who have other medical conditions, such as the danger of retinal detachment. These conditions may be aggravated by vigorous activity. These children can be assigned a program of physical education to minimize or avoid aggravating existing physical pathologies (Buell, 1967, p. 248).

CONTEMPORARY LACK OF PHYSICAL EDUCATION PROGRAMS FOR VISUALLY HANDICAPPED CHILDREN

The reason some blind children are not being offered physical education is the stereotypical attitude of the public concerning the helplessness of the blind. Certainly the loss of sight may curtail activities in some respects for some boys and girls, but this does not mean that they should be neglected or assigned to nonparticipant roles in games or activities. Some common reasons which school personnel give for not offering physical education to visually handicapped children have included the beliefs that they are more prone to accidents, that they cannot participate in activities in physical education, and that they require more supervision (Buell, 1967, p. 249). There are means by which a blind child can achieve a vigorous program of physical education. One noted physical educator with extensive experience with blind found that when blind children were allowed to participate with seeing children their accident rate was no higher than that of their sighted peers. A principal of an integrated program stated: "We've found out that once we convince ourselves that the blind can do these things, then they are quick to grasp this confidence from us" (Buell, 1967, p. 249).

Buell suggests that having a blind child in class need not mean more supervision for the physical education instructor. One method of resolving this problem is pairing a blind child with a classmate who has normal vision. Most classes have a boy or girl who is willing and capable of giving only necessary assistance. It is very helpful to the members of the class to know something of the needs, desires, and abilities of their blind classmates as well as all other classmates (Buell, 1967, p. 251).

The typical general education program of physical education is designed for pupils who have no limitation on participation. Recognizing this fact, two courses of action have commonly been pursued with the handicapped pupils. The first has been to excuse the child, and the second has been to place him in an inappropriate corrective program. Neither course of action has been found adequate in terms of the child's needs or the potentialities of the school for meeting these needs. Excusing the child from physical education has been regarded as a safe way out, but it is costly to the child. One desirable modification for all children with limitations on their ability to participate in physical activity would be the development of programs of adapted physical education (Daniels, 1954). The main objectives of adapted physical education are to develop the physical potential of all children, regardless of physical or other limitations, by tailoring programs to fit their needs. Specific adaptations for physical education with blind children have been developed in elementary as well as high school.

In planning a physical education program for elementary school blind children, it must be kept in mind that the program may be made around the same values and objectives as programs for the sighted. More and more parents are arranging family and community recreational activities which involve their visually handicapped children. It is important that blind boys and girls integrate into the activities of other children at home and in the neighborhood.

ADAPTATIONS

No adaptation is necessary for activities in which the blind person can remain relatively stationary, such as calisthenics, weight lifting, and working with stationary apparatus. Very little if any adaptation is necessary in those activities in which performance is confined or limited in area or where movement is restricted. Gymnastics, tumbling, swimming, dancing, wrestling, and marching would be included here. Little or no adaptations for these activities means that no special equipment is necessary in order for instruction to take place; however, some additional verbal instruction is necessary.

Minor adaptation is necessary for those activities in which there is throwing or kicking of projectiles or relatively unrestricted rapid movement. Skating, hiking, bowling, archery, cross-country, horseshoes, kickball, and track and field would be illustrations of these activities. Minor adaptations means that some modification of the circumstances of participation is necessary, including material aids, but not to the extent that rules for participation are altered. These may mean participation in some special orientation to a spatial area through initial use of a guide, use of cord to guide, buzzers to orient to target, special material for target, guide rails to bowling, or special textured surfaces to delineate foul lines. It should be noted, however, that rules for participation remain the same as for sighted peers.

Major adaptation means substantial changes in conventional rules are necessary in order to participate. This may mean altering rules of play, restricting participation to certain positions, or substantial equipment modification. Any activity which uses a ball of any type which can be thrown at variable velocities through space and can travel in practically infinite directions requires major adaptations. Also included here is any activity in which body contact may occur while participants engage in rapid movement. Baseball, basketball, golf, soccer, volleyball, table tennis, football, softball, and variations of these games require major adaptations. In some instances only a ball with a noise emitter is necessary for participation if the peers are at a low level of skill in the sport. In other instances alteration of game rules may need to be made for a blind participant if other members of the activity are at relatively high skill levels. Game rule change may not be tolerated by peers, which will mean no participation by the visually handicapped in those activities. Frequently, all children engaging in normal play in a part of a sport or game have fun. They might play catch, shoot baskets, have batting, bouncing, or putting practice. All of these activities may be participated in by visually handicapped with little modification. However, as a rule, activities which are best suited and most easily adapted to the visually handicapped are those activities which do not require constant surveillance of a ball or other flying object.

Visually handicapped boys and girls, like most nonhandicapped youngsters, feel more comfortable taking part in activities which need not be modified for them. It should be remembered that an individual attains more physical fitness in those sports in which he can most vigorously participate. A blind child can gain more respect from schoolmates by participating in unmodified activities, although during some periods of his development modified activities are necessary.

It is desirable to begin instruction in physical education of blind as soon as the youngsters enter school. Many of the games and formal physical education activities in the primary grades are new to almost all children and the differences in their initial skills are relatively small. The visually handicapped child may be nearer to the skill level of most of his seeing classmates during these early years and can frequently participate competitively with them. Success and satisfaction in the activity encourages continued physical activity in and out of school.

Physical education should provide for the immediate need of physical exercise necessary for muscle development and coordination, but a program of physical education should also look to the future needs of the child. This requires that a blind child be provided with opportunity to participate in both individual and group games which will develop his long-term interest in physical activity. Hence, there is a responsibility of teachers to cultivate out-of-school contacts which will aid the blind student in continuing participation in activities when not in school. The YMCA, YWCA, Scouts, church groups, and other organized agencies are frequently receptive to blind students. A minimum amount of advice and other aid by a teacher of visually handicapped will often result in the routine participation by these children in various extra-school organizations.

UNUSUAL OPPORTUNITIES
IN PHYSICAL ACTIVITIES

Visually handicapped have repeatedly demonstrated that their aspirations involving vigorous physical activity are very similar to those of nonhandicapped.

For example, consider mountain climbing. It is possible and has been done. Africa's highest peak is located in Tanzania on Mt. Kilimanjaro. Eight blind East African students of the Royal Commonwealth Society for the Blind trained for two weeks at the Outward Bound Mountain School located at Loitokitok at the foot of the mountain. (The Royal Commonwealth Society for the Blind and the Outward Bound Trust are organizations concerned with the interests of young people in East Africa.) They climbed 18,635 feet in three and a half days with four sighted guides. This climb was designed to show that after twenty years of educating the blind in East Africa, the blind man is no longer a beggar, a second class citizen who is forced to sit in the shade in his "shamba" and do nothing all day.

The training course was designed to bring about the physical and mental attitudes vital to mountain climbing. They hiked daily to toughen their muscles for the climb, using back packs and long rough wooden poles used as canes and for measuring the depth of streams and snow. The tropical lowlands surrounding the mountains are just a few miles from the equator; but as they neared the top of the mountain, the students encountered bare rocks, thin air, and sub-freezing cold and needed dark glasses to protect their eyes from the glare of the snow.

One of the students spoke for the group when he said, "I want to prove that I'm just as good as the next man. Because I am blind does not mean that I am dead" (*Ebony*, 1969, p. 52).

A high school geography teacher in Maryland wondered how to get children to observe, really observe. In an attempt to go beyond the usual classroom work, he decided to take his class camping in Utah and Colorado. One of the members of the class was a blind girl.

The group went through twisting caves, rafting on swift streams, swimming in many lakes. The blind girl made the others aware of things they only half-noticed or half-realized, such as the sound of the wind in the treetops, bird and animal sounds, bits of stone falling from cliffs at night, and boulders moving on the bottom of streams. She would say, "Did you notice the air lifting just before the thunder began?" She pointed out that the ground trembles near a rapids, and that grass is softer when there is dew on it. She could identify stones by their texture. Her favorite smells were a newly mown hayfield, the desert after a rain shower, the scent of a pine forest. She had made an important contribution to details of observation which escaped her classmates (Jones, 1967, p. 19).

Another outdoor activity, a specially prepared walk through the woods, can be found in Washington, D.C. The Touch and See Nature Trail at the National Arboretum gives the blind visitor an opportunity to explore and "see" his surroundings on a path through a native hardwood forest. It is neither a fragrance nor a texture garden, not a complicated trail of elaborate design, nor is it planted with exotic shrubs. It is a real walk through the woods.

The trail follows a winding course over undulating terrain. It is 820 feet long and has features pointed out in braille and print at the twenty-four stations on either side of the trail. The visitor is led by a guide rope from one station to the next along one side of the trail and back along the other. The average time required for a blind person to make the round trip is less than two hours.

The trail is kept in its natural state, as undisturbed as possible. Underbrush was cleared to discourage the invasion of weeds, but the wood chips popular in many walkways were not used here because they are not a natural floor cover of the woods. Features were chosen that were easy for a blind person to examine. For example, a large white oak is popular with school children as they are encouraged to "hug" the trunk to estimate its size (forty-eight inches in diameter). The peeling bark of a rotting tree can be felt by curious hands and a text marker at the spot tells the observer that an insect may crawl over his hand as he inspects this insect apartment house. A felled tree can be climbed.

Midway on the trail, beyond the wooded part, a meadow has posted instructions that the visitor can walk freely without fear—he can cross the open grassland free of obstacles and without the use of the guide rope. (A gravel path around its edge limits the area.) At the far edge of the meadow is a boggy spot with a willow tree and cattails (Garvey, 1969, p. 20). Other cities and states also have parks and gardens with both braille and print signs.

A research project at the Georgia Academy for the Blind in Macon, Georgia, resulted in the development of a program to train blind people for employment in the field of horticulture. The program provides different methods of instruction in the growing of bedding plants, cut flowers, bulbs, shrubs, and fruit trees. Facilities consist of a greenhouse, equipment, work and classroom space plus a nursery shade house for growing shrubbery. This is located on the campus of the Georgia Academy for the Blind. The personnel include two horticulturist instructors, a greenhouse attendant, and a secretary. Twelve adult vocational rehabilitation trainees and twelve to fifteen high school students sixteen years of age or older are taught during a twelve-month training period (Clay, 1962, p. 69).

Can a blind person learn first aid? An affirmative answer was found to this question at the Lorain County Center for the Sightless in Elyria, Ohio. In cooperation with the American Red Cross, twelve adventitiously blind people, most of whom were over fifty, were enabled to play an active role in their families and community.

Without an excessive amount of special equipment and without specially trained instructors, these people found their fingers could do much of the work of the eyes. They were able to detect bleeding from a serious wound by the gummy consistency of blood and place a compress over the wound to inhibit bleeding. By touch they could distinguish between punctures, abrasions, incisions, and lacerations. They learned to identify poisons by odor and to identify sprains by feeling for swollen areas, then applying pressure until intense feeling of pain or tenderness is indicated. Shock was recognized by shallow, irregular breathing, weak or imperceptible pulse, vomiting, cold, moist skin, restlessness, loss of alertness, and extreme thirst. They used plastic facsimilies of various kinds of wounds, artificial blood, and mannequins for mouth-to-mouth resuscitation. The twelve students emerged from the course equipped with a new tool which they could use to actively serve their community (DeForest, 1969).

At the South Dakota School for the Blind students have been taught to shoot rifles. They have a rifle club which is chartered by the National Rifle Association and is called the "Sound Shooters Club." The reason for the name "Sound Shooters" is that the students shoot at a sound projected through a bull's-eye. It is produced by an oscillator that emits high frequency beeps from a small amplifier at intervals of four seconds. Single shot lever-action rifles are used to lessen the "didn't know the gun was loaded" danger. Each student is given comprehensive instruction on the proper manipulation of the gun and must demonstrate that he knows the safety rules involved. It is also compulsory for him to load the gun and eject the shell. The danger of reflected bullets is reduced by using the type that disintegrate on striking any object. The targets are set up fifty feet from the firing line, and the students are taught to shoot from the three standard positions—standing, kneeling, and prone. The first attempts at shooting were highly inaccurate because of echoes that made it difficult to determine the direction of the beep from the target. The echo was eliminated by heavily insulating the amplifier. This rifle club not only contributes to good orientation, but provides a good recreational activity for the students (Hack, 1965, p. 24).

There are many other recreational activities in which blind children can participate. It is often stated that blind children should not be overprotected. Dr. Samuel Gridley Howe, the pioneer of the education of the blind, said over 100 years ago, "Do not too much regard bumps upon the forehead, rough scratches or bloody noses, even these may have their good influences. At the worst, they affect only the bark, and do not injure the system like the rust of inaction." (Buell, 1966, p. 3–4.)

As a director of physical education, Buell names many activities which can be enjoyable for blind and other visually handicapped children. For example, blind children can go to a parade and listen to the bands, thus feeling the excitement of the occasion. If there are floats, they can be described to the child—perhaps he can examine a float at the beginning or end of the parade. The same excitement can be obtained by attending a state or county fair. There are many things at a museum, aquarium, or zoo a child can enjoy also.

Blind children can learn to roller skate, ice skate, bowl, and ride horses. (Portable guide rails can be purchased to assist the bowler.) They can be taught social dancing. At the Maryland School for the Blind, Tuesday evening dancing classes are held. Boys and girls wear their good clothes and arrive shining. But, as usual when teenagers gather, there is a huddle of girls and some distance off a group of boys. The rules are few: when the music begins, the boys must ask the girls to dance and a couple may not dance together for consecutive records. The boy always returns his partner to a seat or to the side of the hall at the end of the dance. The girls, due to their tendency to practice with each other, are generally better dancers—this frequently makes them hard to lead, but the teachers work on this. No one is expected to accomplish anything in a given length of time. They are there to have a good time; and they soon learn that the better they dance, the more fun they have (Baird, 1958, p. 85).

Modern dance, as taught at the Kentucky School for the Blind, becomes a personal art form that provides grace and poise, body development, and mental and emotional stimulation. The students learn about movement, about the different kinds of movement, how to move directionally in space, and how to use rhythm, tempo, and pattern to tell a story. The children can then become caterpillars crawling on the ground, butterflies flying through the air, or flowers gracefully spreading their petals. They can be bouncing balls and spinning tops, clocks and melting ice cream cones (Monsky, 1958, p. 86).

Folk dancing is taught at the Ohio School for the Blind as an implement to locomotor movement. Folk dances are based on the fundamentals of locomotion: walking, running, galloping, skipping, hopping, jumping, and leaping. They also teach line of direction. If any student has a foreign background in which folk dances have been prominent, the whole class is taught some of the patterns and movements (Kratz, 1958, p. 88).

Physical education should be included in every blind child's school curriculum. Exercise improves fitness, muscle tone, coordination, posture, and gait. Blind children can play many games played by sighted children and can participate in many sports. But awareness of posture and fluidity of movement depends on the child's attitude toward space. Unless he is sure of his surroundings and feels safe in moving about, he is hesitant and slow in his movements and overly fearful of obstacles. It is important, therefore, to introduce the child to the room, pointing out empty spaces, walls, and furniture, encouraging him to walk around and explore the room, reassuring and vocally guiding him. After this is accomplished the guide should establish one point of reference, a place to start from and to go back to.

Rolling on the floor, walking on all fours, running together, standing and lying down side by side, walking holding hands outstretched are activities that help to evaluate the empty space of movement and the solidity and evenness of the floor.

Blind athletes have participated safely in the most strenuous of interscholastic and intercollegiate competition. More blind athletes have excelled in wrestling than any other sport. It is a sport in which a blind boy can compete on equal terms with high school and college boys with normal vision. In 1968 a blind freshman at the University of California at Berkeley won fifteen bouts, lost none. Football is one of the roughest sports, yet visually handicapped boys have safely played the game. A blind boy at the University of California in Berkeley won letters on the gynmastics team for three years. In ice skating a blind boy placed fifth in the 1964 National Junior Pairs. There are thousands of blind bowlers. At the 1965 International Bowling Congress Tournament, a blind bowler bowled a three-game series of 454 without the use of a guide rail (Buell, 1967, p. 252–53).

A full life with many varied experiences is indeed possible for blind children, but good early training in orientation and mobility is a prerequisite. Physical education has a unique importance for blind in the development of confidence, mobility, and self-esteem.

References

Baird, B. Some values of a social dancing program. *International Journal for the Education of the Blind, 7,* 1958, 85–90.

Buell, C. E. *Active Games for the Blind.* Berkeley, California, 1953.

Buell, C. E. Outdoor education in a school for the blind. *Exceptional Children, 22,* 1956, 266–67.

Buell, C. E. *Physical Education for Blind Children.* Springfield, Illinois, Charles C Thomas, Publisher, 1966.

Buell, C. E. Physical education for blind children in public schools. *New Outlook for the Blind, 61,* 1967, 248–54.

Buell, C. E. The school's responsibility for providing physical activities for blind students. *Journal of Health, Physical Education, Recreation, 41,* June, 1970, 41–42.

Clay, H. Greenhouse and nursery training for the blind. *International Journal for the Education of the Blind, 9,* 1962, 69–70.

Daniels, A. *Adapted Physical Education.* New York, Harper & Row, Publishers, 1954.

DeForest, R. A. Can a blind person learn first aid? *New Outlook for the Blind,* *63,* 1969, 262–63.

Ebony, Blind students conquer Mt. Kilimanjaro. *24,* 1969, 44–52.

Garvey, J. Touch and see. *Parks and Recreation, 4,* November 1969. 20–21.

Hack, W. A. Marksmanship for the blind. *International Journal for the Education of the Blind, 15,* 1965, 24–25.

Halsey, E. and Porter, L. R. *Physical Education for Children: A Developmental Program.* New York, Holt, Rinehart and Winston, Inc., 1963.

Hunt, V. *Recreation for the Handicapped.* Englewood Cliffs, New Jersey, Prentice-Hall, Inc., 1955.

Hunter, W. F. The role of space perception in the education of the congenitally blind. *International Journal for the Education of the Blind, 10,* 1962, 125–30.

Jones, P. L. Sounds and shadows. *Scholastic Teacher,* May, 1967, 19–20.

Kratz, L. E. Folk dancing is fun, too. *International Journal for the Education of the Blind, 7,* 1958, 88–89.

Krause, A. C. Effect of retrolental fibroplasia in children. *Archives of Ophthalmology, 53,* 1955, 522–29.

McCandless, B. R. *Children: Behavior and Development.* 2nd ed. New York, Holt, Rinehart and Winston, Inc., 1967.

Monsky, M. A program based on modern dance. *International Journal for the Education of the Blind, 7,* 1958, 86–87.

Nugent, T. J. Research and demonstration needs for the physically handicapped. *Journal of Health, Physical Education, Recreation, 40,* May, 1969, 47–48.

Oliver, J. N. Blindness and the child's sequence of development. *Journal of Health, Physical Education, Recreation, 41,* June, 1970, 37–39.

Seelye, W. S. and Thomas, J. E. A pattern to promote habilitation of the blind. *International Journal for the Education of the Blind, 16,* 1966, 48–52.

Trevena, T. M. Integration of the sightless student into regular physical activities. *Journal of Health, Physical Education, Recreation, 41,* June, 1970, 42–43.

Williams, F. N. Physical education adapts to the visually handicapped. *Journal of Health, Physical Education, Recreation, 35,* March, 1964, 25–27.

10

Adaptations
in Common
Curriculum Areas

Adaptations of methods and materials for success in some curriculum areas by visually handicapped are relatively minor. Those adaptations which are necessary are in those areas in which tactile examination or manipulation is required. This chapter is devoted to those curriculum areas which require equipment and material use and which involve extensive tactile examination and manipulation.

INDUSTRIAL ARTS

The conventional high school industrial arts program is organized around four basic areas of activity: woodwork, metal work, electricity and electronics, and auto mechanics or transportation. Additions to this framework are drafting, household mechanics, plastics, and certain others. All of these areas can be included in the program of a blind student, with the possible exception of drafting. Equipment used in all of these areas will be the same as that used by sighted students (American Foundation for the Blind, 1960, p. 28). Appendix G contains suggestions for specific adaptations in the four basic areas of industrial arts as developed at the Workshop for Industrial Arts Instructors of Blind Students (Oswego, New York, 1963). These adaptations may be equally useful to both blind and sighted students.

In a local public school program, it would be useful to have the orientation and mobility specialist or the special teacher orient the blind student to the shop areas, after the teacher has learned to identify the equipment and areas by appropriate name. The orientation should take place when no other students are in the shop. The teacher should allow the visually handicapped student sufficient opportunity to identify the location of various stationary machinery as well as basic tools. He can obtain the shop routine from the industrial arts teacher and have the student learn the location of clean-up material, safety lanes, and work stations prior to the first day of instruction. The special teacher should also acquire any books and printed material and provide them in braille or recorded form for the student. The industrial arts teacher should be provided with *Aids and Appliances,* a catalog of special equipment available from the American Foundation for Blind.

Vocational Training

Closely identified with the industrial arts program is vocational training, although the industrial arts program is only one type of vocational training. Plans for appropriate training of blind students in such areas as machine operation have been reported more than three decades ago (Morgan, 1943). The emphasis is to provide training in the operation of as many different machines as possible rather than in one operation. In this manner the blind trainee can acquire more useful skills as a potential employee and can develop good work habits.

A strategy suggested for placing blind students as trainees in trade or vocational schools for sighted includes the following (Quay, 1948, p. 9–13):

1. Place only one blind student per vocational school initially until the school has adjusted to the presence of a blind student.

2. The first student in any school should be totally blind in order to avoid raising unrealistic expectations from experiences with partially seeing students and to allow immediate orientation of the vocational school to the real abilities of blind people in general.

3. Attempt to arrange indeterminate or indefinite periods of training to avoid assuming that competency has been achieved after a predetermined number of hours of instruction. Blind students have a greater variation in ability than seeing students because of the wider differences in experience prior to entering the trade school training program.

4. When an arbitrary time limit for training must be set before training begins, attempt to make it sufficiently long that the blind student can acquire adequate competency. It is suggested that a

time period of twelve weeks (with the possibility of an automatic extension) be arranged. The program should allow for termination of training when competency has been achieved, even if that is before the end of the prespecified training period.

5. A special teacher for visually handicapped, an orientation and mobility specialist, or personnel from a state or private agency for blind should be available at the vocational school to orient the student to the school and to provide necessary material and aid required by the school staff. The presence of a specialist will relieve staff anxiety; he should also encourage them to allow the blind student to perform all realistic operations.

6. A plan should be developed for further advanced training to acquire specialized skills when indicated by earlier performance.

7. The initial training should include use of all reasonable facilities to provide opportunity to learn the operations available in a machine shop, in woodworking, in electrical work, in auto shop, or in other areas.

Shop training in vocational classes is useful in developing general work abilities which can be applied in a variety of situations. The skill necessary to perform successfully on one machine carries over in the operation of other machines and equipment. There are remarkably few industrial jobs which blind persons have not performed at some time (Greater Detroit Society for Blind, 1972). Perhaps the best principle to follow in training blind students in shop activities is to combine a maximum of exploration by the student with a minimum of explanation of the equipment and material to be used (Walter, 1967, p. 56).

ART

It has been suggested that the purpose of art education is to develop an awareness of beauty through the careful observation of form, line, and color, especially in nature, and to give the student a variety of media through which he may be able to share and communicate his personal reactions to the world and his experiences in it (Haupt, 1969, p. 41). Differences in the amount of visual acuity dictate that the media used in art must be specific to an individual visually handicapped child. Those who see only form, but no color, may use the media which are tactile as well as visual. Those with some color vision may even use color in the media. Those totally blind must rely on tactually manipulable media such as clay. A careful determination of manipulative and other skills as well as degree of vision is required in order to initiate art instruction.

A teacher attempting to instruct a visually handicapped child in art activities must be familiar with certain unique emphasis in art instruction. The teacher should know how to help a child to use his hands and fingers efficiently in forming material used in an art program. There should be an awareness that the visually handicapped child, and particularly the blind child, requires more time and opportunity to explore objects than do sighted children. Cursory handling of material is not sufficient as it might be with the normally sighted child.

Special skill is required in the use of generative questions. These questions should encourage imagination and inquiry as the child attempts to discover the intrinsic qualities of an object being explored. The vocabulary used in instruction should be rich in words and phrases which describe experiences in the nonvisual senses. This should involve direct experiences with objects encountered daily, as well as common geometric forms such as cubes, spheres, and cones. It is important that the teacher recognize that many things a sighted child knows, such as sky or shadow, are things which are either out of reach or too tiny or fragile to handle. In these instances skillful use of analogy may be useful. Visually handicapped can learn to explore objects more efficiently it they can observe temperatures, weights, odors, and sounds as well as form and texture (Haupt, 1969).

Art media used with visually handicapped children are varied, with the most common medium being clay (Haupt, 1969, p. 42). To provide variations, wire sculpture has been used with some success (Borodziej, 1964). This project involved building a main armature using soft aluminum wire to which was added copper wire, giving a three-dimensional effect. In this instance, earlier modeling with clay helped the child in developing proportions of animals and recognizing the limitations in the use of wire in sculpture.

Other media used successfully with blind include a sawdust and wheatpaste mixture, clay, plastic coated wire, plastic glue, fingerpainting to music, stitching, and papier-maché (Bains, 1964). Within each medium, there are variations in the value of the changes recognized in the substances used. Clay is a different tactual experience once it is dry or glazed. Glue with dry coral or other substances in it is a more interesting tactual art experience.

Partially seeing children should be encouraged to use the visual arts as much as possible. Material useful as media for partially seeing include most of those used with normally sighted. Of particular value have been some of the novel materials such as cardboard packing for apples, cellulose papier-maché and "clay coiler," which forms water clay into ropes or ribbons with greater tensile strength (Haupt, 1969).

Totally blind children may ask for specific colors or hues they wish to use. It does not mean that colors have an aesthetic impact on them. It may simply be that colors have acquired meaning through verbal association. There may be some attempt by blind to compensate for being different by looking for a highly structured step-by-step art experience and by constructing art objects with a visual orientation. This would not be conducive to creativity and should be discouraged if that is the objective. This does not mean that a blind student should not learn techniques in art; but only that the environment should be used for suggestions and experiences with art, rather than as a rigid dictator of form and content of the creation (Freel, 1969).

To provide extrinsic incentives to excel in an area of art, the works of blind artists should be exhibited along with those of other students. The visually handicapped high school student may achieve considerable sophistication in such areas as sculpture, architecture, ceramics, and design (Freel, 1969, p. 46). He should be provided the opportunity to display this work and receive candid competent judgment as to its quality.

Diagrams, Maps, and Other Tactile Displays

There are many instances in which sighted children are presented visual displays which summarize large amounts of material or in which complex material is simplified. This is particularly true in certain social and physical sciences. The study of geography is replete with maps, charts, and diagrams. History and economics rely heavily on charts and diagrams for summarizing information. In physics, frequent reference is made to diagrams clarifying theories or principles explaining optics, motion, fluids, and other phenomena related to natural forces. These diagrams have not been available to the blind for tactual examination because conversion to a tactile display is laborious and may not be useful.

Perhaps the most persistent attempts at developing tactile displays, such as raised line drawings, have been in the area of geography. The visual map has been an indispensable tool for learning. Simply converting these maps as tactually discriminable relief maps or as raised-line maps conveys relatively little of the information present on a visual map. There is little information conveyed which approximates the data presented through color coding, nor are the geographic relationships as accurate or as perceiveable. However, maps have been of some use in mapping routes of foot travel in orientation and mobility (Gilson, Wurzburger, and Johnson, 1965).

Certain textures and tactile symbols have been identified as useful in coding tactile material. Twelve tactile patterns which are particularly discriminable have been developed using ink and resin compound as the embossing media (Culbert and Stellwagen, 1963). The Roman letters C, I, V, and O are among the easiest to identify in embossed form from among all letters of the alphabet, and continuous embossed lines are more recognizable than geometric figures outlined as raised points (Austin and Sleight, 1952). There is also evidence that in showing directionality with a symbol on a tactile display, a "T" symbol in the shape of a dewdrop is more efficient than the conventional "V" arrow (Schiff, Kaufer, and Mosak, 1964).

There is substantial evidence that blind children cannot identify embossed forms representing perspective (Merry and Merry, 1933). Therefore, there appears to be no effective way of presenting the three-dimensional effect of photographs and pictures. In some instances models, such as those which may be built on sand tables or on the ground, may be useful substitutes. The usual method of resolving the presence of a picture is to give a simple verbal explanation of the contents of a picture or photograph.

In attempting to develop raised maps and diagrams, the teacher should recognize group characteristics of children as affecting efficient use of embossed material. Ability to discriminate tactually appears to develop rapidly through the primary grades and than relatively little improvement appears in later grades (Gliner, 1966). It is therefore possible to use tactile diagrams or maps beginning in the late primary grades without waiting for additional readiness. Intelligence differences among the visually handicapped, within the normal range of intelligence, do not seem to be important as a determiner of who learns to discriminate tactile features quickly (Morris and Nolan, 1961).

There are several methods of producing raised-line drawings (Vermey, 1969). One of the simplest is the screen-board method, which consists of producing raised lines by scratching the point of a standard writing stylus on a sheet of paper lying on a board covered with fine grain mesh screening. The screen is attached to the board with nails or adhesive tape. By varying pressure on the stylus, lines of different prominence are produced. The diagram or picture will appear on the side of the paper facing the screen.

Another method of drawing raised line figures is the use of the Sewell Raised-Line Drawing Kit. This consists of a sheet of cellophane clamped to a rubber padded board. A ball-point pen (without ink) is used to write on the sheet and the resulting drawing is on the side of the cellophane facing the person who is writing. This is easy for a teacher to use in explaining geometric figures.

A sewing pattern tracing wheel or a Howe Tracing Wheel may be used to provide clear perforated lines. The paper to be drawn on should be on a firm but yielding surface such as rubber on a board or balsa wood. The sketch is raised on the side facing the board. This forms an easily discriminable line and is useful in thermoform duplicating.

Whatever the method of developing tactually perceiveable figures, it is important to determine whether the raised-line drawing facilitates learning. It is of little value to diagram information for a blind student if the same information can be conveyed in less time using a written description or verbal explanation. The primary characteristic of raised-line drawings is that they are oriented to the nonsighted viewer. It is at least conceivable that a good embossed diagram may not make much sense to a casual sighted viewer, in the same way that braille cells are incomprehensible to the casual sighted observer.

HOME ECONOMICS AND HOMEMAKING

The area of home economics or homemaking includes some activities which require adaptation for success by visually handicapped. Most of these activities can be completed by blind and partially sighted students without significantly adding to the amount of time required to learn. The primary concern of sighted teachers seems to be the safety aspects of blind students working with sharp implements, hot liquids, and fire.

Foods

In the preparation of foods in class, a number of adaptations have been used to allow visually handicapped to participate successfully (Cumberland, 1950). Adapted utensils which are useful and may be purchased for use in these classes are listed in the *Aids and Appliance* catalog of the American Foundation for the Blind. To function safely, students learn to announce the fact that they are carrying hot liquids or other material. Modern pilot lights in gas stoves mean that students do not have to light stoves with matches. Electric stoves present no particular problem after some initial orientation to the knobs used to set the heat and after location of the burner. Sometimes marking the dials on a stove (as well as dials on other appliances) with braille labels aids in initial learning. Sharp implements such as knives require the same information concerning safety as would be required of a sighted student. The total incidence of minor accidents in these classes does not seem to exceed the number in sighted classes or in a typical home (Cumberland, 1950, p. 239).

Most cooking instructions are given by individual demonstration. Class descriptions of manipulative skills may be presented in lecture, but it is necessary to guide each student's hand in the learning of the various cooking operations. Laying utensils out and organizing materials for cooking in some pattern is important. A utility plate for implements which are not in use aids in locating them quickly as well as maintaining tidy tables and counters. Contents of drawers and cupboards must be returned to the same location following each use. Braille recipes used in class should be memorized as much as possible to avoid the time-consuming necessity of washing hands during the cooking or baking process.

Location of supplies should not be particularly difficult. Fruits and vegetables each have characteristic shapes, textures, odors, and tastes. Containers for baking and cooking ingredients do not necessarily require braille labels. Students can quickly become familiar with many containers such as the round salt box, cocoa containers, and canisters of different sizes for flour, sugar, coffee, and tea. Spices, food coloring, and other identical containers are labeled. Once containers are opened, there is little need for labels on many of these items.

Measuring foods requires some minor adaptations. Distinction between sets of measuring spoons which are joined at the handle are made by noting the largest, which is the tablespoon, and next to the largest, the teaspoon. Metal measuring cups with metal ridges marking each fraction of a cup can be used by noting that the number of ridges in a cup tells the fractional part for each ridge. Placing the forefinger on the proper mark on the inside of the cup allows the blind person to stop pouring when the liquid touches the finger.

Spoonfuls of liquids may be more easily measured if first poured into a dish and then dipped. An eyedropper may be used for measuring a liquid such as food coloring. A round pie crust may be rolled out by using a circular cutting board. Timing cooking or baking is no great problem with today's accurate recipes, easily set stove timers, and braille watches.

Clothing

Sewing for blind students offers teachers many opportunities for developing highly practical skills. Objectives and methods used in classes with blind are substantially the same as with sighted. The *Aids and Appliance* catalog lists devices which can be purchased which make it possible for blind students to perform all necessary tasks in sewing. These devices, together with certain minor adaptations in teaching method, make it possible for blind students to acquire the necessary skills for doing everything from basting to sewing on a sewing machine. A number of adaptations and course emphases have been developed in the instruction of sewing (Welch, 1950).

Initial instruction consists of hand sewing. The students begin practice with large needles and strips of felt, and progress to smaller needles until they have mastered the various common stitches. The sewing machine may be introduced at the junior high school level with orientation to the machine involving manipulating and naming the various parts, threading, and stitching seams. Practice with strips of material is used to build skill and confidence in the student. Again, blind students do not have any more accidents with the sewing machine than do their sighted classmates (Welch, 1950, p. 235).

Teaching aids such as posters showing worked buttonholes, finished seams, and miniature patterns can be developed for tactual as well as visual scanning. Heavy paper patterns from material such as wrapping paper can be constructed as models showing the actual sizes and shapes of patterns for students to examine. When the heavy pattern is understood, tissue patterns can be used, with small patterns used first. The poster teaching aid can also be used to display plackets, buttonholes, and hook and eye fasteners (Welch, 1950).

Colors should be studied visually by those visually handicapped who have residual vision. Blind students also need knowledge about the significance of color in clothing. They must know which colors are the most becoming and also in what combinations these should appear in clothing construction and good grooming practice. Clothing should be labeled for color. An important part of the clothing construction process is the selection of appropriate cloth, and the blind student should participate in the actual purchase of this material.

Good grooming is a necessary part of the instruction of blind home economics students in the clothing unit of instruction. Proper hanging of clothes, pressing, and laundering are all parts of this process. The use of automatic washers and dryers presents very little more difficulty for the visually handicapped student than does use of an electric stove. Dials may be worked with braille stick-on labels initially if desired, but the student soon learns to sense the appropriate degree of turn of the dials.

There is no reason why boys as well as girls cannot participate in some of the home economics activities. Some boys enjoy cooking; it can prove to be a useful practical skill as well as a source of pleasure. Provision should be made in regular high school programs for complete participation by visually handicapped students.

Here again, a special teacher for blind or an orientation and mobility instructor can provide initial orientation to the home economics area at a time when other students are not present. This should include not only the special relationships of furniture and appliances, but also location of utensils and other small items of equipment.

THE PHYSICAL SCIENCES

The modifications of methods and materials used in teaching science consist primarily of those adaptations which make it possible for the blind student to participate in the laboratory experiments and demonstrations. The textbooks can be brailled or recorded and need very little editing except for the diagrams and certain notations. Certain scientific notations have a braille counterpart and can be found in the "Nemeth Code of Braille Mathematics and Scientific Notation" (1973). Either the diagrams must be translated into tactually perceivable form or a description substituted.

Opportunity for meaningful participation of visually handicapped in the laboratory sciences can be provided through properly adapting laboratory experiences. Successful participation by blind students in physics, chemistry, and biology has occurred in the past (Wexler, 1961, p. 9), and with the development of innovations in adapting the manipulative portions for blind, the study of science will become increasingly significant for this population.

Wexler (1961, pp. 9–10) discusses several methods of making science laboratory experiences accessible to the sensory perceptions of blind:

1. Embossed diagrams and three-dimensional models can be used.
2. Apparatus can be audified (modified so its measurement can be heard rather than seen).
3. Electronic light probes can be used for exploring parts inaccessible to fingers.

Since embossed diagrams are discussed in another section of this chapter, only the remaining two methods will be discussed here.

Audification has been used in order to make certain observations possible by blind. Some of these observations and measurements involve convection air currents, electromagnetic induction, motion, temperature, spring balance, microammeter, circuit analyzers, measurement of liquid levels, and voltmeters. Some of these need to be custom-built (Wexler, 1961) and others may be purchased from the American Foundation for the Blind, American Printing House for the Blind, and other agencies. Henderson (1965) has listed additional physical phenomena which may be measured and observed by blind students.

One of the most promising aids to observation of physical phenomena and measurement is the electronic light probe. This device uses a photocell and an optical probe which when moved along a dial of a meter can tell the reading on the dial. A student can listen to the sound frequency instead of using visual observation of the dial. Other devices for converting visual to audio or tactile information have also been developed (Henderson, 1965, pp. 30–47). Light probes using the photo-electric cell are particularly useful because much of the laboratory measurement and observation is done with gauges with sensitive needles, which discourages the students from touching the needles.

Practically any device which relies on an electric light as a signal can be adapted to ring a buzzer or bell. This opens the way to testing for ionization in chemistry experiments, testing electric current in a battery or circuit, and other observations. The periodic table of elements in chemistry provides a useful model for illustrating principles of elementary chemical combinations. Brailling descriptions of each element on individual pieces of cardboard, with the chemical names of compounds on other separate pieces, provides a basis for matching the elements together to form appropriate compounds (Kaufman, 1971). A student can learn to identify many chemicals by odor and touch, when this is done with discretion. It is necessary to clearly label substances which are in similar size bottles, with an added precaution of keeping dangerous chemicals on a specified shelf or cupboard.

Biology laboratory activities require some adaptations. When dissection of animals is necessary, larger animals than frogs or earthworms are desirable because detailed tactile examination of the organs becomes possible. Examination of large organs, such as the heart or head of some livestock or of live small animals, presents useful laboratory experience when done in conjuction with appropriate reading and discussion. Tactile examination of plant structure can also supply profitable experiences to complement reading and discussion.

Science Curriculum Improvement Study Kits have been developed to provide ungraded sequential physical and life science programs for elementary schools. These kits are designed to provide material and a student manual which allow a child to manipulate and discover science principles. Many of these kits do not require adaptation for blind, and others have already been adapted for visually handicapped children. Separate packets of adaptations are available for blind children when needed. This material may be appropriate for junior high school and high school students because of the ungraded nature of the program (Huckins, 1970, pp. 173–76). Development of adaptations for the blind is being continued at University of California, Berkeley.

MATHEMATICS AND ARITHMETIC

The primary adaptation necessary in mathematics is the braille notation. It is necessary to use standard braille symbols for the various mathematical symbols found in print. Hence, the "Nemeth Code of Braille Mathematics and Scientific Notation" (1973) was developed to make possible more precise transcription of print mathematics symbols into braille. This code may be taught children as they need it in their progression through the various arithmetic and mathematic courses, beginning with the primary grades.

Arithmetic

Six calculation methods in teaching arithmetic to blind have been identified (Lewis, 1970). Each calculation method is identified with a specific calculation aid or device, with one exception. This is the use of mental arithmetic or mental calculation. Each of these has been used by teachers of blind children. The six are the braillewriter, braille slate and stylus, cubarithum, Taylor slate, abacus, and mental arithmetic.

The braillewriter is simply a Perkins Brailler or other braillewriter used to set up the problem in braille and follow the arithmetic process by adding the appropriate braille notation as the calculation proceeds. This typically involves placing the braille numbers and signs of operation in the same position on a piece of paper as they would appear in print calculation. The braille slate is used in a similar manner to set up and calculate problems.

The cubarithum has two variations; however, the devices are quite similar in operation. Each involves a frame made of plastic or hard rubber with a matrix of sixteen by sixteen slots into which small cubes fit. Each cube has braille symbols on five of the cube faces which can be positioned to represent the digits 1 to 9 plus 0. These cubes are than positioned into the slots in the frame so that arithmetic problems may be calculated in much the same way as with a braillewriter.

The Taylor slate consists of a frame made of aluminum and a set of plastic or metal type or pegs. One end of each piece of type contains two braille dots and the other end of the type is a solid raised bar. By placing the square type into octagonal holes in the frame in certain positions, numbers as well as signs of arithmetic operation can be represented.

The Cranmer Abacus is a modification of the Japanese abacus (Soroban). The Cranmer Abacus is pocket-size with five beads per column and has a felt backing for the columns of beads so that they will not be moved by the fingers of the operator when reading the results.

Use of mental arithmetic or calculation is an informal collection of techniques used to calculate arithmetic problems without writing them down. This involves recognizing certain principles of grouping numbers as well as noting patterns of digit arrangement which aid in rapid mental calculation. There appears to be no systematic presentation of mental arithmetic which has been developed. Its use is largely dependent on the ingenuity of individual teachers.

The most common method of calculation by blind is the use of the braillewriter, although mental arithmetic is used concomitantly (Lewis, 1970, p. 68). The popularity of the Cranmer Abacus has grown rapidly and now ranks second. (Lewis, 1970, p. 68). A correspondence course in the use of the Cranmer Abacus has been developed for use by blind students at the Hadley School for Blind and has been introduced in the United States as well as abroad (Hattendorf, 1971, p. 113). Because this abacus has not been widely used at the primary grade level (Brothers, 1972), efforts are being made to develop a larger abacus to encourage use by young children as well as those who have manipulation difficulties (Huff, 1972).

Geometry
The primary difficulty encountered in teaching blind geometry involves the inability of the instructor to use print diagrams and drawings. This can be largely ameliorated by use of devices available for presenting geometric concepts in tangible form. A particularly useful device for the sighted geometry teacher is the Sewell Raised Line Drawing Kit, which allows the instructor to draw a diagram and have it immediately available for the student during class. Three dimensional and other devices

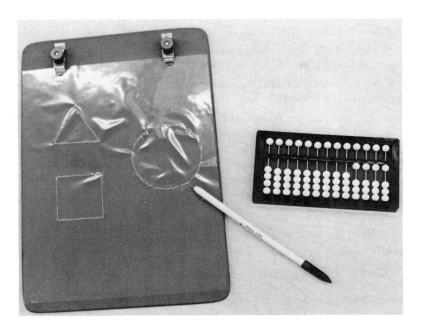

Figure 7. Abacus and Raised Line Kit

for illustrating plane and solid geometry are available from the American Printing House for the Blind (APH).

Common devices for measuring lengths, volumes, temperatures, and other concepts are available from APH or the American Foundation for the Blind (AFB). These may be located and purchased from the *Tangible Aids* catalog of APH or the *Aids and Appliances* catalog of AFB.

References

American Foundation for the Blind. *Industrial Arts for Blind Students.* New York, 1960.

Austin, T. R. and Sleight, R. B. Factors related to speed and accuracy of tactual discrimination. *Journal of Experimental Psychology, 44,* 1952, 283–87.

Bains, M. Art and blind children. *School Arts, 63,* 1964, 3–9.

Bordoziej, I. The visually handicapped youngster in art. *School Arts, 63,* 1964, 27–28.

Brothers, R. J. Arithmetic computation by the blind. *Education of the Visually Handicapped, 4,* 1972, 1–8.

Culbert, S. S. and Stellwagen, W. T. Tactual discrimination of textures. *Perceptual Motor Skills, 16,* 1963, 545–47.

Cumberland, J. H. Foods in classes for the blind. American Association of Instructors of the Blind, *Selected Papers,* 40th Biennial Conference, 1950, 238–42.

Freel, M. E. Jr. Art for visually impaired children. *Education of the Visually Handicapped, 1,* 1969, 44–46.

Gilson, C., Wurzburger, B. and Johnson, D. E. The use of the raised line map in teaching mobility to blind children. *New Outlook for the Blind, 59,* 1965, 59–62.

Gliner, C. R. "A Psychophysical Study of Tactual Perception." Unpublished doctoral dissertation, University of Minnesota, 1966.

Greater Detroit Society for Blind, Catalog of Occupations Performed by Blind, 1972.

Hattendorf, J. K. An abacus update. *New Outlook for the Blind, 65,* 1971, 112–16.

Haupt, C. Creative expression through art. *Education of the Visually Handicapped, 1,* 1969, 41–43.

Henderson, D. R. "Laboratory Methods in Physics for the Blind." Unpublished masters thesis, University of Pittsburgh, 1965.

Huckins, R. L. Current applied research science curriculum improvement study kits adapted for visually handicapped. Association for Education of the Visually Handicapped, *Selected Conference Papers,* 50th Biennial Conference, 1970, 173–77.

Huff, R. Development of an enlarged abacus. *Education of the Visually Handicapped, 4,* 1972, 88–91.

Kaufman, A. S. Tutoring a visually handicapped student in high school chemistry. *New Outlook for the Blind, 65,* 1971, 313–17.

Lewis, M. Teaching arithmetic computation skills. *Education of the Visually Handicapped, 2,* 1970, 66–73.

Merry, R. V. and Merry, F. K. The tactual recognition of embossed pictures by blind children. *Journal of Applied Psychology, 17,* 1933, 148–63.

Morgan, D. H. Vocational aptitudes of the visually handicapped, as demonstrated in trade schools. *Outlook for the Blind, 37,* 1943, 125–29.

Morris, J. E. and Nolan, C. Y. Discriminability of tactual patterns. *International Journal for the Education of the Blind, 11,* 1961, 50–54.

Nemeth code of braille mathematics and scientific notation. 1972 Revision, American Printing House for the Blind, Louisville, Kentucky, 1973.

Quay, W. E. Possibilities in sheltered workshop and home employment. *Seer, 18,* 1948, 9–13.

Schiff, W., Kaufer, L., and Mosak, S. Informative tactile stimuli in the perception of direction. *Perceptual Motor Skills, 18,* 1964, 437–42.

Vermey, G. J. Observations on raised line drawings. *Education of the Visually Handicapped, 1,* 1969, 47–52.

Walter, J. K. A guide for teaching the blind. *Industrial Arts and Vocational Education, 56,* 1967, 55–56.

Welch, M. D. The blind girl and her clothing. American Association of Instructors of the Blind, *Selected Papers,* 40th Biennial Conference, 1950, 235–38.

Wexler, A. *Experimental Science for the Blind.* New York, Pergamon Press, Inc., 1961.

Workshop for Industrial Arts Instructors of Blind Students, State University, Oswego, New York, 1963 (unpublished list of suggested practices with blind high school students in industrial arts).

11

Visually Handicapped Children with Multiple Disabilities

There has been increasing interest in the provision of educational and other services for children who have disabilities in addition to being blind or partially sighted. In recent years it has become apparent that visually handicapped children with concomitant disabilities compose a substantial part of the visually handicapped population, and that there is a general lack of educational services for them (Iverson and Hartong, 1971; Wolf, 1967, pp. 8–9). The American Foundation for the Blind has published the national prevalence estimates of visually handicapped children with concomitant disabilities as 263 per 100,000 of school age population. This multiply handicapped population is expected to increase from about 15,000 in 1965 to 18,000 by 1975 (Graham, 1968, p. 4).

These children have been variously labeled as "multiple handicapped blind child" (Waterhouse, 1964), "multiply impaired visually handicapped" (Hart, 1970), "multihandicapped blind child" (Taylor, 1970) and with other designations reflecting the fact that these children have two or more disabling conditions in the physical, mental, or emotional domains of functioning. All of these designations are approximately synonymous.

DEFINITION OF MULTIPLY HANDICAPPED

Wolf (1967), in reviewing research in this area, concluded that there is "confusion and lack of agreement on definitions, classifications, and terminology" (p. 18). Visually handicapped children with other disabilities will be called "multiply handicapped" children in this chapter and are defined as

> Those who in addition to a visual impairment, have at least one other disability regardless of the extent of either, the combination of which causes such severe educational problems that they cannot receive adequate services in educational programs for visually handicapped children or in those established for other handicapped children (Taylor, 1970).

It should be noted at the outset that there are not only varying combinations of physical, mental, and emotional impairment, but also varying degrees of educational handicap that these combinations impose on children. A partially seeing child with a mild orthopedic impairment and normal intelligence will in all probability present no greater educational problems than a visually impaired child with no other impairments. A visually handicapped child with an orthopedic impairment of such severity that it inhibits mobility and speech presents an educational problem which will require intensive instruction well beyond that required for the visually handicapped child with no other impairments.

Multiply handicapped children have been traditionally considered simply a combination of two or more impairments which include one primary and a secondary concomitant impairment. Thus, subcategories of multiply handicapped children have appeared as hyphenated combinations of deaf-blind, cerebral palsied-blind, orthopedically handicapped-blind, mentally handicapped-blind, emotionally disturbed-blind, etc. Study of multiply handicapped children has sometimes centered around these combinations of disability and have been reported as disturbed blind (Gruber and Moor, 1963), cerebral palsied blind (Frampton, Kerney, and Schattner, 1969), mentally retarded blind (Wolf, 1967), deaf-blind (Curtis and Donlon, 1969), and others. Literature on education of these children has attempted to deal with them in more global terms as multiply impaired visually handicapped children (Regler, 1970; Hart, 1970).

CURRICULUM AND INSTRUCTION OF
MULTIPLY HANDICAPPED CHILDREN

Graham (1968, p. 9) reported that approximately 80 percent of those children who were multiply handicapped had mental retardation as one of the concomitant handicaps to visual impairment, with approximately 40 percent speech handicaps and 35 percent brain damage among the remaining additional handicaps. It would appear that the overwhelming majority of multiply handicapped children are impaired in the cognitive domain of functioning. This implies that the typical additional impairment includes the language development area and suggests that, as a general educational strategy, some procedure for optimal development of language should receive priority.

Curricula have been designed to provide necessary language instruction informally as an incidental component of various motor and social activities. However, the definition adopted here for multiply handicapped (children who cannot profit from the same program as that used by visually handicapped) implies rather severe additional impairments. Hence, the assumption on which this chapter is based is that the combination of disabilities is sufficiently severe that these children should receive their education and training in segregated self-contained rooms or schools.

Training Emphasis

Multiply handicapped children need four areas of emphasis in a training program (Hart, 1970):

1. Speech and language development with a wide range of curriculum objective necessary to changing defective speech patterns, as well as facilitating development of speech and language in a nonverbal child. A unique importance should be ascribed to listening.

2. Self-care skills, which basically cover eating, toileting, walking, and other motor manipulative activities basic to day-to-day functioning.

3. Motor development, including those skills associated with development of orientation, mobility, and body image.

4. Development of adaptive or readiness behavior necessary for entrance into traditional special or general education programs.

A key to success in all areas is the development of adequate language and speech for communication of simple needs. Therefore, the foremost area of concern in this curriculum will be the area of adequate speech and language development.

IMPLICATIONS OF SPEECH
AND LANGUAGE DEFICITS

Multiply handicapped children have been said to use speech and language in two ways (Frampton, Kerney, and Schattner, 1969, pp. 169–81). One is to define what they are doing by talking to themselves or to objects with which they are playing or working. Illustrations of this might be a child speaking to his shoes, saying "Now shoe, stay on my foot." Or he might say "Water, don't get too warm," when getting washed.

Another way of using speech suggests a more sophisticated development of language. In this case, the child uses speech to gain information by asking questions from those around him. When the child asks meaningful questions, the teacher should respond simply and directly to the question. Specific types of speech and language problems identified with multiply handicapped are listed below, with teacher guidelines for resolving them (Frampton, Kerney, and Schattner, 1969, pp. 170–71).

1. Speech apparently unrelated to the activity which is under way. An example of this would be a child persevering in repeating television and radio commercials heard at some earlier period.

2. Undirected speech. In this instance a child talks incessantly, interrupting conversations or discussions going on around him. There appears to be no object or closure to the talking.

3. Use of speech authoritatively. A child may speak in threatening tones to peers or teachers, becoming more agitated as he proceeds, until he may become violent.

4. Use of adult vocabulary without comprehension. Some children may use a sophisticated vocabulary without understanding the meaning of the words.

5. Speech reflecting use of language in fantasy episodes. A child may relate fantasy as though it were objectively real.

6. Abusive language. Some children may use derogatory or obscene language toward other children without understanding the meaning. The children abused by this language react as though the child using this language does understand its meaning.

7. Repetition of questions. Some children persevere in repeating the same questions, even though they do not get any response from others.

8. Speech which is unintelligible but has meaning for the speaker. A child makes a great effort to use speech in communication with people around him, but this speech is unintelligible. A result of this may be frustration for the child.

9. Speech with various infantile qualities. These may be persistent whining accompanying speech, and the sounds are those of a child at a premeaningful speech level.

10. Immature expressions such as those associated with "baby-talk."

11. Stuttering. The child typically does not complete sentences as a result of stuttering.

Speech and Language Instruction Prerequisites

These children should have routine access to the services of a speech therapist and other necessary diagnostic and service staff. The teacher's day-to-day association with the multiply handicapped child provides more opportunity to apply extensive remedial practices than other personnel within a school. Hence, it is possible for practices developed in cooperation with the speech therapist and other professionals to be applied by the teacher over extended periods of time.

It is useful for the teacher to gain some types of diagnostic information concerning the etiology of the condition, such as whether the speech and language problem is related to lack of experience and training, to some physiological pathology, to a search for security, or to some other cause. Diagnostic information can be directly used to develop individualized instructional procedures for resolving the difficulty.

Instruction in Speech and Language

While specific prescriptions for individual children are not possible because of the diversity of each child's speech and language development, some guidelines have been developed which will enhance this curriculum area for multiply handicapped children (Frampton, Kerney, and Schattner, 1969, pp. 171–72). These guidelines are in the form of rules for all teachers in contact with these children.

1. Staff members should consciously use a vocabulary which can be comprehended by the child. The words should be enunciated clearly with a natural rhythm in the flow of words. The teacher should use appropriate expressiveness, including gestures.

2. The teacher should listen to the child when he speaks. The child should be given the teacher's undivided attention until the child has completed a question or statement.

3. The child should be permitted to complete sentences without the teacher anticipating or completing the sentence.

4. The child can gain practice in acquisition of fluent speech and language by deliberately being engaged in conversations on topics which interest him.

5. All adults in contact with these children should present an appropriate language model. Teachers should make a particular effort to address one another and the children courteously, using acceptable vocabulary.

6. Children should not be discussed when they are present.

7. Discretion should be used in correcting speech of children. No child should be constantly corrected in his speech.

Using these guidelines, a structure for developing language and speech can be achieved.

Language and student discussion. The teacher may assemble the children each morning for informal discussions of a wide variety of topics. This may be discussion of the day's schedule of activities, interests of individual students, or items of general interest. A deliberate effort can be made to distinguish a question, answer, or statement for the pupils. The teacher should attempt to get each type of verbal output. Correction of student speech, introduction of new words, and illustration of the use of these new words may be employed during this period.

Many of the same considerations which are used with any child should be exercised during this discussion period. The teacher should insist on orderly discussion with each child allocated a part of the period for talking. The child should raise his hand when requesting the attention of the teacher, and no other child should be allowed to interrupt. The teacher must listen carefully and courteously, encouraging children with all types of speech problems to talk. No child should be permitted to monopolize the discussion, but they should not be abruptly or discourteously asked to terminate talking.

This discussion period should not be considered the only instructional period in language and speech. The teacher can find opportunities for continued use of speech by the students in informal discussions during recess. The teacher should convey to parents or house parents the importance of talking to these children and convey the importance to the children of talking among themselves. The teacher can also design opportunities for development of language and its practical application in social situations.

Language and social graces.   There are many opportunities within the school for instruction in use of language to convey courtesy and cultivate adequate social skills. Multiply handicapped children can learn polite forms of address at some level of usefulness. They may only be able to use a barely intelligible "please" or "thank you," or they may use complete sentences expressing some more sophisticated form of politeness. Other opportunities will be present while eating lunch, in the classroom when requesting material or permission, in greeting peers or adults, and in meeting people new to the school. Deliberately teaching polite forms of address is an important skill in making a handicapped child acceptable to others. Teaching the handshake, smile, to look directly at the person being talked to, and certain gestures such as a wave of the arm are appropriate topics for instruction.

Language and concrete objects.   During regular language instruction, common objects may be examined by the multiply handicapped child and then described to the class. These may include not only paraphernalia within the classroom, but also items brought into a classroom. Plants, including flowers, pets, and items useful in the home may be brought into the room and examined by all the children in a group. This would not only be useful in developing speech, but language would be enhanced because of the relationship between the concrete object and the verbal description. This would also aid in increasing the verbal reality of the children's experiences.

Language and field trips.   Trips away from school provide another source of opportunities for language experiences. Field trips should be a frequent part of a multiply handicapped child's experiences, simply to gain guided experience with the larger world around him. These trips may be used as a source of language and speech practice within the classroom. The children may be taken to places which supply various community services, recreation, and goods. A visit to the grocery store, sheltered workshop, zoo, farm, hospital, and other facilities provides direct information about useful services and also shows the children how they can use the visits as topics in facilitating language and speech development within the classroom.

While a common concomitant handicap to visual impairment is mental retardation, it should not be assumed that every child has a cognitive handicap. Hence, poetry, use of a classroom newspaper, written prose, and other more sophisticated media of communication should not be ignored. The telephone is a uniquely useful device to a blind person. Systematic instruction in its proper use as a source of information and pleasure should be developed. Classroom newspapers can be developed at a variety of levels of reading comprehension, from simple one-word sentences to more complex forms. A newspaper story may be a simple statement of an experience or a more elaborate description of a field trip, vacation, home experience, or some natural phenomenon.

There is little doubt that any program of training must include the development of language. Language is the first step in making the whole world a more comprehensible entity and in viewing it as interesting and nonthreatening.

SELF-CARE SKILLS

Nonhandicapped children learn many, if not most, self-care skills incidentally. For the multiply handicapped these skills must be deliberately and systematically taught and should be included as a part of the school curriculum. Practically any activity which facilitates independent functioning is legitimate curriculum content in this area.

Personal Care

Self-care suggests ability to perform basic tasks of personal care. Typically this includes the abilities to dress, toilet, bathe, and eat. For young children in particular, deliberate instruction in use of buttons, zippers, and shoe laces is necessary. Instruction in use of a bar of soap, washcloth, and towel may be necessary, as well as operation of faucets and toilets. While instruction in some of these activities may not have to be initiated by the teacher, he must be prepared to reinforce instruction begun at home. Both health and social advantages of this instruction should be recognized. A child who is poorly groomed may be offensive to peers and also hygienically unhealthy.

Social Graces

Self-care skills should include various conventional social amenities, deliberate instruction in polite gestures together with manners which do not offend others. Courteous replies or requests and absence of mannerisms which offend others should be given particular attention. Poking fingers in the eye, rocking, and other mannerisms are distracting to the sighted person and only tend to emphasize the differences between him and the handicapped one.

Leisure Time

It has been suggested that few multiply handicapped can maintain themselves completely independently as adults (Helsel, 1965, pp. 262–63). Therefore, the objectives of education should emphasize use of leisure time more than the curriculum for the typical nonmultiply handicapped child. The systematic instruction of leisure time activities is practically endless. One day-activity center has successfully included blackboard play, singing, dancing, rhythms, story telling, simple crafts, pottery, kitchen utensil play, outdoor play with playground equipment, tree climbing, swimming, physical fitness, parties, day and overnight camping, and trips and excursions into the community as a partial list of activities. These events involved children between the ages of fourteen months and fourteen years (Pomeroy, 1972).

Orientation and Mobility

Many of the self-care skills are those learned through orientation and mobility training. Matters of stride, gait, posture, and self-concept may be developed through the use of conventional orientation and mobility practices described in chapter 8. The unique aspects of orientation and mobility with visually impaired multiply handicapped children consist of slower development of motor skills and difference in the kind of activity taught. For example, a visually handicapped child of early elementary school age will usually be able to dress himself if instruction has been initiated in the home. A multiply handicapped child with an orthopedic handicap involving hand use may be in upper elementary grades before he has developed ability to dress himself completely, in spite of home instruction. The teacher needs to constantly observe the stride and posture of those multiply handicapped who can walk and establish a priority for correction of deficiencies in this area. A child should not be demoralized with overwhelming and constant criticism. Continuous instruction in the use of terms denoting relationships of objects in space should be carried on so that a child will automatically recognize "left," "up," "down," "front," "back," and the compass directions. These special relationships terms will facilitate instruction in other areas as well.

Safety

Instruction in safety should be provided in the curriculum of multiply handicapped. A systematic analysis of dangers in the environment should be identified for the individual handicapped child. Some environmental features may present no problem of safety for one child, but will for another child who is multiply handicapped. A pupil who is both visually impaired and has spastic cerebral palsy may suffer injury through the involuntary movement of an arm which a visually impaired athetoid cerebral palsy youngster will not. Common safety practices around tools, kitchens, and playgrounds should be observed as vigilantly with handicapped as with nonhandicapped children.

Adaptive Behavior

Even those children who are rather severely handicapped can achieve some success in their contacts with other handicapped and nonhandicapped children. Therefore, the goal should be to maximize opportunities for meaningful contact with other children. To this end readiness skills in reading, arithmetic, motor activity, and social interaction should be developed. These readiness skills are the same as those used with those visually handicapped who do not have additional impairments, and are discussed elsewhere in this book.

It should be stressed here that great care should be taken to prepare a multiply handicapped child so that he can achieve satisfaction in an integrated program to whatever degree integration is possible. Success is notoriously self-perpetuating. A multiply handicapped student should have many opportunities for contact with nonhandicapped classmates and adults.

EDUCATION AND TRAINING OF ADOLESCENT MULTIPLY HANDICAPPED

Multiply handicapped visually impaired adolescents who are able to follow a high school college preparation curriculum can presumably fulfill substantially the same coursework requirements as their non-handicapped peers. This population, however, is a small minority of as little as 20 percent of a typical residential school population (Clayton, 1972, p. 76). The majority of 60 to 80 percent of a residential school population must prepare for a future without those vocational areas requiring college training. Probably considerably less than 20 percent of the visually handicapped adolescents with additional handicaps, who are moderately to severely handicapped, prepare for full-time gainful employment. Because relatively few multiply handicapped can participate in full-time gainful employment as adults, the curriculum for adolescents may have as its goal development of skills which allow them to function as independently as possible in a nonvocational setting or in a minimal vocational placement. Appendix H outlines a prevocational curriculum for visually impaired multiply handicapped children which may be used in the instruction of adolescents (McDade, 1970, pp. 62–67).

Independent Living

Those multiply handicapped who do not prepare for full-time employment are in the majority; and programs developed for them prepare for activities which strive to provide some satisfactions which to some extent compensate for lack of gainful employment. A comprehensive program for multiply handicapped has been described by Gardner and Nisonger (1962). The adolescent should acquire those skills which allow him to prepare for independent living as much as possible. While this youngster may presently be at home, planning should include consideration for noninstitutional as well as nonhome living. Long-term residential care outside of institutions, while not presently plentiful, does exist in the form of foster homes, group care homes, boarding homes, and half-way houses. The more highly developed the self-care skills are in the multiply handicapped adolescent, the wider the choice of residential settings. A place to live is only one aspect of programming.

Leisure Time Activity

Life-long activity can and should be prepared for with the multiply handicapped. Probably many are capable of some employment in a sheltered workshop or can perform simple tasks around a home or shop for some part of a day. However, there still remains substantial time for other activity.

Social adjustment or day-activity centers serve as a place for instruction in leisure time activities and may be the only activity provided some multiply handicapped. Here a youngster may continue developing hobby and recreational skills as well as social activities. Experienced recreation and day-activity centers provide instruction in a wide variety of activities for adolescents. While these are not located within a traditional school setting, they do provide a basis for a school curriculum. Activities for a teenager's program may include rock dancing, guitar playing, singing, beach or holiday parties, fishing, bowling, boating, swimming, camping, and physical fitness activities (Pomeroy, 1972). Some of these activities, such as camping, may extend over two or more days, and some activities occur during weekends as well as weekdays. Craft activities may be a part of the training program and, in fact, have been a source of saleable items which can not only add small amounts of income for a young person, but provide incentive to pursue these constructive activities.

COMPREHENSIVE CURRICULUM FOR MULTIPLY HANDICAPPED

Some training programs for the severely multiply handicapped have been developed. They are located in centers which have students from four to twenty-one years of age. A representative curriculum for multiply handicapped involves definition of objectives, assumptions about the nature of learning, and methods for achieving the objectives specified. The following discussion illustrates these aspects in an actual program (Lerner, 1966).

The objectives of developing self-care skills, social adjustment, and general independence in areas of activity pertaining to the self and to the home underlie the establishment of the basic curriculum areas for multiply handicapped. The four curriculum areas developed for all of the children in the program are self-management, communication, work, and leisure time. The goals of the program are to teach the students how to take care of themselves, how to use their leisure time wisely, and how to contribute to their environment by help with household tasks and/or participation in sheltered workshop activities.

The needs of the individuals in the program are initially assessed by the use of checklists for evaluation and rating in the completion of basic tasks such as washing one's hands, use of eating utensils, making beds, and ability to get along with peers.

The students are then placed in groups according to the functioning levels indicated on the checklists. The checklists are developed for all of the curriculum areas and a child's progress in each basic task is plotted and dated on these lists. The major areas are broken down into specific and sequential steps, each of which must be successfully performed before progress to the next step is allowed.

The basic assumptions in developing the program are that transfer of learning from one task to another is extremely difficult for the trainable, as is the use of abstractions and symbols. The emphasis is therefore on teaching by doing, rather than by demonstration and lecture.

Each child performs a simple task repeatedly until he demonstrates that he can do it successfully. The trainable possess the potential for social competency, so the approach of the program is group-oriented in order to foster the concept of limits and of skills in relating to peers and adults. The assumption that the possibilities for future placement of the trainable lie in being institutionalized, remaining at home with no program available to them, or remaining at home with daily participation in either special activity programs for the trainable or in sheltered work programs, has led to the formation of the curriculum areas based on tasks of everyday living.

Self-Management

One of the largest curriculum areas is that of self-management. This area is further divided into sections concerning food, clothing, transportation, health, and grooming. Under the section on food, the specific tasks taught are centered around eating meals, planning meals, setting the table and serving the food, preparing the food, and cleaning up. The section on clothing involves the tasks of dressing and undressing, putting clothes away in drawers and closets, choosing clothes, and cleaning clothes. The activities under the section called transportation involve moving in and out of doors, riding on public transportation, and shopping in neighborhood stores. Health activities include sleeping, toileting, exercise, and care of teeth, nose, and eyes. The grooming section emphasizes the care of body, hair, and nails.

In the self-management area, as in the other three areas of the curriculum, the degree of involvement in each task is based on tasks appropriate to each age group. For example, the primary group spends more time learning how to use eating utensils, practice good table manners, set a table properly, and handle the easier aspects of cleaning up than would be true of the teenage group. The teenagers concentrate more on meal planning and preparation, on shopping for more complex items, and on the big tasks involved in clean-up. Even for the teenagers, however, the tasks must be kept simple and basic. Cooking involves the preparation of canned and packaged foods for a long time before the preparation of dishes such as french toast or pizza is taught. The student must first learn how to mix ingredients together with a spoon, use a knife for cutting, regulate the stove, open a can, and so on. One often forgets that even the simplest of tasks must frequently be carefully taught to the multiply handicapped and that a great deal of practice may be required before the task is learned.

Communication

The curriculum area of communication is divided into functional representation of communication, development as a person, basic problem-solving experiences, and symbolizing. The functional representation of communication is evaluated through the media of spontaneous drawing, directed drawing, pasting, cutting, and the combined processes of drawing, cutting, and pasting. In working on the students' development as individual persons, the concepts of personal autonomy and relationship to others are emphasized. The individual is taught to look upon himself as being separate from all other beings, yet having a definite relationship to others such as relatives, teachers, and classmates. The concepts of questioning, categorization, and sequence are handled under the section on basic problem solving.

Work

The work experiences are different for the various age groups. Below eleven years of age, the stress is on giving a group a specific job to do, such as carrying milk, shoveling snow, cleaning toys, and passing out clean laundry. The older students are each responsible for a particular job. The work experiences are geared to the type found either inside or outside of the home. They include such tasks as sweeping floors, washing windows, and other housecleaning tasks, with the goal of each individual being able to clean a whole room completely. Each particular task is handled separately before being combined as required in cleaning a whole room. Other cleaning tasks involve washing and ironing clothes, changing bedding, washing dishes, washing basins and mirrors, and sweeping walks. These jobs are performed at certain times each day. A learner stays with a particular job until he learns it well, after which he moves on to a new task.

Sheltered work experiences are not provided unless an individual is being trained for a particular job that he will handle when he leaves the program, because specific job skills can be handled more effectively in a sheltered work setting. The program aims to help the students develop good work attitudes and habits and teaches them how to work both independently and in a group setting.

Leisure Time

The fourth curriculum area is leisure time. Here the emphasis is on table games, playing with toys, active games, hobbies, gross motor activities, social group activities, and spectator activities. The goal is to provide the students with enough activities to do at home to make life reasonably happy for them and their families. Active games and gross motor activities include kickball, hiking, swimming, and skating. Social group activities include the use of the telephone, parties, and clubs for teenagers. Materials used for hobbies are limited to those that are likely to be found in a home environment. Pets, collecting objects, needlework, woodwork, music, and playing musical instruments such as the bongo drums are among the hobby activities provided.

A large part of the physical setting and activity sequences at this program simulate those found in a home environment. Rooms are set up with living room furniture, carpeting, and curtains. Bedrooms are set up with cots so that the younger children can get undressed, put their clothes away, take a nap, dress again. Bathrooms are equipped with showers, dressing and make-up areas, and hair dryers. The kitchen and laundry areas are completely equipped. The students are thus provided with a realistic home setting in which they can learn and directly apply the skills being taught to them for use in the home.

References

Clayton, I. D. Give a man a fish and he can eat for a day. Association for Education of the Visually Handicapped, *Selected Papers,* 51st Biennial Conference, 1972, 75–81.

Curtis, W. S. and Donlon, E. T. *An Analysis of Evaluation Procedures, Disability Types, and Recommended Treatments for 100 Deaf-Blind Children.* Syracuse University, Division of Special Education and Rehabilitation, 1969.

Frampton, M. E., Kerney, E. and Schattner, R. *Forgotten Children—A Program for the Multihandicapped.* Boston, Porter Sargent, Publisher, 1969.

Gardner, W. I. and Nisonger, H. W. A manual on program development in mental retardation. *American Journal of Mental Deficiency, 66,* 1962.

Graham, M. D. *Multiply Impaired Blind Children: A National Problem.* New York, American Foundation for the Blind, 1968.

Gruber, K. F. and Moor, P. M. *No Place to Go.* New York, American Foundation for the Blind, 1963.

Hart, V. The multiply-impaired visually-handicapped in the day school. Association for Education of the Visually Handicapped, *Selected Papers,* 50th Biennial Conference, 1970, 45–54.

Helsel, E. D. Avenues of action for long-term care of the multiply handicapped. *Rehabilitation Literature, 26,* 1965, 262–78.

Iverson, L. A. and Hartong, J. R. Expanded opportunities for multiply handicapped children. *New Outlook for the Blind, 65,* 1971, 117–19, 125–26.

Lerner, J. A. "A Continuum of Life Services for the Severely Handicapped." Wayne State University, Unpublished master thesis, 1966.

McDade, P. R. The mentally impaired visually handicapped in a non-traditional institutional setting. Association for Education of the Visually Handicapped, *Selected Papers,* 50th Biennial Conference, 1970, 54–68.

Pomeroy, J. Recreation for severely handicapped persons in a community setting. *New Outlook for the Blind, 66,* 1972, 50–55.

Regler, J. The multiply impaired visually handicapped in the residential school. Association for Education of the Visually Handicapped, *Selected Papers,* 50th Biennial Conference, 1970, 30–34.

Taylor, J. L. Educating the multihandicapped blind child. Association for Education of the Visually Handicapped, *Selected Papers,* 50th Biennial Conference, 1970, 1–10.

Waterhouse, E. J. The multiple handicapped blind child. American Association of Instructors of the Blind, *Selected Papers,* 47th Biennial Conference, 1964, 28–31.

Wolf, J. M. *The Blind Child With Concomitant Disabilities.* New York, American Foundation for the Blind, 1967.

12

Teaching Deaf-Blind Children

NATURE AND EXTENT OF THE HANDICAP

A widely accepted definition of deaf-blindness is one developed by the National Study Committee on Education of Deaf-Blind Children in 1960 which states: "A deaf-blind child is one whose combination of handicaps prevents him from profiting satisfactorily from the educational programs provided for the blind child or the deaf child (Graham, 1970, p. 19)." The complexity of this handicap in educational programming, together with the low incidence has resulted in the development of model centers for deaf-blind children on a regional basis in the U.S. (Public Law 90-247, 1978). A conservative estimate of the number of deaf-blind under 21 years of age in the United States range between 2000 to 2500 children (Graham, 1970, p. 12). The definition of deafness used in arriving at this estimate is that the sense of hearing is nonfunctional for the purpose of classroom instruction, and the child is legally blind (Graham, 1970, p. 4).

The complexity of the problem of educating the deaf-blind may be considered in terms of the nature of each handicap separately. The deaf and the blind have in common the loss of one of the two major senses normal in the education of children. This immediately poses the problem of how to circumvent these obstacles to learning. The chief impediment is acquisition of the ability to speak, read, and write.

A deaf child's greatest disadvantage lies in the lack of speech and language development by means of which people enjoy social communication, receive information, express their wants, and acquire information and pleasure through reading. A five-year-old deaf child may enter school unaware of the fact that others have a means of communication that he himself lacks; or he may realize that they do communicate by a means that he knows nothing about. He may not know that he has a name, that everything he sees has a name, that there are words to describe every action that takes place, that people have a way of combining and qualifying these names and actions to express exact ideas. He must acquire the ability to use language.

The acquisition of language through the learning of speech, lipreading, manual alphabet or signing can be a slow process. Each sound and each word must be laboriously acquired through countless repetition, aided by the use of mirrors, mechanical devices, and the sense of touch. Language and speech to the profoundly deaf are always somewhat "foreign," perhaps never completely natural; whereas to the hearing child they surround him and press upon him until he cannot fail to learn them. Learning through speech can never be completely supplanted by the visual impressions upon which the deaf child depends largely for the learning of language.

EDUCATIONAL CHARACTERISTICS OF DEAF-BLIND

The problems faced by the blind child are also diverse (French, 1932, pp.25-26). The blind child lacks the motives that prompt the seeing child to explore and to learn. The bright color of beads or a rattle, the shine of a silver spoon, the appealing variety of colors of foods, arouse the curiosity of the normal child and induce him to further investigation. This visual incentive for curiosity is absent for the blind child. He may learn to sit and day-dream in solitude if other incentives are not provided. Other senses must be developed that will lead the blind child to an interest in life and the things about him.

The educator of the blind child begins immediately to develop the other senses and the joys that they may bring. Objects of every sort are presented for his enjoyment. He learns to spin a top and to feel and hear the whirr as it revolves. He learns the many properties of objects through touch—cold, heat, smoothness, roundness, flatness, bluntness, roughness, silkiness, and many others.

He also becomes aware of the odors of things. Odors which have little or no significance to the seeing child become of great importance to the blind. The odor of his rubber ball may become one of the pleasant associations with this object. He notes the odor of paper, of pencils, of the cosmetics that friends use, of food, of his pets; and he interprets these odors into terms of emotions just as we interpret our visual impressions. The teacher talks to the child, helping him to understand further about his surroundings and the things that he is feeling, smelling, tasting, and hearing. This child learns language through speech almost as does the seeing child. There is one exception to this statement: Many words have little meaning to the blind child because of his handicap. For example, names of colors convey little of the meaning seeing children attach to them. Such words as shadow, reflection, shining, glow, do not mean the same to blind as those with vision.

The education of the deaf-blind is hampered by a serious lack of ability to substitute one of the two major senses for the other. The education of the deaf turns persistently to the development of language through the use of sight. The education of the blind depends in a large part upon the development of language through the sense of hearing. In teaching the doubly handicapped child who is deaf and blind, it is impossible to employ either the methods primarily used in teaching the deaf or the methods used in teaching the blind. The teacher of the deaf-blind child cannot turn to the use of a second major sense as can the teacher of either the deaf or the blind. It should be noted that while the deaf-blind person is physiologically capable of learning to speak, they rarely learn to speak intelligibly to the casual listener. Hence, the expression "deaf-mute" is often (erroneously) used synonomously with deaf-blind.

From the educational standpoint, all of those children who lack sufficient hearing and vision to progress with peers require instructional methods and material unique to their combined impairment. In a great majority of cases the individuals are not totally deaf and totally blind. More commonly, these children have vestigial hearing or vision (Graham, 1970, pp. 7-8). This does not, however, ease the problem of educating them. A relatively small combined loss can pose substantial problems to learning.

THE FIRST SUCCESSFUL TEACHING OF DEAF-BLIND

Any discussion of educational needs and teaching methods with deaf-blind must begin with the first successful instruction in their use of language. Dr. Samuel Gridley Howe is credited with teaching the first deaf-blind person to acquire language (Richards, 1928). Howe had already devoted himself to the education of blind in 1837 when he was brought into contact with Laura Bridgman, a deaf-blind child. Several cases of deaf-blind adults who were uneducable had come to his attention, and it was popularly considered impossible to educate persons with this double handicap. Howe wanted an opportunity to educate a deaf-blind person when his attention was drawn to Laura Bridgman.

The first pupil that Dr. Howe found available for his experiment was the seven-year-old Laura Bridgman. On a farm near Hanover, New Hampshire, this child was spending an almost sedentary existence. The mother was occupied with countless duties of a farmer's wife: Knitting, sewing, churning, weaving, cooking, candle-making, and the raising of bees, lambs and chickens. She found little time to devote to her handicapped child. Laura had suffered a severe illness in infancy that had deprived her of the senses of sight, hearing, taste and smell. The girl's father considered Dr. Howe's proposal to teach his daughter a foolish idea, but the mother regarded the plan more favorably. Howe was able to convince the parents of the necessity of attempting to educate Laura and she was brought into the home of Dr. Howe as his first deaf-blind student. How does one begin instruction of a deaf and blind child?

With no precedent to follow, Dr. Howe began the work which has since been recognized as one of the most significant educational undertakings. The first step was to train the child to use her muscles, particularly those of her hands. The objective was to prepare her to learn finger-spelling. Then labels, printed with raised letters, were pasted on familiar objects such as a key, a knife, and a book. Over and over the child felt of these labels. Later she was given a set of the labels to match with the objects. When the ability to perform this task was learned, the labels were cut up so that she must now assemble the words and match them to the objects. During all of this process the interest of the pupil was maintained, although she had no idea of the ultimate goal. Along with this work, Laura was also learning the letters of the words by having them spelled into her hand with the same signs as are still commonly used in the teaching of the deaf. Then came the moment when Laura suddenly discovered that she herself could express a word; that there was a practical use for these things she had been practicing so painstakingly. From then on, progress was comparatively rapid, although Dr. Howe said that when Laura was nine years old she had no greater knowledge of language than a child of three. Laura's education progressed steadily for many years. From the learning of nouns she went on to other parts of speech, to the expression of abstract ideas, to the study of arithmetic, geography, history, astronomy, and nature study. She learned to do fancywork of various kinds, making gifts for friends or selling the work for "pin money."

Dr. Howe and Horace Mann made a trip to Europe in 1843 where they had an opportunity to see speech being taught to the deaf in Holland, Switzerland, and Germany, and they resolved that such work would be done in this country. Laura was never taught speech, although Dr. Howe himself said that this could have been accomplished had there been more time to work with her on this skill. Up to this time, no deaf-blind person had ever been taught to speak.

While Laura Bridgman was still at Perkins Institute, and during the lifetime of Dr. Howe, four other deaf-blind pupils came to the school. None of these pupils approached Laura in ability or achievement (Fish, 1934, p. 16).

THE SECOND SUCCESSFUL TEACHING OF DEAF-BLIND

While Ragnhild Kaata, a deaf-blind Norwegian child, is generally considered the first to learn speech with this double handicap (Farrell, 1956, p. 88), perhaps even more famous as a deaf-blind child who was successfully educated is Helen Keller. It must be kept in mind, however, that this individual is not typical of the deaf-blind any more than Abraham Lincoln may be said to be typical of Americans. Each rather epitomizes a goal for the group he so ably represents.

Perhaps no deaf-blind pupil has ever had the opportunities that were offered Helen Keller (Brooks, 1956). From the time her education was begun until far into adulthood, Helen had an understanding teacher. This one teacher was with her for twenty-four hours a day, ready to answer questions, even in the middle of the night, should the pupil desire. Money was always available for care, travel, and education. Helen's intelligence was of a high order, and her determination to succeed was indomitable. She learned the sign language, learned to read braille, to write, to speak, and to understand the speech of others through the sense of touch. She graduated from Radcliffe College, and in addition to the A.B. degree there, she later received several honorary degrees from other institutions. She wrote a number of books, lectured, and wrote for various publications. Some of her works have been translated into other languages so that people throughout the world know of her accomplishments.

The history of the education of the deaf-blind is not only the story of a few outstanding pupils, but is also the story of almost unknown children and their teachers scattered here and there about the country. Some of the pupils attained moderate success in the acquisition of speech and language; some learned to do useful work and became partially or entirely self-supporting; some had to discontinue their education through lack of educational facilities, health, or finances; some were required to return from school to their homes because the progress they made did not seem to justify the expenditure of effort that was being made in their behalf.

CONTEMPORARY METHODS AND MATERIAL

During the brief history of the education of the deaf-blind, a number of methods have come into use. No one method has become generally accepted as the best; a fact that perhaps works for the best interests of the pupils. Teachers do experiment with methods in an effort to determine which method or methods in use will be best for their pupils; or they may even embark upon new and untried combinations. Factors to be considered in the selection of the method are: age of the pupil, age at which each handicap was acquired, home training, interests, amount and type of previous educational experience, and native ability. The type of training the teacher has acquired will also be a determining factor.

Each case of deaf-blindness constitutes a unique teaching problem. If the pupil has some vision, the teacher endeavors to train him to utilize this residual vision to the greatest possible advantage. The pupil is helped to use remaining vision to get around without bumping into objects. He can be aided in some cases to learn to distinguish colors and to recognize them by name. He can be taught to recognize shapes and objects by using gross visual cues. If the pupil has some hearing, a comparable utilization of the remaining portion of that sense is undertaken. The hearing may be used for obtaining better voice quality, for the teaching of individual speech sounds, words, and even connected language. Amplifying instruments such as hearing aids may be used in some cases for these purposes. All of the techniques used by teachers of the deaf in training residual hearing may be employed (Robbins, 1964).

A consideration of previous training is important in determining the method of teaching a deaf-blind pupil. A pupil who has started his education as a deaf child and who later loses his vision presents both a problem and advantage to instruction. If that pupil has learned sign language (or a manual method) and appreciates its use, this may be continued.

On the other hand, if a pupil has been educated as a blind child and eventually loses his hearing, a different approach may be indicated.

Since the pupil is already using speech he would be encouraged to continue to do so, and he may now be taught to understand the speech of others through the sense of touch. Even in such cases, however, there may be reasons for teaching the manual alphabet in addition to the use of speech. The pupil's own aptitudes and desires may help to determine the course to be pursued. The child who has lost both sight and hearing early in life, likewise presents a variety of new options to the teacher.

Oral speech may be taught to pupils of this type, although speech intelligible to a casual listener may not be achieved. Some individuals object to the placing of another's hand on their face, and it may seem desirable to give the deaf-blind child some additional means of communicating. There are several mechanical devices which are useful in communicating with deaf-blind by people who do not know any manual signing methods. Among these are the Electro-Braille Communicator and the Braille Communicator. These are both mechanical devices through which deaf-blind who read braille can communicate with nonhandicapped who have no special knowledge of deaf-blind communication methods.

The Electro-Braille Communicator contains a standard typewriter keyboard to enable someone who has no knowledge of Braille to talk with a deaf-blind person. When a letter is pressed on the keyboard, a corresponding braille character appears in a small cell attached to the machine. This cell is a flat disk with six perforations through which metal dots appear. The deaf-blind person feels these dots with the tips of his fingers. The deaf-blind person cannot, however, respond to the communication with this machine unless he has speech.

The Braille Communicator is similar to the Electro-Braille Communicator, but simpler in mechanism. It contains a braille writer keyboard instead of a typewriter keyboard and can be operated by a person who knows braille. If the blind person has no speech, he can respond through the keyboard since both "speakers" must know braille (Dinsmore, 1953).

There have been devices for communicating with the deaf-blind which have been used but are not widely employed. Letters cut out of sandpaper or cardboard have been used to teach the alphabet to deaf-blind pupils. Sometimes corresponding braille symbols are placed on the letters, so that the pupil learns both simultaneously. The Morse Code has also been used by the deaf-blind speaker, tapping out the words in the palm of the handicapped person.

A one-hand manual alphabet is a special method in use in the U.S. which is somewhat difficult to learn. In this method a pattern of letters is formed with the fingers on the hand of the listener. There is also a two-hand manual alphabet which is popular in many English-speaking countries outside of the United States. This method involves using both the "listener's" and "speaker's" hands in the formation of letters (Kinney, 1969).

Another method by deaf-blind persons are words written with the index finger on their palm or wrist by one wishing to speak to them. A rather widely used systematic communication method of print letters have been learned by deaf-blind; the pocket-sized alphabet plate that bears raised letters easily recognized by touch. This involves placement of the deaf-blind person's index finger on the desired letters as the words are spelled. Once a person learns to use this fluently they may begin finger-writing capital or block letters on the palm of the deaf-blind individual as a means of communication (Kinney, 1969).

Alphabet gloves have been used by deaf-blind who would memorize the location of each letter on the glove. The deaf-blind person puts on the glove while the one wishing to communicate with him touched the letters in succession to spell out the message he wished to give. In some cases the letters have also been put on the glove in braille, so that another blind person might use the glove in talking to a deaf-blind person (Kinney, 1969).

The usual devices that the blind employ in reading and writing may be used by the deaf-blind. Typewriters, braille writers, grooved writing boards, and the slate and stylus. The latter device is less popular now with the deaf-blind because mechanical braille writers are a common substitute.

The Tadoma Method of teaching the deaf as well as the deaf-blind has been used with some success (Alcorn, 1932). This method teaches pupils to learn to speak and to understand speech by vibration. At first the pupil is allowed to place his thumb on the teacher's upper lip, while the fingers rest lightly on her cheek. Later the thumb is removed from her lip, and the pupil relies entirely upon the vibrations felt on the cheek (Alcorn, 1932). More recent instruction has refined the Tadoma Method and developed a wide variety of situations in which speech is practiced (Robbins, 1963).

No matter which means of communication is used, every deaf-blind person needs a quick signal for "yes" and "no." These signals can serve to facilitate conversation. For example, the deaf-blind person can anticipate a word or sentence before it is given, and a quick signal for "yes" eliminates the necessity for completing the word or thought. "Yes" and "no" are especially useful to a deaf-blind person with limited understanding of language (Dinsmore, 1953).

Teachers of the blind as well as of the deaf-blind are concerned with the problem of verbalism. Persons who do not see are the recipients of countless verbal descriptions from those who do see. The blind person may soon acquire a manner of using such descriptions in his own speaking and writing. This makes it difficult distinguishing accurately between the things that they have sensed and the things someone related to them. Deaf-blind pupils, likewise, learn to use words applicable to visual and auditory experiences that are descriptions which have no meaning in reality for them. The use of such words and phrases gives an air of insincerity and unreality to their expression. The pupil must be taught to differentiate between those things that he has experienced, those things that he has read, and those things that he has been told. There will be experiences in which they cannot participate.

In general, those attitudes and methods of teaching most desirable in the teaching of normal children apply in the teaching of the deaf-blind. The relationship between teacher and pupil is always important. Those who have worked with the deaf-blind stress the importance of the pupil's trust in and obedience to the teacher. Upon this attitude the child's health and safety depend. Regardless of the ability and training that a deaf-blind person may possess, his dependence upon others will probably remain greater than that of other people.

In contrast to Helen Keller, few present-day deaf-blind will have the wonderful opportunity of twenty-four hour instruction which Ann Sullivan provided her. Greater effort is made now to assist parents in facilitating the development of their deaf-blind child. Readily available are printed materials providing instruction on the care and training of these children at home (Esche & Griffin, 1970; Robbins, 1963). Consultation is provided nationally through the regional centers for deaf-blind as well as state departments of education.

References

Alcorn, S. "The Tadoma Method." *Volta Review*, 1932.

Brooks, V. B. *Helen Keller*. E. P. Dutton Co. New York, 1956.

Cutsforth, T. D. *The Blind in School and Society*. American Foundation for the Blind, New York, 1951.

Dinsmore, A. B. *Methods of Communication with Deaf-Blind People*. American Foundation for the Blind, New York, 1953.

Esche, J. and Griffin, C. *A Handbook for Parents of Deaf-Blind Children*. Michigan School for Blind, Lansing, Michigan, 1970.

Farrell, G. *The Story of Blindness*. Harvard University Press, Cambridge, 1956.

Fish, A. G. *Perkins Institute and Its Deaf-Blind Pupils*. Perkins Institution, Watertown, Mass., 1934.

French, R. S. *Homer to Helen Keller*. American Foundation for the Blind, New York, 1932.

Graham, M. D. *The Deaf-Blind: Some Studies and Suggestions for a National Program*. American Foundation for the Blind, New York, 1970.

Kinney, R. "Touch Communication" excerpted from *Independent Living Without Sight and Hearing*. Hadley School for the Blind, Winnetka, Illinois, 1969.

Public Law 90-247, 90th Congress, HR7819, Jan. 2, 1968. *An Act to Strengthen, Improve and Extend Programs of Assistance for Elementary and Secondary Education*.

Richards, L. E. *Laura Bridgman*, D. Appleton & Co., New York, 1928.

Robbins, N. *Auditory Training in the Perkins Deaf-Blind Department*. Perkins School for the Blind, Watertown, Massachusetts, 1964.

Robbins, N. *Speech Beginnings for the Deaf-Blind Child*. Perkins School for the Blind, Watertown, Massachusetts, 1963.

13

The Structure and Function of the Eye

ANATOMY OF SEEING

The language of the medical sciences can be very technical. Therefore, the aspects of the subject that are most commonly met in daily life are emphasized, and the terminology is simplified and selected rather than technical and comprehensive.

Objects can be seen only when light reflected from them passes through the eye and is perceived by the brain. The pathway of reflected light entering the eye can point out the many parts of the visual mechanism involved in the marvelous sensation of sight. The light reflected from some object first passes through the cornea. The cornea is normally transparent, and curved out over the pupil. (See Figure 8.) The cornea is made up of several layers pressed close together, each of which has a function in seeing, either as protection for the interior of the eye, as a supply of nutrition for nearby layers, or the beginning of bending (refraction) of light rays toward correct focus for sharp vision.

Next, the light continues through the anterior (front) chamber, the space between the back (posterior) surface of the cornea, and the pupil. This chamber is filled with a water-like fluid called aqueous humor, which circulates through the anterior chamber. The aqueous is normally transparent, as is the cornea. Light passing through the aqueous is not changed in quality, but only slightly in direction, as it travels toward the back of the eye. The next part of the eye through which the light passes is the pupil, the space between the ends of the circular muscle called the iris. The iris is the part of the eye that appears colored blue, brown, etc. (See Figure 8.) Under conditions of dim light, the pupil ordinarily grows larger, and in bright light, the pupil normally becomes smaller. These pupillary changes, which regulate the amount of light entering the eye, are the result of changes in the size of the iris. The iris is made up of two types of muscle which control these changes. If the pupil is to enlarge, the iris is forced away from the center of the pupil by muscle fibers radiating like rays of the sun. These fibers form the radial muscle. If the pupil is to become smaller, the iris is pulled toward the center of the pupil by circular muscle fibers. These fibers form the circular muscle.

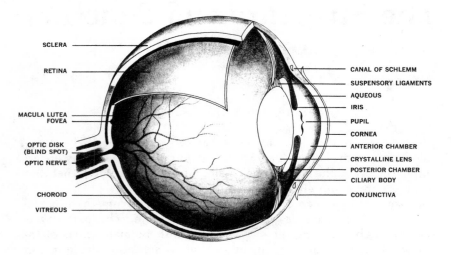

Figure 8.   Diagram of the Human Eye.

Once through the pupil, light rays immediately enter the lens, which is held in place behind the pupil by suspensor ligaments. The lens is made up of many layers, much like an onion, and being transparent in normal health, it does not diminish the light, but makes delicate, automatic adjustments to cause accurate focusing on the back of the eye.

The light then leaves the lens and continues to travel toward the back of the eye through a chamber larger than the anterior chamber. This large space is filled with gelatin-like fluid (vitreous humor).

Normally, this material, too, does not affect the course of the light. The next surface reached by the light is the retina.

The retina forms the inner lining of the back four-fifths of the eye, and acts much like the film of a camera. It is formed by the endings of thousands of nerve fibers, which are sensitive to light. These many nerve fibers converge from all parts of the retina toward an area near the back of the eyeball or globe called the optic disc. This area is the head of the optic nerve, through which the fibers extent to the brain.

Directly in line with the centers of the cornea and the pupils is an area of the retina which is more sensitive than the rest of the retina. This small area, called the macula, is used for vision that demands sharp focusing, while the rest of the retina is used for "side" or peripheral vision. A small spot, the most sensitive, is called the fovea.

This light-sensitive tissue, the retina of the eye, is a most fascinating formation of specialized tissues, each having a definite purpose in the accurate transmission of impressions of light. First, light passes through a thin layer of pigment cells which lines the retina. Then the light reaches the nerve-ending layer of cones, for daytime light, including elements responsible for color vision, and another kind of nerve-ending, rods, which have a lower threshold of sensitivity and are used in dim light, as in night vision. Eight other layers relay the light impulse through the retina, for a total of ten layers.

Up to this point the refractive system of the eye has been discussed and includes the cornea, aqueous humor, lens, and vitreous humor which causes light entering the eye to focus on the sensitive central area, as well as peripherally.

The retinal nerve endings have connected to them long neurons, or strands of nerve tissue, which carry visual impulses out of the eye to brain centers of vision. These neurons all leave the globe of the eye through the optic nerve as a bundle of neurons which travel back from the eye about an inch or two. Here the optic nerve branches from the main bundle of neurons. This branching or partial crossing-over (decussation) will be described later in this chapter. Each new visual image, one from each eye, now goes to a center of the mid-brain where the optic neurons end. Here relays take place. Some impulses go directly to neurons which cause physical muscular reactions to light. These reactions can be called reflex motions such as closing of the pupil by the iris, blinking, whole body movements out of the way of danger, etc. These actions do not need thought by higher brain centers before they take place, although only the pupil reflex is a true reflex in a technical sense. Most of the visual impulses are relayed via other neurons to the occipital lobes of the brain, left and right posterior brain portions, where sensations of light and images are registered.

From here the visual impulses are again relayed from both sides of the occipital lobes to a single center in the frontal portion of the brain cortex (the most highly specialized brain tissue), where the most complex neural interplays take place, and "thought" is carried on. It is in this context that the expression, "Looking is done with the eyes, and seeing is done with the brain" can be understood.

The parts of the eye directly in the path of entering light have been described, but there are many other parts of the globe of the eye which are necessary for the support of the shape of the eye, nutrition of the eye tissues, and protection of the inner structures. The entire globe is covered by a tough elastic, white membrane called the sclera, except for the cornea anteriorly, and the exit of the optic nerve posteriorly. Lining the inside of the sclera is a layer of tissue rich in blood vessels, both arteries and veins, which provide the bulk of the nutrition for the eye. This "coat" is the choroid which begins around the head of the optic nerve and continues forward past the central portion of the globe until it becomes continuous with the ciliary body. The ciliary body continues forward becoming ciliary muscle which in turn is continuous with the iris. The choroidal coat, then, consists of choroid, ciliary body and muscle, and iris.

The third and innermost "coat" of the eye is the light-sensitive retina which has been described. It is usually transparent so that if one were to examine the inside of the eye, the color seen would be that of the choroid, reddish in appearance, the retina ends anteriorly at the area where the choroid meets the ciliary body. This area is called the ora serrata.

There are two other points of interest in this efficient, optical instrument called the eyeball. One is the fibers which hold the lens in its proper position and regulate its function in focusing light. These zonular fibers are attached to the lens at one end and to the ciliary muscle at the other end.

The other point of interest is the course of the aqueous fluid which flows from behind the iris, through the pupil, and through the anterior chamber. This fluid is produced by the ciliary body and has as its main source of exit openings in the angle between the iris and cornea. These openings are known as Canals of Fontana and another canal in the scleral tissue near the same area known as the Canal of Schlemm.

In order for the two separate eyes to produce a single, unified image, the eyes must be moved in unison. Each eye is moved by six small, powerful muscles which operate in groups. (See Figure 9.) Along with these muscles, eye movements are limited by various check ligaments attached to surrounding bone structures.

The eyeball itself is enclosed in a thick layer of fatty tissue which is in turn surrounded by various bone structures which protect the globe. The top of the orbit, or hollow eye socket, into which the globe is set, is formed by part of the frontal bone which underlies the forehead and forms the brow; the lateral side is formed by part of the cheek bone or superior (upper) maxillary. The medial, or nasal, side is formed by several bones in the midline, common to both orbits, the lacrymal, sphenoidal, ethmoidal, and malar bones. The inferior (lower) side is formed by part of the superior maxillary bone. The orbit is shaped roughly like a cone narrowing toward its apex at the back. It has openings for the entrance and exit of various nerves and blood vessels.

The remainder of this discussion is directed toward answering the question: How do these many structures contribute to the phenomenon of vision?

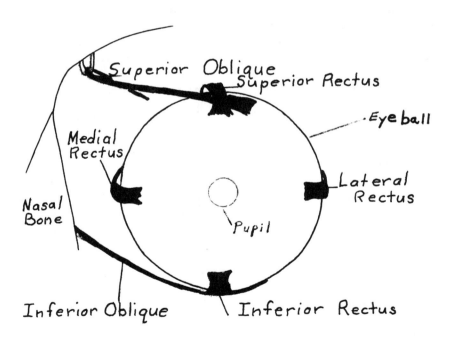

Figure 9.   Attachment of the Six Extra-ocular Muscles

PHYSIOLOGY OF SEEING

One of the most obvious external features of the eye is the eyelid. This structure serves both to protect the sensitive tissues of the eye itself from dust and other foreign bodies and to lubricate the front surface of the globe when necessary. Its muscles have nerve connections for both voluntary and involuntary or reflex actions. The lashes of the eye also serve to exclude foreign bodies. The eyelids help control the amount of light that is allowed to enter the eye by starting to close automatically when light becomes brighter, and opening when light becomes duller.

Once light gets into the eye the process of refraction begins. From whatever direction the light comes, it is bent so that it can become part of the pattern reaching the retina. The cornea is the first structure to bend light, and in cases where the cornea is not evenly curved, the eye usually cannot compensate for the blurred impressions resulting on the retina. As the intensity of light varies, the iris changes its size so as to control the amount of light that enters the posterior portion of the eye by using alternately its radial and circular muscles.

Just behind the iris the lens is in constant change in order to keep the focus on the retina as sharp as possible. If the focus of light were to fall behind the retina (as would happen if the cornea did not bend the light rays sufficiently or the eyeball were too short), the lens mechanism would try to allow the lens to thicken, and thus bring the focus forward. Note that the thicker a convex lens, the shorter is the distance of the focus of light through it. (See Figure 8.) Also, if the focus of light were to fall in front of the retina the lens mechanism would try to flatten the lens so as to move the focus back to the retina if possible. These marvelous, automatic adjustments are made whenever vision changes from an object at one distance to an object at another distance. Objects beyond twenty feet distance cause very little change in the size of the lens. The twenty-foot distance is known as optical infinity.

The liquids inside the eye serve to maintain constant pressure so that the various organs stay in their relative positions. The aqueous humor, circulating from the posterior chamber (among the zonular fibers) through the anterior chamber (between the iris and the cornea) contains a weak solution of various elements of nutrition needed by surrounding tissues as well as antibodies to counteract infectious organisms which may accidentally enter the eye. The vitreous humor is a more gelatin-like substance and serves to keep the retina pressed smoothly against the back of the eye for the best possible visual reproduction.

When light reaches the retina a substance in the rods called visual purple (rhodopsin) is bleached and this photochemical action starts an impulse along the nerve pathway to the brain. The impulse passes through the various layers of the retina along the neuron to the optic nerve where it joins other neurons, also carrying impulses. The neurons from the nasal half of each retina cross over (decussate) to the opposite side at a point called the optic chiasm and join neurons from the lateral half of the other retina. In this way the left side of the retina in each eye is represented in the left side of the brain, and the right half of each retina in the right side of the brain. Both sides are united in a single center in the frontal cortex of the brain for purposes of interpretation of the image seen.

Now it is possible to understand why seeing can be called a function of the brain. Until the visual impulse reaches the higher brain center in the cortex, no interpretation is made of the object from which the light originated.

Single vision with two eyes can be accomplished only if both eyes work in close-to-perfect harmony. The function of the eye muscles is to keep the two eyes in position continuously so that a stimulus from an object can affect corresponding points on each of the retinae. To accomplish this the muscles work in various combinations as shown in the following example. (See Figure 9.)

If both eyes want to turn right, the lateral rectus muscle of the right eye and the medial rectus muscle of the left eye shorten (contract). The medial rectus muscle of the right eye and the lateral rectus of the left eye lengthen to allow the turning to the right. Since the action of the superior oblique muscle is both down and in, because of the point at which it is attached on the eyeball, for a right turn the superior oblique of the left eye would be partially used. The same muscle of the right eye would have to be relaxed or lengthened. Since the action of the inferior oblique muscle is up and out, for a right turn the inferior oblique of the right eye would be partially used. The same muscle of the left eye would have to be relaxed.

The signals to these various muscles to make their proper movements together come from the brain, another aspect of the brain in the seeing process. The brain, however, cannot overcome many of the defects in the physical apparatus of the visual system. Thus, it is necessary to consider several of the commonly seen types of abnormal visual conditions.

PATHOLOGY OF SEEING

It is not difficult to conceive of many types of obstructions that could interfere with light reaching the retina. Any scars from injury or disease which might be formed on the central part of the cornea, the lens, or the retina would prevent light from making a normal impression on the retina. Any foreign body which enters the anterior chamber or the vitreous chamber would also block out part of the light.

Active infection is accompanied by clouding of the tissues and liquids in the eye and may cause more or less permanent interference with the entry of light. Severe nutritional deficiencies could cause clouding of the normally transparent tissues. Normal senility often has associated with it a loss of the transparency of the lens called cataract. Cataracts can also be congenital (present at birth).

Another area of impairment in the visual cycle can be described as extending from the retina to the visual area of the brain. The retina may be pushed away from its normal position by a tumor pressing against it, a scar tissue on the surface of the retina pulling it from its moorings, or a sudden blow to the head near the eye which tears the retina loose. A tumor may press against the nerve pathway, or an injury may sever its fibers anywhere along its length to the brain center. The visual symptoms would depend on the exact location of the trauma (wound or injury).

Infections may attack the visual nerve pathway, or nutritional upsets may take place. Once these nerve tissues die, there is almost no regeneration in contrast to other body tissues which do. Visual impairment resulting from destroyed nerve tissue is typically permanent.

Hemorrhages and other conditions of excessive fluid pressing against the visual pathway may also cause visual disturbances.

Eye conditions that would attract attention by their appearance are relatively easy to discover and should be referred for appropriate professional attention. Examples of these are: (1) Albinism, which is a lack of pigmentation or color, sometimes accompanied by nystagmus (constant involuntary movements of the eyes), photo-phobia (extreme sensitivity to light), and high errors of refraction; (2) Aphakia, or the absence of the lens; and (3) Coloboma, in which a portion of a structure in the eye is missing.

Other visible conditions of the eye may be disease conditions as differentiated from structural defects, e.g., congenital or traumatic. Some of these have the suffix "itis" to the name of the structure to denote inflammation. Illustrations of this condition are: (1) Iritis, or inflammation (swelling or discoloration of the iris); (2) Choroiditis, which is inflammation of the choroid; (3) Conjunctivitis, or inflammation of the conjunctiva, which is the thin mucous membrane covering the outside of the cornea and extending along the inside of the eyelids. This latter condition may be called "pink eye"; (4) Ptosis, drooping of the eyelid due to faulty or damaged muscle control; and (5) Styes, infections of the roots of the eyelashes which may reappear frequently if not controlled. The most common eye pathology associated with fluid pressure is glaucoma. Glaucoma is not as visible to the observer as the eye conditions mentioned above, but often presents the victim with visible warnings of an increase of fluid pressure in the eye in the form of halos around lights. Other symptoms of glaucoma include periods of pain deep in the eye itself and narrowing of the visual field. The cause of the fluid pressure in glaucoma is an obstruction to the exit of fluid from the eye. If the obstruction is partial, the condition may be chronic, lasting over a period of years. If the obstruction is great, vision may be lost in a few weeks. Eye fluid normally leaves through spaces at the angle between the cornea and iris, and may be interfered with by a swollen iris, scar tissue after an accident or disease in that area, or other reasons.

Traumatic and disease conditions can also affect the muscle and nerve mechanism which moves the eyes. If the energy through a nerve to a muscle is interfered with abnormally, the movements of one or both eyes controlled by the muscle or muscles involved can no longer be coordinated. Consequently, vision itself, which must be single and clear, may not remain normal. Conditions of this kind, when extreme, result in tropias such as strabismus resulting in the failure of two eyes to simultaneously direct their gaze at the same object. This is known to the layman as crossed eyes.

There is a large classification of visual defects which are due to improper curvatures of the refractive mechanism (cornea, lens, etc.) of the eye. These errors of refraction are the most common causes of visual difficulties. They are generally classified in three large groups; myopia or near-sightedness; hyperopia or far-sightedness, and astigmatism.

In myopia, light rays are focused before the retina. To correct this condition a lens may be needed which will move the focus of light back to the retina. The lens which has this effect is concave so that the center is thinner than the edges. (See Figure 10.)

In hyperopia, light rays focus "behind" the retina, and for mild amounts of error, the lens of the eye can adjust itself to become thicker and correct the error by bringing the focus forward to the retina. A more satisfactory solution to mild hyperopia, and a necessary solution for extreme error, is a glass lens which acts in a way similar to the action of the lens of the eye. This lens (convex in shape) has a center that is thicker than the edge. (See Figure 10.)

In astigmatism, the surface of the cornea is unevenly shaped, and light rays passing through are focused at many different points near the retina, some in front and some behind. The lens of the eye cannot resolve this problem and spectacle lens usually can.

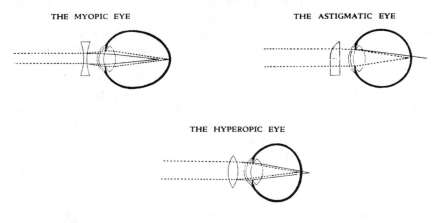

THE MYOPIC EYE

THE ASTIGMATIC EYE

THE HYPEROPIC EYE

Figure 10.   Errors of Refraction

For persons, both children and adults, who have a combination of refractive visual problems, multiple focal length spectacle lenses may be prescribed, including bifocals and trifocals. The most common pathology associated with multiple focal length lenses is presbyopia, or the inability of the natural lens to focus.

We have discussed normal and abnormal vision on the basis of physical make-up. As is true of all systems involving the brain, psychology plays a vital part in the functioning and efficiency of the seeing mechanism.

An important basic principle underlying the process of seeing is that it is learned. Looking, or directing one's attention to an object, comes early in learning. Seeing, or the ability to comprehend what one is "looking at," comes somewhat later in life. We note this as we observe the newborn infant gazing without apparent recognition as he makes random movements. Later in his development, we observe him looking purposeful, with accompanying attending behavior predictive of comprehension of his surroundings. This psychological component of vision is much less amenable to treatment when a pathology occurs than the physiological part. It is this psychological component, and its accompanying perceptual disability which is more common as an obstacle to learning than deprivation of vision per se.

References

May, C. H. (Revised by Charles A. Perara), *May's Manual of the Diseases of the Eye* (22nd Ed.), Williams and Wilkins Co., Baltimore, 1957.

Vaughan, D. and Asbury, T. *General Ophthalmology* (7th Ed.), Lange Medical Publications, Los Altos, California, 1974.

14

The Future
and Education of
Visually Handicapped

There continues to be considerable interest in developing methods and materials which will help the blind and severely visually handicapped in acquiring academic and environmental information. Better methods of using the senses other than vision are needed to cope with the imperfect translation of visual phenomenon by the other sensory channels. Attitudes of adult relatives and friends which are debilitating to blind children must be recognized and changed. Lack of visual acuity must not be routinely accepted as prima facie evidence that the visually impaired person lacks vocational competency. Technology needs to be exploited to solve problems of information acquisition by visually handicapped.

TECHNOLOGY AND BLINDNESS

Reading Machines

Technology is used in many spheres of a blind individual's life. Of particular interest to the teacher and parent are the intensive attempts to develop a machine which can instantaneously convert printed books and other printed material into either sound or tactual output. The federal government in one recent year allocated more than $1,500,000 in contracts through one agency to deal specifically with the development of reading machines for the blind (American Association of Workers for the Blind, 1971). These efforts have been productive, and functional machines are being field tested.

Attempts at developing machines which can optically scan a printed page and produce sounds which are intelligible to the listener date back to 1919, when the optophone was demonstrated in England. This machine had the capacity to scan a page and produce coded sounds which correspond to the printed letters (Jameson, 1966). Few people ever learned to use the machine because of the difficulty in learning the sound code and slow reading speed, however. This was the most highly developed print-to-sound machine for blind until after World War II.

More recently efforts have been directed to correcting the limitations of the optophone so that reading speeds can be increased and training time is minimized. An interim word-reading machine has been developed which stores and retrieves prerecorded words. The problems presently being investigated include the very difficult one of recording the words to sound like sentences in which appropriate syllable stress is present. The prototype machine planned for this project is not designed for portability at the present, but will be one which is suitable for a central reading facility such as a library (Gaitenby, 1969).

A successor to the optophone was developed in 1964 (Batelle Optophone); and at the present time the Visotoner, which is a third generation optophone, is being field tested. This print-to-sound conversion machine contains a vertical column of nine photo cells, an optical system, and electronic circuits which generate a different audible tone for each photo cell. Hence, the machine presents the letter shapes as patterns of tone. This hand-held reading machine fits into a specially designed attaché case and weighs about eleven pounds. Reading speeds on the Visotoner are reported as being as high as thirty-seven words per minute (Lauer, 1969, p. 259).

The Cognodictor, which may also be considered a successor to the Batelle Optophone, is a machine which spells words audibly but can be modified to give tactile braille output. This machine is approximately the size of a portable typewriter and can identify most common types of printing. Both the Visotoner and Cognodictor have been found useful in field testing for such tasks as reading correspondence, bank statements, labels, and other brief narratives or phrases (Lauer, 1969, p. 259).

Print-to-touch conversion reading machines have also been tested. One of these machines is the Optacon, a device which allows a blind person to read ordinary print by sensing the letters tactually on a matrix of vibrating pins. The reader moves a small hand-held scanning device along the lines of print while one finger of the other hand rests on the vibrating pins and senses the letters. Results of the use of the Optacon with elementary and junior high school blind students indicate a reading rate of about six to eight words per minute after twenty hours of instruction (Weihl, 1971, p. 161). Higher rates have been achieved with adults.

Another print-to-touch conversion reading machine is the Visotactor. Two mechanical vibrators are felt by each of the four fingers of the right hand as the output of the device. The size of this machine is approximately the size of the Visotoner. Reading rates of between five and fifteen words per minute have been reported (Lauer, 1969, p. 259).

Each of these machines is an important step in the development of machines which can instantaneously convert printed material to an audible or tactile output which a blind person can use. While the problems of relatively slow reading rates, expensive equipment, and difficulty in providing the audible machines with human-like speech persist, these seem to be sophisticated enough to suggest that reading machines will become an important device in the education of blind children before very long.

Orientation and Mobility Devices

Attempts at improving on the long cane and guide dog as mobility aids continue to occupy much of the attention of those who develop tangible aids for blind. These efforts are directed toward providing a convenient method of protecting the blind traveler from objects which cannot be detected by the long cane. One new device is the Laser Cane.

This cane is similar in appearance to the familiar long cane and emits pulses of infrared light. This light is reflected from an object in front of the user and provides a warning in the form of a high pitched tone. Three beams are emitted simultaneously: down, straight ahead, and up. The downward channel warns of any drop-off larger than nine inches, such as stairs, which may appear approximately two paces in front of the traveler. The maximum range of the straight-ahead beam is ten feet from the cane top. Presently this device is being field tested (Nye, 1971, pp. 9–16).

Another mechanical mobility aid which has been used is the "Sonic Glasses" or the Kay Ultrasonic Binaural Sensor. This device is similar to a common pair of spectacles which transmit high frequency sound pulses. The reflected echo is then used to identify and warn the user of impending obstacles. Like the Laser Cane, the Sonic Glasses are used to supplement the information gained with the long cane. The user is alerted to obstacles by tones heard through inconspicuous earphones (Nye, 1971, pp. 17–25).

A third mobility aid is the Pathsounder, which is about the size of a 35 mm reflex camera and is worn on the chest by means of a neckstrap. This device directs an ultrasonic beam in front of the person using it. When an obstacle is detected within six feet, a ticking sound is first emitted. The ticking later turns to a beeping sound, as the user comes within thirty inches of the obstacle. It is designed to be used with a long cane; only objects above the waist level are detected (Nye, 1971, pp. 33–42).

It is interesting to note that the long cane, when used properly, remains the best aid to independent travel for blind. Machines to aid pedestrian travel are designed to complement the long cane, and not to replace it. Perhaps the next generation of mobility machines will provide not simply a supplement to the use of the long cane or dog, but to substitute completely for these methods of independent travel. At the moment, there appears to be no device which can serve as a complete substitute.

EFFICIENT USE OF INTACT SENSES

Everyone obtains information about his environment through "perceptual systems." These systems may be thought of as using the human senses in various combinations to achieve comprehension. When one of the senses does not function adequately, as in the case of visual impairment, the individual must obtain the same or equivalent information by means of alternative perceptual systems. Deliberate investigation of alternative perceptual systems is underway at the Perceptual Alternative Laboratory, which has as its primary thrust the investigation of these systems as they relate to orientation and mobility and to reading alternatives ("The Blind in the Age of Technology," 1970, pp. 207–8).

The investigations in the area of mobility will attempt to define the perceptual basis of mobility. This information will be useful in aiding blind pedestrians in determining the states of the environment which make for safe and successful travel. This investigation is also designed to provide data on the perceptual systems a blind person uses, through the intact sensory channels, in traveling on foot.

Reading alternatives include both the auditory and tactile modes of information acquisition. Specifically, the Perceptual Alternatives Laboratory investigates the relationship between man's perceptual capacity and the kind of dot patterns that occur in the braille code and "time compression" or compressed speech, which increases the rate at which recorded material is presented to a listener. The compressed speech concept has resulted in the development of a center which produces time-compressed recorded material.

This one facility is intended as an example of the contemporary interest in systematically investigating those factors which allow blind to function in day-to-day life. Evidence of intensive research and development activities in many areas of education by a wide variety of types of institutions should provide optimism concerning the solution of educational problems of blind children. Perhaps special note should be taken of the continuing research and development at the American Printing House for the Blind, which continues to develop and test useful education devices as well as to investigate psychological problems related to education.

ATTITUDES TOWARD THE BLIND

One of the most difficult obstacles confronting the visually handicapped child is the attitudes of parents, teachers, and other adults which hamper them in their normal development in education and other areas of life. Parents can, and sometimes do, become overprotective or rejecting of their blind child. Teachers excuse poor achievement with the erroneous notion that because the child is blind he cannot achieve in the various educational tasks. Other adults have biases which lead to condescension, unrealistically simple expectations, and other actions which tell the blind child that he is different and that therefore he does not need to achieve in those tasks in which other children must demonstrate competency.

Attempts continue to be made to change those attitudes which are detrimental to the self-esteem and morale of the blind individuals. The most notable example of a systematic approach to elimination of negative attitudes toward blind was initiated in 1971. The National Invitational Symposium on Attitudes Toward Blindness set as its goal the design of a methodology for use by local communities to translate the "realities of being blind in today's society in order to create a more realistic awareness and acceptance of blind persons, and to develop a body of knowledge that could be exploited on the local level" (Lukoff et al., 1972, p. vi). Several regional symposiums were concluded during 1972 to further develop strategy for changing the biases of society which hamper the social and educational development of both children and adults who are blind. Additional planning meetings will continue both at national and local levels to develop methods of removing the effects of public bias toward blindness.

There is good reason to be optimistic about the technical progress in minimizing the effects of blindness through the development of machines and other gadgetry. There is somewhat less optimism about any rapid changes in the very complex area of human interrelationships and the attitudes which develop as a result of these associations. However, even in the area of attitudes, progress has been made to the extent that a large proportion of blind children attend integrated schools and obtain employment in occupations which have been historically closed to them. Blind children, as all children, need a basis for being optimistic about their futures. A teacher's or parent's optimism, based on reality, is one of the most important assurances that a visually handicapped child can receive to help face the future confidently.

References

American Association of Workers for the Blind, Inc. *Blindness.* Washington, D.C., 1971, 222–25.

The blind in the age of technology. *New Outlook for the Blind, 64,* 1970, 201–18.

Gaitenby, J. H. The machine conversion of print to speech: Two papers. *New Outlook for the Blind, 63,* 1969, 114–26.

Jameson, M. The optophone: Its beginning and development. *Bulletin of Prosthetics Research.* Washington, D.C., Veterans Administration, Spring, 1966, 25–28.

Lauer, H. Personal reading machines: How they work, what they can do. *New Outlook for the Blind, 63,* 1969, 257–62.

Lukoff, I. F., et al., *Attitudes Toward Blind Persons.* New York, American Foundation for the Blind, 1972.

Nye, P. W. (Ed.). *Proceedings of the Conference on Evaluation of Mobility Aids for the Blind.* Washington, D.C., National Academy of Engineering, 1971.

Weihl, C. The optacon reading program at the Monroe Public School. *New Outlook for the Blind, 65,* 1971, 155–62.

Appendix

List of competencies of teachers of blind children which are considered "very important" by 100 teachers of blind children. These are ranked in importance from 1 (most important) to 34 (least important).

Rank order of importance	Knowledges and abilities
	The ability—
1	to help blind children develop acceptable patterns of personal hygiene and behavior.
2	to recognize individual differences in each blind child and to make provisions for them.
	A knowledge or understanding of—
3	the significance of the possible effect of the socioeconomic conditions and emotional climate of the home on the blind child's social, emotional, and intellectual development.
	The ability—
4	to create a classroom atmosphere that is conducive to good mental health.
5	to help blind children with respect to their personal attitudes toward their physical handicap.
	A knowledge or understanding of—
6	the medical, emotional, psychological, social, and educational implications of blindness.
	The ability—
7	to help blind children use the senses of touch and hearing in analyzing a situation.
8	to recognize possible causes of social and emotional maladjustment of blind children and to

Excerpt from: Mackie, R. P. and Dunn, L. M. *Teachers of Children Who are Blind.* U.S. Office of Education, 1955, 24–26.

participate in planning courses of action aimed at alleviating them.

The ability—

9   to encourage and create situations in school in which blind children have an opportunity to associate naturally and freely with children of normal vision.

A knowledge or understanding of—

10   the significance of amount of usable vision.

The ability—

11   to enunciate clearly and pronounce correctly in a pleasing voice.

A knowledge or understanding of—

12   the importance of initiating all experiences in the program within the arm's reach of each blind child, and being ready to interpret that which he cannot reach.

The ability—

13   to recognize symptoms that suggest the need for referral to medical personnel.

A knowledge or understanding of—

14   factors related to readiness for braille reading and writing.

15   methods and techniques of teaching the socially and emotionally disturbed child.

The ability—

16   to help blind children with respect to their social problems.

17   to help parents with their child's limitations and potentialities.

18   to organize and plan field trips for blind children which bring as many objects as possible within their arm's reach.

19   to develop the blind child's skill in using special aids and appliances which will help him to operate more efficiently, such as talking books, special educational models, barometers, rulers, and braille writers.

A knowledge or understanding of—

20   the most efficient use of hearing and vision with the least amount of fatigue for blind children.

The ability—

21   to teach braille (when necessary).

to provide blind pupils with opportunities in the curriculum for experiences in—

22   health education.

23   physical education (skill in orientation and travel including recreational activities).

24   to cooperate with other special teachers and regular school personnel in developing an integrated educational program for each blind child.

25   to help blind children with respect to their educational problems and the relationship of the educational program to future placement.

A knowledge or understanding of—

26   types, sources of procurement, and uses of special equipment and materials for writing braille.

27   methods and techniques of teaching the normal child.

The ability—

28   to coordinate the learning process around socially meaningful central themes.

A knowledge or understanding of—

29   the significance of age at onset of blindness.

The ability—

30   to help blind children with respect to their vocational problems and life goals.

31   to interpret special educational programs for, and the problems and abilities of, the blind to the general public.

32   to work as a member of a team with other professional workers, such as medical and psychological personnel, in making a case study of a blind child aimed at planning a program suited to his needs and abilities.

33   to make educational interpretations from psychological reports.

A knowledge or understanding of—

34   methods and techniques of teaching the partially seeing child.

B

Sample Lesson Plan in
Visual Discrimination Training

LESSON 6

Object: To teach discrimination and recognition of circles, squares, and triangles presented in solid black.

Materials
  A. Large chart containing a row each of solid black squares, circles, and
      triangles in diminishing sizes from 2" to ¼".
  B. Large chart containing assorted sizes of each shape in scrambled order.
  C. Individual cards containing all sizes of the three shapes in solid black.

Procedure
  A. Teacher presents child with 2" size of each shape. As child traces each
      with his finger, teacher calls attention to hand movements in terms of
      corners, points, curves, etc.
      1. Teacher gives child other cards with assorted sizes and asks him to
          separate according to shape.
  B. Discrimination of size differences.
      1. Child chooses the largest one of each shape, etc.
      2. Child arranges his cards in rows according to shape, and increasing
          in size from smallest to largest.

Excerpt from: Barraga, N. *Increased Visual Behavior in Low Vision Children.* New York,
American Foundation for the Blind, 1964, p. 118.

C. Matching
   1. Present child with large chart in size sequence, and ask him to match his cards to those on the chart.
   2. Present chart with scrambled shapes and sizes, and ask child to match the appropriate one.
   3. Matching game—each child presents one card and partner matches with same one.

Conclusion
   A. Teacher asks child to select shape with no corners or points; shape with corners and straight lines; shape with points, etc.
   B. Plan for next day and remind child of time.

Sources of
Reading Materials for the
Visually Handicapped

Sources of Reading Materials for the Visually Handicapped is a series of 21 leaflets prepared by the Publications Division of the American Foundation for the Blind, Inc. Included in the series are lists of library and reference services, sources of various types of recreational and educational reading materials, and names and addresses of publishers. The complete series includes leaflets on the following topics:

Agency publications
Braille publishers
Educational materials
Learning braille
Library of Congress
Library reference services
Nation-wide agencies
Periodicals (Braille)
Periodicals (Large-type)
Periodicals (Tape)
Producers of spoken word
    recordings

Publishers of large-type books
Reading aids
Reference books in braille and
    large type
Religious materials
Sources of braille music
Talking book topics and braille
    book review
Talking books for sale
Technology and research
Volunteers

The complete series may be ordered at nominal cost from:
Publications Division
American Foundation for the Blind
15 West Sixteenth Street
New York, New York 10011

THE AMERICAN PRINTING HOUSE FOR BLIND
(APH)

Of special significance to teachers is the American Printing House for the Blind. This printing house provides a wide variety of services to education throughout the United States, and its operation is subsidized by the federal government. Under a quota allotment system, this agency provides educational material to visually handicapped children in local schools, as well as residential schools, at no cost to the schools concerned. Among the services provided to visually handicapped in public schools are:

1. Braille publications including textbooks, standardized exams, and reference books.
2. Large-type publications including textbooks, standardized exams, and reference books.
3. Tangible apparatus which are educational aids to achievement in academic and nonacademic areas.
4. Talking book publications.
5. Braille music publications.
6. Recorded educational aids to learning (tape recordings).
7. The Instructional Materials Reference Center, which provides comprehensive reference services for teachers.
8. An educational research and development component which continues research related to problems of educating visually handicapped children.

Catalogs of material and information on services are available from APH without cost by writing to:
American Printing House for the Blind
1839 Frankfort Avenue
Louisville, Kentucky 40206

A list of the eighteen visual training categories, together with a definition of each, which are used in the Visual Efficiency Scale.

Form Discrimination
The child is able to distinguish differences and/or similarities among FORMS (geometric or contour).

Light-Dark Density Discrimination
The child is able to match forms according to their DENSITY.

Position Discrimination
The child is able to distinguish differences in POSITION of similar figures.

Inner-Detail Discrimination
The child is able to distinguish differences of DETAIL within configurations.

Size Discrimination
The child is able to distinguish differences in SIZE of similar figures.

Size and Position Discrimination
The child is able to distinguish differences in SIZE and POSITION of similar figures.

Detail Discrimination
The child is able to distinguish DETAILS between similar figures or outlines.

Position in Space Discrimination
The child is able to distinguish differences and/or similarities among figures which are ALTERED IN POSITION.

Pattern Detail Discrimination
The child is able to distinguish a specific PATTERN from among similar patterns.

Excerpt from: *Workshop Coordinator Guide.* East Lansing, Michigan, U.S. Office of Education/Michigan State University, 1971, Appendix 1.

Object Unification
The child is able to UNIFY a set of object parts to form a complete object.

Visual Closure
The child is able to distinguish a COMPLETE OBJECT from an incomplete picture or set of picture parts.

Spatial Perspective Discrimination
The child is able to distinguish differences and/or similarities among figures which are ALTERED IN POSITION and/or PERSPECTIVE.

Figure Detail Discrimination
The child is able to distinguish DETAILS between similar FIGURES.

Object Discrimination
The child is able to distinguish differences and/or similarities among OBJECTS.

Hidden Figure Discrimination
The child is able to distinguish specific FORMS which are integrated WITHIN a more detailed picture.

Symbol Position Discrimination
The child is able to distinguish between like SYMBOLS which have DIFFERENT POSITIONS in space.

Symbol Sequence Discrimination
The child is able to distinguish differences in the ORDER of groups of SYMBOLS.

Configuration Discrimination
The child is able to distinguish differences in the OUTLINE SHAPE of the configurations of symbol groups.

Outline of a
Listening Curriculum for
Grades K–6

Kindergarten–Grade 2

Specific objectives
1. To learn the names of simple objects in the immediate environment.
2. To follow simple directions.
3. To listen willingly to what others have to say.
4. To use new words learned in speaking, listening, and reading activities.
5. To explain an idea or opinion.
6. To learn sequential order through listening.
7. To recognize words that begin with the same sound, end with the same sound.
8. To discriminate sound differences.
9. To recall experiences (a story, an event).

Classroom skill or activity	Definition of the skill or activity
Directive listening	Encourage children to pay attention to the speaker. Listen to directions and follow them. Learn to give directions to others.

Excerpts from: Rathgaber, J. M. *A Sound World, Experimental Listening Curriculum.* Dominican College of Blauvelt, Blauvelt, New York, U.S. Office of Education, Project #6–8477, 1969.

Social listening	Pupils listen to stories and cooperative compositions. Favorite library books, fairy tales, nursery rhymes are read or recited.
Listening and speaking	Children compose original stories using new words. Several children read stories aloud for enjoyment and reinforcement of learnings.
Sequential listening	Listen quietly and attentively to a story. Elicit order of events according to the story. Have children retell the story.
Tactual and sound discrimination	Find things which sound and feel the same. Introduce word families, rhymes. Indicate similarities and differences in sound. Match textures: smooth, rough, sharp, hard, fuzzy—note effects of texture on sound.
Listening and recall	To strengthen memory span have children recall past experiences. Have children tell stories heard in previous sessions.

(K-2) Mobility and Orientation Listening

Specific objectives
1. To aid the child in becoming a silent and attentive listener.
2. To develop ability to identify simple sounds.
3. To foster development of self-care habits.
4. To strengthen ability to localize sounds.
5. To encourage sensitivity to sound signals.
6. To use sounds as clues in mobility.
7. To develop good posture.

Classroom skill or activity	Definition of the skill or activity
Nonvocal sounds	Objects such as whistles, bells, clappers, drums, horns, cymbals, and other noisemakers are assembled. The children learn to listen to, experiment, and practice with the sounds.
Classroom sounds	Children are asked to identify familiar sounds such as tapping on desk, striking piano, ringing bell, opening and closing doors, chair movements, clock ticking, braille writer, stylus, paper.
Environmental sounds	Each day the child should be asked to sit quietly and listen to the various sounds heard: cars passing by, steps on stairs and in corridors, noises from buses, trucks, fire engine, police cars, ambulances,

	garbage-disposal trucks, lawnmowers, construction sounds. Have the children discuss specific sounds and their use in mobility.
Body orientation	In order to enable the child to understand terms such as up, down, forward, backward, left, right, low, high, narrow, wide, soft, hard, big, little, front, back, near, far, inside, outside, short, long, heavy, light, stop, go, and wait, play "Simon Says."
Directional sense	Familiarization with classroom arrangement will help children develop a directional sense.
Tactual discrimination	In order for the children to have a knowledge of different types of materials and to be able to discriminate between them, objects of varied dimensions and textures should be brought to the classroom and handled by them.
Physical activity	To develop good posture, activities such as standing, stretching, running, jumping, bending, skipping, hopping, and climbing should be enjoyed in early school years.

GRADES 3 AND 4

Specific objectives
1. To improve listening comprehension.
2. To associate the spoken word with the printed word.
3. To relate important ideas gathered from listening to a story.
4. To develop ability to relate happenings in an intelligible and interesting manner.
5. To extend knowledge of new words in speaking, listening, and reading.
6. To listen for specific information.
7. To listen for directions in making things: carpentry work, sewing, constructing model planes and automobiles, constructing paper figures.
8. To follow travel directions.
9. To make relevant contributions to group discussion.

Classroom skill or activity	*Definition of the skill or activity*
Selecting main ideas	A record or tape may be played or a story read by the teacher. Encourage children to listen attentively and select a good title for the story.

Finding specific information	Afford children an opportunity to explain some event or happening to the class, giving data as to time, date, location.
Following travel directions	Give clear, precise directions with few or no repetitions.
Increasing vocabulary	Practice new words learned in speaking, listening, and reading activities.
Associating braille with spoken word	Excite interest through "Show and Tell" type games. Mark object with braille word to associate written and spoken word.
Listening for instructions	Give clear, precise directions with few or no repetitions.
Relating ideas	Listen to discover the most important facts in a paragraph.
Relevant contributions to group discussion	Topics relevant to present-day happenings may be introduced. Stimulate interest and encourage group discussion through appropriate questioning.

(Grade 3 and 4) Mobility and Orientation Listening

Specific objectives

1. To instill in the child an awareness of how words can serve his demands as he proceeds through life.
2. To promote growth of discrimination necessary for success in mobility.
3. To maintain a classroom atmosphere that will be conducive to listening.
4. To provide auditory memory and to strengthen motor coordination.
5. To provide ample opportunities for good posture.
6. To inculcate awareness of position while traveling.
7. To introduce concept of distance in relation to sound and movement.

Classroom skill or activity	*Definition of the skill or activity*
Sounds about us	Present and review environmental sounds (K–2 level) to insure identification of sounds already learned and to learn new ones.
Tones	To become aware of tones and intensity, high and low pitch notes may be played on the piano, record player or tape recorder.
Sounds which identify	Identify people through the sound of the human voice. The teacher touches a child and

	asks him to say something. Other children guess who he is.
Distance	Ability to gauge distance is a necessary skill which must be developed to afford the blind child a measure of safety. Facility in this skill can and should be correlated with physical education activities such as relay races, baseball, and dodge ball.
Directions	Skill in responding to directions is built by graduating the difficulty and complexity of the given command. In the first instance, one command is given—"Go to the nurse's office." After ability to respond on this level is achieved, two or more directions are given— "Take this message. Deliver it to the principal's office and await a reply."
Auditory memory	Practice in attentive listening must be a part of effective mobility because it is important for the blind person to recall information and develop memory span.

GRADES 5–6

Specific objectives
    1. To recognize sequential happenings.
    2. To identify and correct one's own poor listening habits.
    3. To form mental images when traveling directions are being given.
    4. To form mental images when directions for constructing or making something are being given.
    5. To understand how a person explains or directs through the use of *what, where, when, why.*
    6. To be alert to propaganda methods.
    7. To show how opinions have been helpful in establishing scientific facts.
    8. To develop discriminative directive listening.
    9. To listen and to do.

Classroom skill or activity	*Definition of the skill or activity*
Listening habits	Administer listening tests to diagnose weaknesses and strengths.
Sequential order	Students note the order of happenings in terms of before, after, or at the same time.

Traveling directions	Discuss alternate routes to all locations within the school building. Revise directions if response is inadequate. Relate to games which require knowledge of environment and environmental clues.
Listening and speaking	Discuss techniques for beginning, changing, and closing conversation.
Telephoning	Demonstrate appropriate telephone experiences.
Propaganda	Listen to opposite views about current controversial issues. Compare methods used to influence opinions.

(Grades 5 and 6) Mobility and Orientation Listening

Specific objectives

1. To reinforce knowledge of sounds already acquired.
2. To identify sounds in their environment at certain times of the day and to evaluate them in terms of their orientation.
3. To improve ability to concentrate attention on oral directions.
4. To foster ability to repeat directions and to mentally identify clues used in a given area.
5. To provide activities that will further the development of the child's motor dexterity, balance, and directional sense.
6. To promote the growth of echo perception and spatial orientation.

Classroom skill or activity	Definition of the skill or activity
Sequence and direction	The children have become aware of many sounds about them. To develop sequence in direction and to reinforce knowledge previously learned in the earlier grades, the children should spend time outdoors, whenever possible, listening for sounds.
Localization	To foster development of localization of sound, the teacher must arrange listening situations on the level of the pupil. Drop articles on the floor in the classroom, in the corridor, in play area, and suggest aids in determining relative position in order to help the child retrieve the articles.
Noting and remembering	In order to note and remember important facts regarding orientation and mobility, the entire physical plant of the school must be explored. Ask the children to relate some of the sound

clues they use outdoors to find pathway and
play apparatus and to avoid crevices and
pitfalls. What are some of the sounds that tell
you when the school bus is nearing home?
What do some of the various sounds in your
neighborhood tell you? What does speed do to
sound?

Echo perception

To improve echo perception, have the students
determine the difference in quality of echoes
produced by various sounds such as clapping
hands, vocal calls, stamping feet. So that the
children will acquire the ability to determine
the relative position of objects from the echo,
have a child stand in a certain spot on the
playground and let him walk toward the
direction of the object producing the echo.
Compare the quality of the echo from various
distances.

Description of
Specific Orientation and
Mobility Techniques

ORIENTATION AND MOBILITY SKILLS

Formalized mobility skills are referred to (here) as basic skills rather than pre-cane skills. These basic skills can be taught by the teacher in cooperation with the mobility instructor whenever one is available. For some children with limited ability, these skills constitute all of their formal training. They should not be given the idea that they are receiving only a part of something; but rather, something which is in itself complete. For the majority of children, basic skills provide a solid foundation for cane travel.

To all visually handicapped children, the goals of mobility training are safer, more efficient, more graceful, and relaxed travel.

The amount of formal training needed by an individual child depends on a number of factors: the amount of residual vision, visual memory, intellectual ability, self-concept, sensory efficiency, previous sensory learning, other handicaps, and prognosis. Determining the needs of each child requires careful judgment.

Learning mobility skills should begin as soon as possible. Even very young children can use trailing and direction taking, coupled with auditory clues. It is difficult to enforce the use of techniques in an area in which the child is familiar. Elementary school children can take turns being the leader when going to the

Excerpt from: *Mobility Training for the Visually Handicapped, A Guide for Teachers.* Springfield, Illinois, Illinois Department of Children and Family Services, 1968, 24–34.

washroom, with the other children following in single file. As the children become more familiar with the building they can take longer trips, and may eventually be messengers for the office.

The degree of success that the child ultimately achieves with the mobility instructor depends upon the foundations laid by parents and teachers.

Secondary school children not previously exposed to basic orientation and mobility techniques need the same introductory training as the elementary school child. In the adolescent group, social pressures to conform have an effect on mobility performance. This may cause reluctance on the part of the youngster to use good travel techniques, such as the hand and forearm techniques or the cane. It is the teacher's job here to convince the student that he makes a better and more graceful appearance with proper mobility techniques. This is particularly hard for high school students.

Using the Sighted Guide

The roles of the student and the guide:

1. A greater degree of independence should be the goal in teaching the use of the guide. The student must make his needs known and be responsible for the way the travel proceeds. He should be aware of the route being taken as well as the significant landmarks, buildings, and points of interest along the way. If possible, the student should determine the route to be followed. When he is

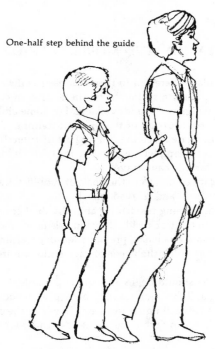

One-half step behind the guide

FIGURE 8.   Use of Sighted Guide

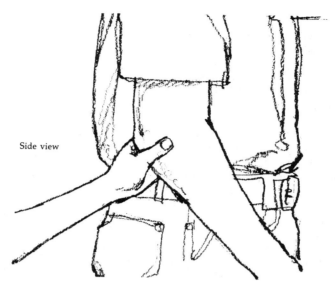

Side view

FIGURE 9. Grip Used with Sighted Guide

with a guide, he should speak for himself in all matters that concern him and not be just a passive follower.

2. The guide's function is to be a substitute pair of eyes. It is important that he be open, direct, and unobtrusive in imparting information. He must antici-pate situations in advance and be prepared for appropriate actions. As they go along, the guide can give information about the route and the surroundings in an interesting manner. A patronizing manner should be avoided at all times.

The Guide Technique

This technique is the logical beginning for mobility training to familiarize the student with his surroundings. It is also used later with other techniques taught by the mobility instructor. Dog guide agencies recommend the guide technique as a prelude for using a guide dog.

1. The student takes the guide's right arm with the left hand, or vice versa, just above the elbow, with the thumb on the lateral side (outside) and the fingers on the medial (inside). Younger children who cannot comfortably hold the guide's arm in this way can grasp the wrist. The upper part of the student's arm should be parallel and close to his side. The forearm should be parallel to the ground. This position will automatically place him one-half step behind the guide for normal walking.

2. Dealing with doorways, narrow openings, crowded or dangerous places:
    a. The guide indicates to the student the approach of a doorway by clasping his arm against his side or by moving the arm back slightly. This is a signal for the student to extend his arm straight out and move directly behind the guide. This increases his distance from one-half step to one

full step. At the beginning verbal directions are necessary, but these can be gradually eliminated.

b. Until the student can distinguish for himself, the guide should indicate whether the doors open to the right or left, in or out.

c. In passing through a doorway, the student may hold the door for himself by placing the palm of his free hand against the center of the door.

d. If the door is on the wrong side to be properly held, i.e., the student is holding the guide's left arm and the door is on the right, he should switch to the guide's other arm. This is done by letting go of the arm that he is holding and moving across the back of the guide, picking up his opposite arm with the other hand.

e. The guide should be careful not to swing the student around abruptly into a wall or post and should exercise particular caution when going through a narrow opening.

3. Using washrooms:

a. *Washbowl.* After approaching the washbowl, the guide moves one of the student's hands forward a few inches to touch the front edge and places the other hand on the spigot and the handles. He also shows the student the towels and wastebasket, touching the containers with the back of his hand.

b. *Commode.* The guide leads the student until his legs come in contact with the front edge and then tells him where to locate the paper and the flush handle. It may be necessary to place his hand on these objects.

4. Using chairs:

a. In an open area the chair is approached from the back, and the guide touches the student's free hand to the back of the chair. To avoid an awkward appearance, the student should move to the side and check the seat with the back of his hand for contour, objects, and armrests. He can then move around to the front and sit down.

b. Along a wall, the approach is from the front until the student's legs touch the front of the chair.

5. Ascending and descending stairways. Until the children have developed confidence in themselves and in their guides, they may be hesitant. Practice should begin on a good, indoor stairway, perhaps one with which the student is already familiar.

a. *Ascending.* The stairway is approached squarely so that the toes of the guide are near the bottom riser. The guide stops and allows the student to move forward until his toes are near the riser. The guide then steps upon the first step while the student hesitates. As the guide ascends the second step, the student steps up on the first. They continue up the stairs together, with the student remaining one step behind the guide and in step with him. Upon reaching the top, the guide hesitates long enough to allow the student to step up the last step. In continuing, the guide steps out and the student resumes the normal walking position, one-half step behind the guide. Again, with some students it may be necessary to inform them that the top of the steps has been reached. If necessary, the child can hold the guide's wrist instead of the elbow, while ascending the stairs.

b. *Descending.* Again, the stairs are always approached squarely. In this case, as in many others, the guide must think ahead and anticipate what is to be done as well as what the student may do. In a cautious, but normal, manner the guide moves up to the edge of the first step so that the student's toes are near or just over the edge. The student then hesitates to allow the guide to step down the first stair and begins down as the guide starts on the second. If necessary, the student may slide his hand up the guide's arm to descend more comfortably. The guide hesitates at the bottom to allow the student to take the last step. They then continue on in a normal manner. Though these techniques must be used cautiously and with explanation at first, as the student gains familiarity with the technique and the guide, the pace may be speeded up. The student learns to take many clues from the movement of the guide, allowing some of the detail in these techniques to be eliminated. The deciding factor here, as always, is the needs of the student.

Basic Skills of Independent Travel

Trailing

1. Trailing is primarily an indoor skill. It is defined as the act of using the back of the fingers to follow lightly over a straight surface (i.e., wall lockers, desks, tables) to determine one's place in space, to locate specific objects, and to get a parallel line of travel (direction-taking).

2. *Position.* The body is about eight inches away from the wall for normal walking. The arm to be used is raised forward about 45 degrees and kept straight at the elbow. The fingers are relaxed but almost fully extended (straight), with the thumb against the hand to prevent catching. If the wrist is bent down slightly, the tips of the fingers will not strike or catch objects.

3. *Procedure.* The student walks at a fairly normal rate, maintaining good posture. The end portion of the last two or three fingers should slide lightly along the wall and desk. This trailing technique is also used to take a direction from known objects, to cross open areas, as in using the teacher's desk to locate one's seat.

4. Negotiating curbs: The procedure for curbs is exactly the same as for ascending and descending stairs. One additional problem may be caused by rounded curbs. It may be necessary for the guide to turn or detour a few steps so the student can approach the curb as squarely as possible. This gives the student an exact knowledge of the location of the curb. Additional information about a broken curb, or a higher than normal step may be given. In preparation for future travel with a cane, traffic patterns can be discussed; and the student can decide when it is safe to cross.

5. Entering a car: The student can engineer his own actions if he is told which way (right or left) the vehicle is facing and if one hand is placed on the door handle and the other on the top of the car to inform him of head clearance. If confusion occurs, more information can be given.

The Role of the Family in Basic Skills

Without cooperation and reinforcement on the part of the parents, little progress can be expected. Techniques taught to the child should be shown to the parents so they can follow through at home.

Arm and forearm (cross-body technique)

1. This technique affords protection for the upper trunk and the head in dangerous situations, as well as in uncontrolled areas, such as hallways where any number of doors could be open or opening. It may also be used in conjunction with trailing and later with the cane.

2. *Position.* The arm is held horizontally even with the shoulder, with the upper arm sticking straight out in front. The elbow is bent so that there is about a 130 degree angle at the elbow. The palm of the hand faces outward, away from the student. The arm then acts as the bumper of a car. The fingers and thumb should be kept together. The tips of the fingers must extend far enough over to protect the opposite shoulder. Initially, it may be necessary to place the child's arm in proper position. Continual verbal reminders are necessary during practice until muscle memory has been developed (i.e., "Move your arm a little higher," "Bend the elbow a little more").

Arm in lower position (the dropped-hand technique)

1. This is used to locate walls, tables, chairs, and other objects when walking toward them. In some instances, it may be substituted for the arm and forearm technique, particularly when the student is trying to locate or avoid low objects, such as desks and chairs in a classroom. It should not be used in unfamiliar areas, since it does not afford the amount of protection provided by the hand and forearm technique.

2. *Position.* The arm is lifted upward about 45 degrees as in trailing. With the elbow kept straight, the arm is moved so that the hand is in the center of the body. The hand is held limply with the back facing outward (forward).

3. *Procedure.* Once the desired object is located, the trailing position may be easily assumed.

Additional Basic Skills

A great deal of danger and insecurity may result from improperly offered help. When the child is pushed along in front of someone, he has no idea of what is being approached. Impress upon the student that it is his responsibility to take the initiative in getting assistance in the proper way. When help is offered, it should be accepted properly and graciously. Politeness would dictate some comments, such as, "Please let me take your arm," or "It's better if we do it this way."

Techniques for Getting Directions

1. Squaring off:
   a. The student aligns his body to an object for the purpose of getting a line of direction and establishing a definite position in the environment.
   b. *Procedure.* The student places his back or heels against a straight-edged object such as a table, sofa, or wall to establish a definite position of departure and to determine the angle leading to a desired location.

2. Direction-taking:
   a. The student gets a line or course from an object or sound to facilitate traveling in a straight line toward an object.
   b. *Procedure.* Using the trailing technique, the student follows an object, such as a table or wall, to the end and continues along an imaginary projected line from that object. He uses the arm and forearm technique for additional safety.
3. Other directional devices are following a shoreline, staying on the line of a string of lights overhead or along windows, and being guided by sounds.
4. Picking up dropped objects: The student should listen and turn in the direction of the object. If possible, he should move toward it while auditory clues are still present, being sure to use adequate protection at all times. He then bends down, using the arm and forearm technique, or squats down keeping the head vertical. The object is located by placing the outspread hand on the floor in front of the body and moving it in an expanding circular pattern. If the student is not successful, he should turn right and check; and if the object is still not found, then check to the left. There should be no prodding or poking around, because that method is inefficient and gives the appearance of incompetence. If necessary, the student should take a step forward and repeat the circular pattern. To reverse directions, he should turn around and move forward, using proper protection rather than stepping backward.

FURTHER FORMAL MOBILITY TRAINING

Good training in basic skills gives a student the background and foundation he will need for advanced formal mobility training. The two formal programs currently recognized involve the use of canes or dogs.

Training in and facility with a cane is the result of an intensive course of study involving independent movement, travel in unfamiliar areas, use of public transportation, and advanced levels of all basic mobility skills. The instructor who works with the student must be a trained mobility specialist who understands not only the physical problems involved, but also the emotional problems the student faces.

Another aid to travel used by visually handicapped individuals is the dog guide. Though the dog is well-trained, the student who works with the dog is responsible for making decisions and knowing the routes to be followed. It is generally recommended that individuals, before entering into a dog guide program, have a good background in mobility and an understanding of all basic travel techniques.

In recent years there has been considerable research in developing effective electronics devices to aid the visually handicapped individual in travel. Although these devices hold promise for the future, they are still in the experimental stage and not currently recommended for universal use.

Full view   Side view

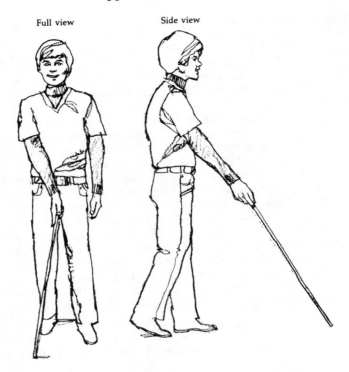

FIGURE 10. Use of Long Cane

Workshop for
Industrial Arts Instructors of
Blind Students

SUGGESTED TRANSPORTATION TEACHING
TECHNIQUES FOR BLIND STUDENTS

1. Cut-aways and mockups of all types of components on the automobile and small engine are essential to teaching the student the parts of the automobile.

2. A thorough orientation to all the component parts of the automobile and engine and their relationships to each other is essential before attempting to teach the student about various parts of the automobile.

3. Ignition. In checking point gap, the knife or blade-type feeler gauge is easier for the student to use than a wire feeler gauge. Braille dymo tape should be applied to gauge blades.

4. Assembling an ignition system using a dry cell battery, coil, and distributor is an effective teaching device for teaching the ignition system.

5. Students can be taught to clean and gap spark plugs, but we do not have an effective device adapted for telling when the plug is clean. The adapted wire feeler gauge is used in checking gap on the plugs.

6. Students can effectively tear down and reassemble small motors (one and two cycle). To assist the student in keeping parts separated and in order, a compartmented cupcake tin might be used. The student should be taught to place parts in separate compartments as they are removed. When reassembling, they can be removed from the compartments in reverse order.

Developed at State University College, Oswego, New York, 1963.

7. In working on jobs or problems, students may work in teams of one to three. It is better if they work alone if there are enough separate jobs. If there are partially sighted students in the class, place a partially sighted student with a totally blind student to work.

8. Students should be encouraged to use a normal working posture; so that they develop stance, stability, and comfort while working in handling tools and parts.

9. Compression checks can be performed by adapting a standard gauge so that it can be read by feel by removing cover glass.

10. Setting of tappets can be performed with the motor running (hot setting) or with the motor cold, by using a jumper lead to the battery to turn the engine over. Use cam angle plate to locate piston position.

11. Bicycle work can be performed satisfactorily by blind students, but it is desirable to have a partially sighted or sighted person work with the student.

12. In checking timing on an engine, cellophane can be placed between the points and the distributor rotated until the points open and cellophane can be pulled out.

13. Start outboard motor and small engines and allow student to run and adjust carburetor settings to develop interest.

14. When student works on parts of engine on a bench, make sure parts are anchored on a base or placed in a vise to enable student to concentrate on what he is doing rather than on holding parts in position.

15. Have a work table with a well in the center to collect all pieces which might drop or roll off the bench and get lost. Other means might be the use of magnetic table top or a cloth or canvas apron to catch small parts.

16. Tire changing is a reasonable and simple operation that can be performed by a blind student.

17. In providing orientation to the automobile, place a car on a hoist and allow the student to become familiar with the underside of the car.

18. Adjusting automobile brakes can be done very satisfactorily (if student is made familiar with auto brake assembly) by use of cut-away or mock-up first.

19. It is important to have a mock-up or cut-away of the principle parts of the automobile and engine if the student is to be able to understand their operation.

20. To hold small parts in position, a small dab of grease provides tack. Use #2 permatix on gaskets.

21. Spring-type clothes pins with braille markings should be used to mark spark plug wires.

22. Torque wrench may be marked with brads or small rivets for touch identification.

23. Care must be taken that the student follow operation by tactually examining all parts under discussion.

24. Point out danger in working on a motor-running engine; stress using safe method of adjusting an engine.

SUGGESTED METAL TEACHING
TECHNIQUES FOR BLIND STUDENTS

1. When teaching cutting sheet metal with snips, scribe metal heavily so student can feel line with snips or fingernail. Nick the edge of the metal to locate starting point if needed.

2. Perforated sheet metal is a good material to use for early experience. The pattern is useful in guiding cuts and provides decorative appearances.

3. In using square sheers, replace standard scale with brailled or notched ruler and proceed in usual manner.

4. A raised line drawing of the sheet metal layout enables the student to find out what the pattern will look like.

5. Soldering can be performed more readily by use of electrical soldering iron or soldering gun, depending on size of job and thickness of metal.

6. Soldering with propane torch is practical with some practice. Torch with button balbe is recommended. Student should orient himself to joint with unlit torch for practice.

7. The end of a soldering gun may be wrapped with asbestos rope to reduce student's fear of burns, but he should be taught to use soldering gun in normal manner if possible.

8. Spot welding is an ideal method for joining sheet metal and lightweight wrought iron.

9. Table model hand-operated sheet metal shears are easier for the blind student to use and operate than the floor model foot-operated models.

10. The braille rule is most effective in layout work on sheet metal. It is used mainly on flat work.

11. Introduce student to the metal lathe and show student the main parts of the machine with the motor off. Instructor should mount work in lathe for students as an introduction to what it does.

12. Start student on the lathe by using horizontal cuts with the apron hand-wheel used manually.

13. Bending wrought iron to a 90-degree angle may be accomplished by bending metal in a vise with the metal parallel to the top of the vise jaws and using side of vise for squaring off bend.

14. All wheels on the lathe or any machine can be operated more effectively when the student understands one complete turn of the wheel is one hour on a clock, one quarter turn being fifteen minutes on a clock, etc. Also he should know the amount of travel of one complete revolution.

15. If repeating a certain cut on the lathe or milling machine, it is advantageous for the student to count the number of revolutions of the apron hand wheel to find his starting and stopping points.

16. When working on the metal shaper, the student can better understand the operation of the machine and can more easily tell the progress if he keeps one hand riding safely on the clapper-box and the other hand on the clutch.

17. Finish cuts and adjustments of the tool cutter on the shaper and milling machine can be determined by use of paper between work and tool bit.

18. The student should become familiar with the sounds and vibrations of a normal operating machine and be ready to stop the work immediately when a drastic change takes place.

19. When setting a cutting tool for lathe work, it is much easier if student uses the dead center on tail stock to adjust tool on center.

20. When using the bar folder, the way to measure depth of fold is by making trial folds, measuring them, and then adjusting machine to proper setting.

21. Student should keep scrap metal clear of all working surfaces as soon as metal is cut. This can be done easily if the teacher attaches a scrap bin to sheet metal benches.

22. Putting a stopping block on the lathe bed for making horizontal cuts will prevent the student from running cutting tool into the lathe chuck.

23. Aviation-type sheet metal snips are easier to use and more practical than straight tinner's snips.

24. When making adjustments on metal-working machinery, place a hand, outstretched, with thumb on the work to be moved, such as a lathe tailstock or milling machine adjustments, etc., to reach for the work.

25. To check a lathe spindle for direction of rotation or to tell when it has stopped, place the left hand on the headstock and move slowly to the outboard or left end to feel spindle rotation.

26. To determine whether a lathe has power lead or cross feed engaged while machine is idle, engage clutch and turn hand wheels. The one that doesn't move has the power. If both wheels move, there is no power lead or cross feed.

27. Since students cannot see chips or dirt, they should be taught to wipe surfaces that are to be joined or assembled.

28. Local tool panels should be utilized whenever possible so that a student can return tools to the proper place more efficiently.

SUGGESTED ELECTRICITY TEACHING TECHNIQUES FOR BLIND STUDENTS

1. All electrical supplies should be stored in definite marked location so students can easily locate. Students should also be taught color code for resistors.

2. Arrange spools of hook-up wire in color code order with braille labels so students can easily select the color of wire he is to use.

3. Stress the importance of exactness to the student. Proper connections and tight windings are necessary to achieve success.

4. Complicated coils should be bought. Don't waste time winding big coils; however, a student should be taught to wind a simple coil. One of the easiest to wind is a crystal coil (about 150 turns on 1½" tubing).

5. Create situations which cause questions to arise in the student's mind. They may be answered as the student works on his experiment project.

6. Have at least two sets and if possible three sets of 2,000 ohm highly sensitive head phones [1–102 impedance 1,000 ohm or 2,000 ohm–1 high impedence (crystal ear-phone)].

7. Formvar (GE) wire should be purchased for winding coils. With ordinary enamel-covered wire, the insulation breaks off in process of winding and unwinding.

8. Use a crystal set in good working order so that the student may follow plans to a successful experience. This means a good aerial and ground as well as head set. A raised line diagram of circuit should also be provided.

9. When building a crystal set with a loop stick, use approximately ten–twenty turns of #20 plastic insulated wire wound over the loop stick with ends hooked to aerial and ground to improve selectivity and sensitivity. Wound coil over loop stick increases selectivity.

10. When explaining a transformer, have a small one that works a buzzer for sound or a light bulb that heats up enough for the student to feel; or have student use auditory circuit analyzer to measure voltages.

11. Use bases to mount all materials whenever possible. When using circuits, it is necessary to have components firmly mounted so the student can trace the circuit without pulling connections apart or damaging them. Standard connections should be used.

12. Have student check all soldered joints as completed with the audio circuit analyzer.

13. Before soldering, double check connections and solder as many connections as possible before placing them into complicated areas like radio chassis.

14. Purchase an audio circuit analyzer as soon as possible. Let the student test as many things as possible (even body resistance). Adapt audio circuit analyzer with braille dials.

15. Success is one of the best drivers. Let the student gain confidence in his work by experiencing success with his first experiments. Work from the simple to complex.

16. A mock-up board showing the various means of producing electricity—electrolitic, magnetic, heat, etc.—is most useful in explaining electricity to the beginner.

17. Shock hazard can be minimized by touching only one wire at a time. Also use nonconductor floor mat in electrical area.

18. Electronic kit L-100W (Science Electronics Inc.) is a durable commercial kit for use in teaching principles. Needed units can be made for a good project. Pegboard base should be thicker and prongs on units should be longer than usual.

19. Component parts mounted on pegboard bases enable students to assemble simple circuits and test operation without wasting time on construction problems.

20. Circuits using lights for resistances should have buzzers or other auditory devices substituted or lights that produce enough heat to feel.

21. Electrical symbols or braille labels should be made large, for identifying parts of a circuit when using the raised line kit for drawing schematics.

22. Beginning students in electricity should mount components on one side of a base and do all wiring and soldering on the same side, in the case of small radios, etc.

23. In making small radios, use of sheet plastic or metal which can be bent perpendicular to form a panel for mounting control knobs, switches, etc., enables the student to confine wiring and work to one surface.

24. A parts compartment to hold various small parts of a project can be of help to the student to keep track of pieces.

25. If student is wiring a particular project, he should be taught to cut the wire from the spool as he needs it rather than pre-cut several wires at once.

26. Solder lugs should be used in conjunction with fahnestock clips for ease in making solder connections.

27. Student should be taught to arrange his tools in an orderly manner or have tool panel at his work station to avoid confusion and the danger of injury or burns when working in electrical area.

28. When using resistors, the leads should be shortened before they are inserted into position for soldering.

29. Small fahnestock clips should be used when mounting transistors. If mistakes are made, they can be easily remedied by moving the leads on the transistor.

30. Wire strippers that can be set for size are better than those with no adjustment for size.

31. Students should be taught to use a braille drawing of the schematic diagram of an electrical circuit as a reference to guide them in their work.

32. Use tape-recordings of related information to brief a student on material or work to be accomplished the next day. Such topics as transistors and theory of radio are most useful. Brailled questions could be referred to while listening to tapes.

33. To strip lamp-cord wire, insert scribe in end and open insulation; then tear down and cut off (use Sterrett pocket scriber).

34. To strip solid wire, hold in hand against thumb by knife blade.

35. When soldering wire splices, wrap needed amount of solder around the connection before applying heat (for students that have poor coordination).

36. A series of small electrical experiments may be assembled in small boxes containing necessary parts to perform experiment, accompanied by a tape with brailled questions or directions to serve as a complete learning unit.

SUGGESTED WOODWORKING TEACHING TECHNIQUES FOR BLIND STUDENTS

I. General

1. Blind students should be thoroughly acquainted with all braille tools and those tools used extensively in their shop work.

2. Templates of plywood, sheet metal, etc., should be used whenever duplicate parts need to be made.

II. Safety

1. Students should practice emergency shut-off of machine tools, and teacher should periodically simulate emergency conditions to check the students' reactions.

2. The four-point safety pattern should be reviewed and each student made aware of it for each new machine to which he is introduced. Special emphasis should be placed on the nature of the cutting edge or dangerous part of the machine tool, and the establishment of a safe tactual path to its location.

3. Safety zone markings of abrasive tread material should be placed on the floor around all machines and their use strictly observed (use 3-M Tape on Ferrox).

4. Instructors should make sure that "shorts" or scraps of wood should be placed in a scrap box or supply area immediately after cut-off operations are completed.

III. Bench work

1. Make marks with a scratch awl tangible enough for students to follow in measuring and laying out. Scratchlines should be used instead of a dot only when scratch marks will be cut away.

2. A small notch may be used on edge of work to mark location for starting a cut.

3. For beginning students, hand sawing and planing operations can be achieved successfully with the aid of a straight-edge attached to the work as a guide.

IV. Machine tools

1. A feather board to hold in position should be used whenever possible when operating the circular saw.

2. The wood lathe tool rest should have stops or adjustable metal pins attached to limit the traverse of the turning tool.

3. Use thumb on top of turning tool to hold down against tool rest, while index finger curves over the work, touching lightly in line with cutting edge to follow tactually the work being done.

V. Planning

1. Student should be introduced to simple raised-line drawings as soon as possible to get used to reading a plan (use AFB raised line kit or perforating wheel and braille paper).

2. Full size models and full size line drawings should be used with beginning students. After students gain proficiency and understanding, scale models should be introduced.

3. Use thin metal strips on heavy solder wire for students to bend in designing original shapes for portions of their projects.

VI. Related material

1. Student should be taught to identify woods by smell, feel, density, and weight.

VII. Finishing

1. Rub-on, fast-drying finishes such as Seal-o-Cell are more practical than brush-on finishes.

An outline of a prevocational curriculum for adolescent visually handicapped who have concomitant disabilities.

PREVOCATIONAL TRAINING PROGRAM
AT THE GREENE BLIND UNIT

Purpose

This aspect of the program has been designed and developed to provide prevocational training in those areas which have been deemed necessary to insure an individual's maximum possibility for successful adjustment to job placement within a sheltered, semi-sheltered, or independent setting within or out of the state institution.

The amount of training each individual may receive will be based upon his needs. Program flexibility insures opportunity for maximum growth, including areas relating to overall function as an independent or semi-independent adult. Some of these areas are described briefly below.

Techniques of Daily Living

T.D.L. is a vital component in any habilitative or rehabilitative program. Mastery of self-help skills, which leads to good personal hygiene and grooming, makes the individual more acceptable to society and future vocational placement. The objectives of the T.D.L. course are to teach each resident to be clean and well-groomed; to acquire good manners so that he can live with others and practice effective habits in their presence; to build up a self-image and self-identity; and also to give learning experiences for the betterment of his own being.

Self-help skills are stressed and encouraged according to the individual's needs, including ability to bathe, ability to tie one's shoes, ability to clothe oneself (zippering, buttoning, putting on stockings), ability to brush and comb hair well, ability to brush teeth effectively, ability to use deodorants, ability to eat using acceptable table manners, and of course, the use of good toilet habits.

Excerpt from: McDade, P. R. The mentally impaired visually handicapped in a non-traditional institutional setting. *Selected Papers,* Association for Education of Visually Handicapped, 50th Biennial Conference, 1970.

Household Management

The household management phase of the program is devoted to the development of skills essential for successful independent living. They include cooking
—the functional application of the culinary arts with the use of various modern
kitchen facilities; understanding of basic tools and their application to minor
home repairs; basic household chores such as cleaning, dusting, vacuuming,
laundering, ironing, sewing, and pouring, and basic home arrangement and
decor.

Communication Skills

Communication is an essential skill which enables individuals to acquire basic
knowledge about the physical and social environment. Communication includes not only the ability to understand language via the auditory sense but
also the spoken and written modes. Therefore, communication must be functional and realistic with ample opportunity to foster achievement and satisfaction.

1.   Controlling the volume of the voice when speaking.
2.   Developing skill in facing the individual to whom one is speaking.
3.   Learning to make introductions in various social situations.
4.   Developing skill in use of appropriate vocabulary in specific situations
such as greetings, telephone conversations, asking for information, order-
ing in a restaurant, handling a variety of situations concerning transportation, and responsible behavior during emergencies.
5.   Utilizing the tape recorder as an instructional aid.
6.   Developing acquaintance with interviewing procedures.

Written Communication

Written communication includes a variety of media to provide each individual
with a mode of expression. Instruction stresses practical usage based upon
individual abilities.

1.   Braille medium-writing letters to friends and mailing procedures.
2.   Care of and mailing procedures for talking books and tape recorders.
3.   Writing an acceptable signature for banking and legal purposes.
4.   For advanced and capable individuals, budgeting and in writing
checks.
5.   Using typewriter as another medium for communication with sighted
friends.
6.   Written communication for business purposes, including proper letter
headings and envelope addressing.
7.   Developing a personal communication system including addresses,
telephone numbers, and memoranda.
8.   For the non-braille trainee, using as the mode of communication the
tape recorder. (Instruction is essential in care and operation of cassette and
reel recorders.)
9.   Wrapping and mailing packages.

Listening and Current Events

The media for listening skills pertaining to the physical environment includes a variety of mechanical instruments: radio and television, newscasts, talking books and tapes, movies and speakers. These provide ample opportunity for individuals to know more about the physical world and the problems therein —political, social, and economic.

Concept Development

The concept development program involves development of those basic concepts essential to independent mobility and a knowledge of one's environment. A knowledge of body concepts as described by Bryant Cratty is essential for the beginning phase of this program. Terminology must be consistent and meaningful for conceptualization in a variety of experiences. These experiences can involve tactual aids such as maps, scale models, and actual objects.

Orientation and Mobility

The objective of the orientation and mobility program will be development of skills that will enable an individual to be a safe, efficient, independent traveler during training and in future vocational placement. Such skills include: independent travel to and from classrooms and training areas; moving safely within the classroom or training areas; negotiating special areas such as the employee's cafeteria, recreational areas, public restrooms; as well as any other situation a resident encounters during training.

The orientation and mobility program will also include *sensory training*— training of the tactual, auditory, kinesthetic, vestibular, and olfactory senses as they pertain to independent travel; *concept development*—development of basic concepts essential to independent mobility and a knowledge of one's environment; and *body image*—awareness and knowledge of one's body and the relationship of one's self to other objects in the environment. It is apparent that these are not only essential to orientation and mobility, but complement the other areas of training.

All orientation and mobility training will be done on an individual basis by professional trained peripatologists. An initial evaluation will be made of each resident to determine the specific needs of the individual and a program planned accordingly.

Task Management

The main purpose of the task management phase of the program is to provide residents with a series of structured, stimulating experiences in a controlled setting. The primary goal is to foster acceptable social and personal attitudes by means of related activities which are essential to successful habilitative adjustment. The tasks themselves are of secondary importance, but are structured to provide a variety of skills necessary for further habilitative development. Various materials and equipment are utilized to provide instruction in terminology, tactile discrimination, following directions, spatial concepts, accuracy, speed, and the necessity for safety precautions.

Healthy work attitudes of major concern are: (1) cooperation with authority figures and acceptance of rules and responsibilities; (2) cooperation with fellow trainees; (3) concentration, perseverance, and pride in work completion; (4) control of unacceptable mannerisms; and (5) safety in handling materials.

Specific projects are presently being incorporated because of their utilitarian value at Fernald, such as making cotton swabs; making laundry tags; folding diapers, towels, and face cloths; folding letters and inserting them into envelopes; packaging elastic bands one hundred per envelope, packaging safety pins seventy-five per envelope; and sorting materials of various sizes and shapes.

Vocational Placement

The objective of vocational placement is to enable the individual to experience various aspects of vocational placement, allowing for the development of healthy attitudes toward on-the-job training and future employment. With the Greene Blind Unit as a focal point, it is possible to utilize numerous opportunities on the Fernald grounds for vocational training. The staff of Fernald is receptive to allowing these training opportunities to the blind and appreciate the assistance given them by trainees. At the present time, a number of residents work in various buildings on the grounds, performing essential functions similar to those done in the community. They function quite adequately in roles such as dishwashers, porters, laundry assistants, and supply clerks. In these placements a member of the staff remained with the trainee until it was decided the individual could function effectively without supervision.

Opportunities for other types of employment are limited only by the capabilities of the individuals entering the program. At present, there is a list of other possibilities for job training at Fernald which will not be fully explored until trainees are capable of fulfilling the requirements. All in-service training is realistic, and trainees are given experience in jobs in which it is felt they will be able to find successful employment in their home communities. For this reason it is essential that the staff of the Greene Blind Unit establish and maintain close communication with the counselors of the Commission for the Blind.

Leisure Time Activities and a Recreational Program

Since no individual devotes all of his energy to a vocation, it is apparent that he will have leisure time. What to do with this leisure time is the goal of this phase of the program. The ultimate goal is to develop and foster activities which enable an individual to make better use of his leisure time during training and in the future. Included in the activities will be games and hobbies as well as exploration into other personal interests expressed by the trainees.

Field trips, while mentioned last, are equally vital to the overall success of the program. Various trips shall be planned that will provide opportunities for the trainees to participate in the cultural, social, and recreational programs in the community. As well, a number of trips to shopping centers and a variety of stores will be planned to expose each individual to as much as the community has to offer during the time the trainee actively participates in the entire program.

Index